Teach Yourself®

Complete Italian

Elena Borelli and Giulia Baronti

First published by Teach Yourself in 2025

An imprint of John Murray Press

1

A CIP catalogue record for this title is available from the British Library

Trade Paperback ISBN 9781399818612

ebook ISBN 9781399818636

Typeset in FS Albert Pro light 10.5/12 by Integra Software Services Pvt. Ltd. Pondicherry, India.

Printed and bound by Oriental Press, Dubai.

John Murray Press policy is to use papers that are natural, renewable and recyclable products and made from wood grown in sustainable forests. The logging and manufacturing processes are expected to conform to the environmental regulations of the country of origin.

John Murray Press	Teach Yourself
Carmelite House	123 S. Broad St., Ste 2750
50 Victoria Embankment	Philadelphia, PA, 19109
London EC4Y 0DZ	

www.teachyourself.com

The authorised representative in the EEA is Hachette Ireland, 8 Castlecourt Centre, Dublin 15, D15 XTP3, Ireland (email: info@hbgi.ie)

John Murray Press, part of Hodder & Stoughton Limited

An Hachette UK company

Contents

Resources available online at library.teachyourself.com:

- Audio
- My takeaway study guide
- Assessments for A1, A2 and B1 levels
- CEFR and ACTFL can-do statements
- Grammar summary
- Glossary – English to Italian
- Glossary – Italian to English
- In my own words writing prompts

Meet the authors

Elena Borelli and Giulia Baronti have extensive experience teaching Italian as a foreign language.

Elena says: 'In 2004, I moved to the United States as a Fulbright scholar. I soon began teaching Italian classes at various institutions. I lived in Germany for two years, became a professor in New York, moved back to Italy, and eventually relocated to London, UK, where I am currently Lecturer of Italian at King's College London. Throughout those years, I followed my two passions: learning languages (I am fluent in five, and a beginner in two more) and teaching languages to a variety of students, with different backgrounds, motivations, and needs. Being a learner and a teacher at the same time made me aware of how language students learn, and what they need to progress. With this book, I hope to inspire students to enjoy learning a foreign language as much as I do.'

Giulia says: 'Since my childhood, I have always been fascinated by languages and cultures, beginning with classical antiquity. Being born in a small town in the Tuscan countryside, my biggest dream was to one day immerse myself in a bustling, intercultural city. After obtaining my degree in Classics and spending two years as a professional photographer, this dream blossomed into reality when I moved to London in 2013, embarking on my journey as a language educator. My experience as a lecturer of Italian for one of the most prestigious universities in the UK has filled me with the joy and enrichment that come from sharing one's language and culture with others. My motto embraces Seneca's timeless wisdom from his Letters to Lucilius: "Homines dum docent discunt," meaning "Men learn while they teach." Over the years, as I've taught and learned simultaneously, I've developed a deep appreciation for cultures worldwide, lovingly shared by my students. With this book, I aspire to ignite a passion for learning the Italian language among students from diverse backgrounds. My aim is for them to not only grasp the language but also to comprehend the culture it embodies, all while enjoying the learning process to the fullest.'

Acknowledgments

Now that *Complete Italian* has finally become a reality, we would like to express our sincere gratitude to Ana de Medeiros, the director of our Language Centre, for her continuous support and encouragement throughout the process of writing. We extend our heartfelt thanks to our colleagues whose enthusiasm and expertise have inspired us to strive for excellence.

We are also deeply thankful to our partners, Giovanni and Francesco, for their understanding, patience, and unwavering support during the demanding periods of writing and editing. Their support kept us motivated and focused on our goals.

Special appreciation goes to our friends in Italy whose first-hand experiences and insights have helped us create authentic characters and vivid descriptions of life in Italy. Their contributions have added depth and richness to the narrative of Annalisa and Cristian's adventures.

With heartfelt gratitude,
Elena and Giulia

Welcome

Congratulations on deciding to learn (or refresh) Italian and thank you for choosing Teach Yourself. This book was designed specifically with the independent student in mind, with features to provide as much motivation and support on your learning journey as possible. Join Annalisa and Cristian, two roommates who are as different as they can be: he is from the autonomous region of Bolzano in the far North of Italy and is an introverted teacher and lover of art history, with a particular passion for Venice. She is a Neapolitan engineer working on the MOSE project, a system designed to protect the city of Venice from floods. Cristian becomes obsessed with the portrait of a woman he finds hiding behind some furniture in the attic, and you will help them solve the mystery of her identity. Together with Annalisa, Cristian and their friends Aicha and Matteo, you'll get an authentic glimpse into modern life and society in Italy as you build and expand your knowledge of the language.

What's in the book?

WARMING UP

This book begins with an introduction to the Italian alphabet which will familiarize you with the basic sounds and rhythms of Italian and give you a chance to warm up and practice your pronunciation. As you practice, you'll get a few **Key expressions** under your belt before you begin. In **First things first**, you'll get comfortable with a few basic features of Italian before you dive into the units.

CORE UNITS

The core of the book are **20 units**, designed to help you communicate in practical, everyday situations and steadily build your knowledge and facility with Italian. Each unit is structured in a way to make it easy to follow and consists of two parts, each with the following features:

Culture point introduces the theme and provides a context for the unit. It presents practical information about the way things work in Italy and introduces you to the rich tapestry of Italian culture—food, music, art, architecture, literature, social traditions, and more—and useful, related words and phrases. Many Culture points also feature a QR code, which you can scan to learn more about the topic. This is a window into authentic sources and will let you explore the language and culture beyond the borders of the book.

Vocabulary builder introduces key unit vocabulary, accompanied by audio. Listen to the recording several times, repeating each word. Then do the **Vocabulary practice**. Return to the list to review as often as you can, covering up one side and then the other. Use the vocabulary builder for reference as you work through the Builder that follows.

Conversations are the cornerstone of each unit. This is where you will follow the adventures of Annalisa, Cristian, Aicha, and Matteo. Who is the mystery woman whose portrait Cristian and Annalisa find in the attic? As the story unfolds, you will join our friends in common, everyday situations and learn to participate in similar situations. The conversations are recorded so that you can listen to them, practice your pronunciation, and even role play. Listen first and try to get the gist of the conversation, don't get hung up on understanding every word. Focusing questions and follow-up activities are there to guide you. Work with the conversations as much and as often as you can. And if you really need help with understanding, translations are available online at library.teachyourself.com, or can be accessed via the Teach Yourself Library app.

Language builders (four in each unit) introduce key language points you encounter in the conversation and explain how the language is used in practice. Each topic opens with a **Language discovery** activity, designed to help you notice patterns and usage on your own. Read more about the benefits of the **Discovery method** of learning later in **How to be a successful language learner**.

Throughout the units, you will find **Tips** with study shortcuts, additional explanations, and cultural tidbits to enhance your learning.

Language practice offers a variety of exercises, including speaking opportunities, to give you a chance to see and use words and phrases in their context. The **Skill builder** section at the end of each unit provides additional practice, and you will have ample opportunity for **Speaking, Listening**, **Reading**, and **Writing practice.**

Test yourself puts together everything covered in the unit and helps you assess what you have learned. Try to do the tests without consulting the text and check your answers in the Answer Key. If you are happy with your results, move ahead to the next unit. Otherwise, go back and review the unit once more before moving on. There are also three assessments available online, at A1, A2 and B1 CEFR levels (Intermediate Low, Mid and High ACTFL levels) to help you gauge your overall progress at key junctures.

In the back of the book, you'll find the **Answer key** to all the exercises and tests, in the book. Look up the language topic you need in the **Index** to find the relevant units where it's covered.

Online resources are available at library.teachyourself.com. Look up any word in the course in the two-way **Glossary**, and quickly access key grammar patterns in the **Grammar summary**. Take the assessments to gauge your CEFR level and see which CEFR and ACTFL outcomes are covered in each unit. Finally, use the **My takeaway** template to reflect on your learning journey and make the process personal.

How to use this book

A LITTLE GOES A LONG WAY!

Try to use the book little and often, rather than for long stretches at a time. This will help you to create a study habit, much in the same way you would practice a sport or musical instrument.

MAKE A PLAN, TRACK YOUR PROGRESS, AND REFLECT ON THE PROCESS!

Setting goals affects the programming of your brain, strengthening neural pathways and ultimately making it more likely that you will achieve those goals. Before you begin, think about how much time you want to devote to learning, which skills or areas you want to focus on, and identify specific ideas you want to be able to communicate or activities you want to engage in. **In this unit you will learn** will help you identify what you should be able to do in Italian by the end of the unit and will help you set your personal goals for each unit. Each unit opens with a dashboard where you can note your personal goals.

Studies show that holding yourself accountable is another great way to stay motivated. Use the **Progress tracker** at the beginning of each unit to help you keep track of your progress and the work you do. Personalize the tools. You can use the progress tracker to keep track of the date or day, or you can enter an increment of time (15 minutes, 30 minutes...). Add columns for culture, vocabulary, grammar, or any other area you wish to focus on. Give yourself a star when you feel you've done particularly well. Make it your own! Review your tracker regularly and see which areas could use more practice.

At the end of each unit, you can review your progress and reflect on the learning experience. Use the **Self check** to assess your progress. You will need to go back to the unit opener page to do this and to review your progress against your goals and the unit objectives. A **My takeaway** template page is available online. Here you can jot down things you noted about your study habits in **My process**—What worked? What would you have done differently? Is there a new strategy you want to try? Note the highlights of the unit in **Best of...** (favorite word or phrase, important language rule). Are there any questions you still need answered? Finally, make the language your own! Try to write a few personal sentences by responding to the prompts in **In my own words**, also available online. Don't worry about making mistakes. Use the language to talk about yourself and your life.

My progress tracker

Use the progress tracker to keep a record of what you've accomplished. The first column tracks time, and the remaining five columns represent the skills you'll be working on: listening, pronunciation, reading, writing, and spoken interaction.

In this unit you will learn how to:

Each unit begins with an overview of the language you will be learning and skills you will be acquiring.

1

In this unit you will learn how to:

» Talk about where you are from and the languages you speak.
» Say how old you are using the verb **avere**.
» Briefly introduce someone you know.

Amici

My goals

Make a note of your goals. They can be general (*I want to be able to say three sentences about myself in Italian*) or specifically related to the topic at hand (*I want to be able to order breakfast at a café.*) At the end of the unit, take a look at your goals and see if you feel you've accomplished them.

My study plan

I plan to work with Unit 1

- ○ Every day
- ○ Twice a week
- ○ Other ________

I plan to study for

- ○ 5–15 minutes
- ○ 15–30 minutes
- ○ 30–45+ minutes

My progress tracker

Day / Date	Listening	Pronunciation	Reading	Writing	Spoken interaction
	○	○	○	○	○
	○	○	○	○	○
	○	○	○	○	○
	○	○	○	○	○
	○	○	○	○	○
	○	○	○	○	○
	○	○	○	○	○

My study plan

Use My study plan to plan how often and for how long you plan to study.

My goals

What do you want to be able to do or say in Italian when you complete this unit?

		Done
1	....	○
2	....	○
3	....	○

My review

SELF CHECK

	I can ...
●	... say my nationalit(ies) and the language(s) I speak.
●	... say how old I am and ask someone for their age.
●	... briefly introduce someone and say where they are from.
●	... briefly introduce someone and say where they live and work.
●	... ask simple questions regarding people's basic biographical information.

My review

Use this checklist at the end of each unit to review your progress and to reflect on what you can do and what you need to look at again.

Try to practice each skill every day

The icons in the progress tracker are used throughout the book to help you easily identify and locate the skills you want to practice:

 Listening skills

 Speaking – pronunciation skills

 Speaking – conversation skills

 Reading skills

 Writing skills

Remember, there are many ways to build your skills in addition to those provided in this book: use a language-learning app, listen to music or podcasts, watch TV shows or movies, go to a restaurant, follow social media accounts in Italian, read blogs, newspapers or magazines, switch the language settings in your apps to Italian, or sign up for a language exchange or a tutor. And remember to keep a record of them on your Dashboard!

Above all, talk to other Italian speakers or learners, if at all possible; failing that, talk to yourself, to inanimate objects, to the imaginary characters in this book (warn your family and friends!). If you can find someone else to learn along with you, that is a great bonus. Do all the exercises, and do them more than once. Make maximum use of the audio: play it as background, even when half your mind is on something else, as well as using it when you are actually studying. The main thing is to create a continuous Italian "presence," so that what you are learning is always on your mind. Finally—enjoy yourself and celebrate your progress!

How to be a successful language learner

The Discovery method

There are lots of philosophies and approaches to language learning, some practical, some quite unconventional, and far too many to list here. Perhaps you know of a few, or even have some techniques of your own. In this book we have incorporated the Discovery method of learning, a sort of DIY approach to language learning. What this means is that you will be encouraged throughout the course to engage your mind and figure out the language for yourself, through identifying patterns, understanding grammar concepts, noticing words that are similar to English, and more.

Simply put, if you figure something out for yourself, you're more likely to understand it. And when you use what you've learned, you're more likely to remember it. And because many of the essential but (let's admit it!) dull details, such as grammar rules, are introduced through the Discovery method, you'll have more fun while learning. Soon, the language will start to make sense and you'll be relying on your intuition to construct original sentences independently, not just listening and repeating.

Everyone can succeed in learning a language—the key is to know how to learn it.

Learn to learn

There are many strategies that can help you become a successful language learner. Different people have different learning styles and some of these approaches will be more effective for you than others. Use this list as a point of inspiration when you want to find the most effective ways to advance your skills and begin your journey to fluency.

VOCABULARY

Words are the building blocks of language. The more you use the words you're introduced to, the more quickly they'll lodge in your memory. These study tips will help you remember better:

- Say the words out loud as you read them. Listen to the audio several times.
- Write the words over and over again. Create flash cards, drawings and mind maps.
- It helps to group new words in categories, like food or furniture, or according to the situations in which they occur, e.g., restaurant, hotel, sightseeing, or their functions, e.g., greetings, thanks, apologizing.
- Cover up the English side of the vocabulary list and see if you remember the meaning of the word. Then cover up the Italian side and see if you can remember the word itself.

- Use mnemonic tricks for the words with similar sounding words in English, e.g., think of people talking in a parlor to remember that parlare means ***to talk***.
- Write words for objects around your house and stick them to objects.
- Pay attention to patterns in words, e.g., adding -mente to an adjective turns it into an adverb in much the same way that we add *-ly* in English: probabile > probabilemente (*probable* > *probably*).

GRAMMAR

Grammar gives your language structure. It allows you to experiment with the vocabulary you learn because you'll understand how they work together to create meaning. In other words, you'll begin to develop a feel for the language. Here are some tips to help you study more effectively:

- Write your own grammar glossary and add new information and examples as you go.
- Experiment with grammar rules. Use old vocabulary to practice new grammar structures.
- Try to find examples of grammar in conversations or other articles.
- When you learn a new verb form, review other verbs you know that follow the same pattern.
- Compare Italian structures with your own language or other languages you may already speak. Try to find out some rules on your own and be ready to spot the exceptions.

PRONUNCIATION

The best way to improve your pronunciation is simply to practice as much as possible. Study individual sounds first, then full words and sentences. Don't forget, it's not just about pronouncing letters and words correctly, but using the right intonation. So, when practicing words and sentences, mimic the rising and falling intonation of Italian speakers.

- Repeat all of the conversations, line by line. Listen to yourself and try to mimic what you hear.
- Record yourself and compare yourself to the recordings.
- Make a list of words that give you trouble and practice them.

LISTENING AND READING

The conversations in this book include questions to help guide you in your understanding. But you can go further by following some of these tips.

- Imagine the situation. Try to imagine where the scene is taking place and who the main characters are. Let your experience of the world help you guess the meaning of the conversation, e.g., if a conversation takes place in a café, you can predict the kind of vocabulary that will be used.
- Concentrate on the main part. When watching a foreign film, you usually get the meaning of the whole story from a few individual shots. Understanding a foreign conversation or article is similar. Concentrate on the main message and don't worry about individual words.

- Learn to cope with uncertainty—don't over-use your dictionary! You don't have to look up every word you don't know—try to deduce the meaning from context. Concentrate on trying to get the gist of the passage and underline the words you don't understand. If after the third time there are still words which prevent you from getting the general meaning of the passage, look them up in the dictionary.

WRITING

You'll have plenty of writing practice using this book. Creating vocabulary lists, grammar summaries and taking good notes as you study is another great opportunity to practice writing.

If you're keeping your lists or notes on your smartphone, computer, or tablet, remember to switch the keyboard language to be able to include all accents and special characters. Here are some other ways to practice writing:

- Write out the answers to all Practice and Test Yourself questions.
- Create your own vocabulary lists and a grammar summary.
- Look up writing prompts for language learning or write a daily gratitude journal in Italian.
- Write out your To Do and shopping lists in Italian.
- Join online forums and discussion groups about or in Italian.

SPEAKING

The greatest obstacle to speaking a new language is the fear of making a mistake. Keep in mind that you make mistakes in your own language—it's simply part of the human condition. Accept it. Focus on the message. Most errors are not serious, and they will not affect the meaning: for example, if you use the wrong article, wrong pronoun or wrong adjective ending. So, concentrate on getting your message across and use the mistakes as learning opportunities.

Here are some useful tips to help you practice speaking Italian:

- When you're going about your day, e.g., buying groceries, ordering food and drinks, do it in Italian in your mind! Look at objects around you and try to name them in Italian. Look at people around you and try to describe them.
- Answer all of the questions in the book out loud. Say the dialogues out loud, then try to replace sentences with ones that are true for you. Role play different situations in the book.
- Keep talking. The best way to improve your fluency in a language is to talk every time you have the opportunity to do so: keep the conversations flowing and don't worry about the mistakes. If you get stuck for a particular word, don't let the conversation stop; simplify what you want to say; paraphrase or replace the unknown word with one you do know.

Learning a language takes work. But the work can be a lot of fun! So, let's begin!

The Italian alphabet and pronunciation

The Italian alphabet has 21 letters: 16 consonants and five vowels (a, e, i, o, u).

Letter	How to spell the letter	Sound	Example
A, a	a	/a/	sof**a**
B, b	bi (*bee*)	/b/	**b**ottle
C, c	ci (*chee*)	/tʃ/, /k/	**ch**ip, **k**ip
D, d	di (*dee*)	/d/	**d**ot
E, e	e (eh)	/e/	**e**lephant
F, f	effe (ehffeh)	/f/	**f**ive
G, g	gi (jee)	/dʒ/, /g/	**g**elato, **g**irl
H, h	acca	mute	**h**our
I, i	i (ee)	/i/	**i**ntelligent,
L, l	elle (ehlleh)	/l/	**l**oop
M, m	emme (ehmmeh)	/m/	**m**other
N, n	enne (ehnneh)	/n/	**n**ew
O, o	o (oh)	/o/	**o**pera
P, p	pi (pee)	/p/	**p**ond
Q, q	cu (ku)	/k/	**q**uarter
R, r	erre (ehrreh)	/r/	**r**ota
S, s	esse (ehsseh)	/s/, /z/	**s**oap, ri**s**e
T, t	ti (tee)	/t/	**t**op
U, u	u (ou)	/u/	p**u**t
V, v	vi (vee)	/v/	**v**ine
Z, z	zeta (tsehta)	/ts/, /dz/	**ts**ar

There are five additional letters that are used to spell loan words, and that are now part of the dictionary.

Letter	How to spell the letter	Sound	Example
J, j	i lunga (ee loonga)	/i/, /ʒ/, or /dʒ/	*Juventus, abat-jour, job*
K, k	kappa	/k/	*kite*
W, w	doppia vu	/v/, /w/	*whisky*
X, x	ics (eex)	/x/	*xenophobia*
Y, y	ipsilon (eepsilon)	/y/ /i/	*yoga*

Italian pronunciation consistently follows the spelling of words. While you can consult the table above for the pronunciation of individual letters, it's important to note that exceptions may arise when two or more specific letters are combined. Once you familiarize yourself with the rules governing the sounds of letters and vowels, you'll discover that the pronunciation of new words becomes quite straightforward.

COMBINED LETTERS

Group of letters	Sound	Example
ce ci	/tʃe/ as in **che**stnut /tʃi/ as in **chi**p	**ce**na (*dinner*) **ci**ao (*hi*)
ca chi che co cu	/ka/ as in **ca**t /ki/ as in **kee**n /ke/ as in **ke**ttle /ko/ as in **co**ver /ku/ as in **cu**ckoo	**ca**sa (*house*) **chi**tarra (*guitar*) an**che** (*also*) **co**lore (*color*) **cu**rioso (*curious*)
ge gi	/dʒe/ as in **je**alous /dʒi/ as in **ji**ngle	**ge**lato (*ice cream*) **gi**n (*gin*)
ga ghi ghe go gu	/ga/ as in **ga**p /gi/ as in **gi**ft /ge/ as in **ge**t /go/ as in **go**t /gu/ as in **goo**d	**ga**tto (*cat*) **ghi**ro (*dormouse*) **ghe**pardo (*cheetah*) **go**la (*throat*) **gu**sto (*taste*)
gl	/ʎ/ as in torti**ll**a	a**gl**io (*garlic*)
gn	/ɲ/ as in lasa**gn**a	ba**gn**o (*bathroom*)
sci sce	/ʃi/ as in **she** /ʃe/ as in **she**lter	**sci**are (*to ski*) **sce**na (*scene*)

Group of letters	Sound	Example
sca	/ska/ as in **sca**r	**sca**tola (*box*)
schi	/ski/ as in **ski**	**schi**ena (*back*)
sche	/ske/ as in **ske**ptical	**sche**letro (*skeleton*)
sco	/sko/ as in **sco**rn	**sco**po (*scope*)
scu	/sku/ as in **school**	**scu**ola (*school*)

STRESS

Most Italian words have stress or emphasis on the second-to-last syllable, as in "ar-ri-ve-**der**-ci" (*goodbye*).

When the stress falls on the final syllable, an accent is added, as in cit**tà** (*city*), universi**tà** (*university*), caf**fè** (*coffee*).

However, sometimes stress falls on the third or fourth syllable from the end, without a fixed rule. In these cases memorization is necessary: **le**ggere (*to read*), **Na**poli (*Naples*), **ti**pico (*typical*).

KEY PHRASES

hello	ciao
good morning	buongiorno
good afternoon	buon pomeriggio
good evening	buonasera
good night	buonanotte
see you later	arrivederci, a dopo
no	no
yes	si
please	per favore
thank you	grazie
you are welcome	prego
excuse me ...	scusa (informal) / scusi (formal)
sorry	mi dispiace
OK	okay, va bene
My name is ...	Mi chiamo...
What's your name?	Come ti chiami? (informal) / Come si chiama? (formal)
Nice to meet you	piacere

First things first

in this unit you will learn how to:

- Greet people and introduce yourself.
- Say where you live and which city you are from.
- Describe people and places with the verb **essere**.
- Ask questions with **dove**, **quale** and **come.**

Ciao!

My study plan

I plan to work with Unit 1

- ○ Every day
- ○ Twice a week
- ○ Other ___________

I plan to study for

- ○ 5–15 minutes
- ○ 15–30 minutes
- ○ 30–45+ minutes

My progress tracker

Day / Date	Listening	Speaking	Reading	Writing	Conversation
	○	○	○	○	○
	○	○	○	○	○
	○	○	○	○	○
	○	○	○	○	○
	○	○	○	○	○
	○	○	○	○	○
	○	○	○	○	○

My goals

What do you want to be able to do or say in Italian when you complete this unit?

		Done
1	....	○
2	....	○
3	....	○

My review

SELF CHECK

	I can ...
●	... greet people formally and informally.
●	... introduce myself.
●	... spell my name and ask others to spell theirs.
●	... say where I am from and where I live.
●	... ask and give my phone number.

CULTURE POINT 1

Regioni e province d'Italia *Regions and provinces of Italy*

Italy may seem small on a world map, but its geographic position—stretching from the Alps to the Mediterranean—makes it extremely diverse in terms of landscapes, climates, food, and cultures. Its 20 regioni (*regions*) are very different from each other. Cinque (*five*) of these regions—Friuli-Venezia-Giulia, Trentino-Alto Adige, Valle d'Aosta, Sicily, and Sardinia—have semi-independent status and linguistic minorities. For instance, in Trentino-Alto Adige, the region of Bolzano, tre (*three*) quarters of the population speak German as their first language. Due (*two*) of the regions are islands (Sardinia and Sicily). Each region is divided into province (*provinces*) and every province and region has a capoluogo (*regional capital*). The capitale (*capital*) of Italy is Roma (*Rome*).

Take a look at this map of Italy or explore an interactive map of the regions by scanning the QR code. Identify:

a At least quattro (*four*) capoluoghi di regione

b Cinque (*five*) regions that do not face the sea

c The number of provinces in Lombardia

d The region of Torino

VOCABULARY BUILDER 1

Look at the words and phrases and complete the missing English words and expressions. Then listen and try to imitate the pronunciation of the speakers.

SALUTARE	*TO GREET SOMEONE*
buongiorno	....
buonasera	....
buonanotte	*good night*
arrivederci	....
ciao	....
Come stai?	*How are you?* (informal)
Come sta?	*How are you?* (formal)
Bene, grazie.	*I'm well, thank you.*

PRESENTARSI	*TO INTRODUCE ONESELF*
io sono	*I am*
io mi chiamo	*my name is ...*
io	*I*
tu	*you* (informal)
Lei	*you* (formal)
signore	*Mister*
signora	*Miss/Mrs/Ms*
nome	*first name*
cognome	*last name*
Piacere!	*Nice to meet you!*
Diamoci del tu!	*Let's be informal! (lit. Let's call each other "tu"!)*
Io sono di + (città)	*I am from + (city)*
Come si scrive?	*How do you spell ...?*
Scusi	*Excuse me* (formal)
indirizzo	*address*

The Italian word ciao is very well known, having spread into at least 38 languages. Outside of Italy, ciao is used when people part ways in an informal manner. Ciao stems from an expression in the Venetian dialect meaning "I am at your service." In Italian, it is used both to greet people and to say goodbye, but only among friends, as it is very informal. To be formal, use buongiorno or buonasera (*good morning/good evening*) when greeting people, and arrivederci (*goodbye*) when leaving.

Vocabulary practice 1

Match the sentences below with the pictures.

1 Ciao, Carlo!

2 Piacere, signora, come sta?

3 Io mi chiamo Sara.

4 Buonanotte!

a

c

b

d

Pronunciation practice

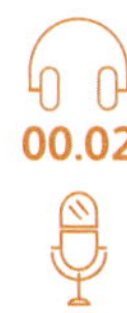

00.02

1 Listen to the pronunciation of the following words or expressions, paying attention to the underlined syllable. What do you notice? How do you pronounce the letter c when it is followed by an i or an e? And when there's an h in between?

arriveder**ci** **cia**o io mi **chia**mo diamo**ci** del tu pia**ce**re

- CI is pronounced like the English *chin*.
- CHI is pronounced like the English *zucchini*.
- CE is pronounced like the English *cherry*.
- CHE is pronounced like the English *chemistry*.

2 Practice pronouncing the following words.

a Cina

b chimica

c schema

d ceramica

e cappuccino

f cemento

g macchina

h macchiato

i eccellente

CONVERSATION 1

Piacere! *Nice to meet you!*

00.03

1 Here are a few words and expressions to help you understand the conversation.

insegnante	*teacher*
Chiamo per l'appartamento.	*I'm calling about the apartment.*

00.04

2 Listen to the conversation without looking at the text. Play it a few times and see whether you can make out a few new words and phrases each time. Then listen to the conversation again and read the text.

Annalisa has just moved to Venezia (*Venice*) and rented an appartamento (*apartment*) in the centro città (*city center*), but she wants a roommate to share the costs. She placed an announcement online and today someone calls about coming to see the apartment. Pay attention to how they introduce themselves and say where they are from.

Cristian	Buongiorno. Mi chiamo Cristian Steiner. Chiamo per l'appartamento...
Annalisa	Buongiorno! Io sono Annalisa.
Cristian	L'appartamento è in centro città?
Annalisa	Sì. L'indirizzo è via Garibaldi 10.
Cristian	Perfetto!
Annalisa	Scusi, il Suo cognome è Steiner? Come si scrive?
Cristian	S-T-E-I-N-E-R.
Annalisa	Steiner. Okay. Lei è italiano?
Cristian	Sì, sono di Bolzano. E Lei?
Annalisa	Io sono di Napoli.
	A little later, Cristian comes to see the apartment.
Cristian	Buongiorno. Sono Cristian. Come sta?
Annalisa	Bene, grazie, e Lei?
Cristian	Benissimo!
Annalisa	Ma diamoci del tu ... Tu sei studente?
Cristian	No, sono insegnante di storia dell'arte.
Annalisa	Interessante!

3 Answer the questions.

a Who suggests switching to informal speech?
b Where does Annalisa come from?
c What word is Cristian spelling?

LANGUAGE BUILDER 1

Language discovery 1

Look at these phrases from the conversation and match the people/places in the left column with the correct word or expression in the right column. Can you find the phrases that mean *I am* and *you are*?

1 io
2 tu
3 io
4 Napoli
5 Venezia e Napoli

a sono differenti
b sono Annalisa
c sei italiano?
d sono di Napoli
e è una bella città

Saying who you are and where you are from

In Italian, there are two ways of giving your name: io mi chiamo (literally: *I am called*) or io sono (*I am*): io mi chiamo Annalisa or io sono Annalisa.

In fact, like in English, the verb essere (*to be*) can be used to express a variety of things, such as:

- where you are from: io sono di Napoli (*I am from Naples*)
- what you do: sei studente, sono professore
- to describe something or someone: l'appartamento è in centro città (*the apartment is in the city center*).

Did you notice that the forms of essere are different, depending on the subject? In English, most verbs only change for the *he/she/it* form (*I know*, *she knows*), but in Italian, the verb changes for each subject. Most verbs are regular and follow a set pattern, but essere is irregular. Look at the forms of essere in the table below. For the moment, just focus on the io, tu, and lui/lei/Lei forms.

essere (*to be*)

I am	io **sono**	*we are*	noi siamo
you are (informal)	tu sei	*you are*	voi siete
he/she is	lui/lei **è**	*they are*	loro **sono**
you are (formal)	Lei **è**		

Note that Italian has two ways of saying *you* when talking to one person: tu (informal) and Lei (formal). Lei is used when addressing someone you're meeting for the first time or don't know well; in business environments, especially with supervisors; and with elders. Tu is used among young people and when addressing children. Tu is increasingly used among adults even on initial meeting, as in a shop or café. Knowing when to use tu and Lei can be challenging, but the rule of thumb is: when in doubt use Lei and wait for someone to suggest diamoci del tu (literally *let's give each other* **tu**). In the conversation, Cristian and Annalisa first use Lei because they don't know each other. Typically, the older person (in this case Annalisa) suggests switching to tu.

For *he* and *she*, the pronouns are lui and lei, respectively. Note that lei meaning she is lowercase, while Lei meaning *you* is capitalized. In Italian there is no neutral pronoun for objects like *it*, and so far, there is no gender-neutral pronoun for people ... but they are working on it! (*They* is loro, but it is not used in the singular.)

Language practice 1

1 Complete the sentences with the correct form of the verb essere and say them out loud.

- **a** Ciao! Io .... Chiara!
- **b** Ma tu .... di Milano?
- **c** Io .... di Roma.
- **d** Buongiorno, signora, Lei .... italiana?
- **e** Roma .... una bella città.
- **f** Io .... [nome e cognome].
- **g** Io .... di [città].
- **h** Gina .... di Napoli.
- **i** Tu .... di New York.

2 Give it a try! Tu or Lei? How would you greet...

- **a** your mother-in-law when you two first meet?
- **b** your teacher (imagine you are a schoolchild)?
- **c** the operator of a call center?
- **d** a waiter who looks in their early twenties (and you are of the same age)?
- **e** your line manager, who is younger than you?
- **f** someone in the club where you are dancing?

3 Now use essere to say your name and where you are from. You can also say that you are a student of Italian—studente d'italiano!

LANGUAGE BUILDER 2

Language discovery 2

00.05 **Listen to the conversation again without looking at the text and repeat each line in the pauses provided. Try to imitate the phrasing and intonation you hear. Can you figure out how to spell Cristian's name?**

Spelling your name in Italian: the alphabet

In Italian, to ask someone to spell a word, say Come si scrive? (*How is it written?*). Italian is a phonetic language, with not much difference between the sound and the spelling of words. However, especially when speaking on the phone, people indicate the lettere (*letters*) of the alphabet using the names of cities or words that start with that letter: M (emme) come Milano.

00.06 Listen to the alfabeto (alphabet) below and note how the letters are pronounced.

ALFABETO ITALIANO

Lettera	Pronuncia (pronunciation)	Città / Oggetto	Lettera	Pronuncia (pronunciation)	Città / Oggetto
A, a	a	come Ancona	N, n	enne	come Napoli
B, b	bi	come Bari	O, o	o	come Otranto
C, c	ci	come Como	P, p	pi	come Palermo
D, d	di	come Domodossola	Q, q	cu	come Quarto
E, e	e	come Empoli	R, r	erre	come Roma
F, f	effe	come Firenze	S, s	esse	come Sassari
G, g	gi	come Genova	T, t	ti	come Torino
H, h	acca	come hotel	U, u	u	come Udine
I, I	i	come Imola	V, v	vu/vi	come Venezia
J, j	i lunga	come jolly	W, w	vu/vi doppia	come Washington
K, k	cappa	come kursal	X, x	ics	come xilofono
L, l	elle	come Livorno	Y, y	ipsilon	come yogurt
M, m	emme	come Milano	Z, z	zeta	come Zar

As you can see, almost all the terms are Italian cities, except for j, k, w, x, and y, which are not Italian letters and have been added to the alphabet only in recent years.

Introduce yourself in Italian and say where you are from. Come si scrive? Practice spelling your name, last name, and the city you are from.

CULTURE POINT 2

Le città d'Italia *Cities of Italy*

Now that you are familiar with Italy's regions, let's get to know some of the major città (*cities*). Roma (*Rome*) is the capital, and it is one of the oldest capitals in the world, as well as the biggest city in Italy. Milano is the second largest, and it is the capital of industry and fashion. Venezia (*Venice*) is a magical city built on a lagoon. Other famous cities include Firenze (*Florence*) and Napoli (*Naples*). However, almost all Italian cities are ancient, with a historical and picturesque centro (*city center*) featuring a main piazza (*square*) and old vie (*streets*) often built during the Roman Empire or the Middle Ages.

Rome was not always the capital of Italy. When Italy became a unified country in 1861, the first capital was Torino (*Turin*) and then Firenze. Roma was annexed in 1871, when it became the capital of the Kingdom of Italy, and, in 1946, of the Repubblica Italiana (*The Italian Republic*), which is the official name of Italy.

VOCABULARY BUILDER 2

00.07

Look at the words and phrases and complete the missing English words and expressions. Then listen and try to imitate the pronunciation of the speakers.

NUMERI DA 1 A 10	*NUMBERS FROM 1 TO 10*
1 uno	*one*
2 due	*two*
3 tre	*three*
4 quattro	*four*
5 cinque	*five*
6 sei	*six*
7 sette	*seven*
8 otto	*eight*
9 nove	*nine*
10 dieci	*ten*

INFORMAZIONI IMPORTANTI: INDIRIZZO E NUMERO DI TELEFONO	*IMPORTANT INFORMATION: ADDRESS AND PHONE NUMBER*
dove	*where*
quale	*which*
appartamento	....
Qual è il tuo indirizzo?	*What is your address?*
via	*street*
piazza	*square*
coinquilino/coinquilina	*roommate* (masculine/feminine)
io abito	*I live* (I reside)
Qual è il tuo numero di telefono?	*What is your phone number?*
Puoi/Può ripetere?	*Could you repeat?* (informal/formal)
senti	*listen*
Noi siamo in due.	*It's two of us.*
da solo (masculine) / da sola (feminine)	*on one's own*

Vocabulary practice 2

00.08

Write down the numbers you hear. Then practice saying them out loud.

a .... d ....

b .... e ....

c .... f ....

CONVERSATION 2

Indirizzo e numero di telefono *Your address and phone number*

00.09

1 Listen to the conversation without looking at the text. How much can you understand? Play it a few times and see whether you can make out a few new words and phrases each time. Then listen to the conversation again and answer the questions below.

After agreeing to share the apartment with Annalisa, on his way back Cristian meets a friend he had not seen in a long time, Matteo. He lives in Mestre, the "new" part of Venice on the mainland. They decide to go for a drink in one of the pubs of Venice, and they talk about Cristian's new living arrangements. Pay attention to how they say their address and how Matteo asks for Cristian's phone number.

Matteo Dove è l'appartamento?

Cristian È in centro città, in via Garibaldi 10.

Matteo Wow! Io abito a Venezia, ma a Mestre, in piazza Ferretto 7.

Cristian Da solo?

Matteo No, siamo in due, io e il mio coinquilino Giorgio, uno studente di Napoli.

Cristian Ah! Annalisa, la mia coinquilina, è di Napoli.

Matteo Interessante! Senti, quale è il tuo numero di telefono?

Cristian 3-3-9-1-8-7-9-4-2-0.

Matteo Un momento... puoi ripetere?

Cristian 3-3-9-1-8-7-9-4-2-0.

2 Answer the questions.

a Who is Giorgio?
b Where is Cristian going to live?
c Where do Italians normally put the house number in the address?

LANGUAGE BUILDER 3

Language discovery 3

Complete the sentences from the conversation with the missing words. When do we use a or in? When do we use di?

a L'appartamento è .... via Garibaldi, 10.
b Io abito .... Mestre.
c Annalisa è .... Napoli.

Saying where you live

The preposition a means *to* or *in*, and is used to say which city you live in:

Io abito a Roma. *I live in Rome.*

But when you want to say which city you are *from*, use di:

Io sono di Roma. *I am from Rome.*

To say an address, use the preposition in followed by via or piazza and the house number. Notice the different word order in Italian: the house number comes after the street name.

Io abito in via Bellini 9. *I live at 9 Bellini Street.*

Language practice 3

1 Create three sentences using the words below. You can use some words more than once.

abito	io	a	via	Venezia	da solo	sette
Garibaldi	tu	Napoli	di	sei	in	

....

....

....

LANGUAGE BUILDER 4

Language discovery 4

00.10

Listen to the conversation again and repeat each line in the pauses provided. Try to imitate the phrasing and intonation you hear. Then match the questions from the conversation with the answers.

a Dove è l'appartamento?
b Da solo?
c Quale è il tuo numero di telefono?

1 No, siamo in due.
2 3-3-9-1-8-7-9-4-2-0
3 È in centro città, in via Garibaldi 10.

What do dove and quale mean?

Asking questions

When asking yes/no questions in Italian, you can simply raise your voice at the end of the sentence:

Tu sei studente?	*Are you a student?*

For information questions, use a question word, like dove (*where*), quale (*which, what*) or come (*how*), at the beginning of the sentence.

Come stai?	*How are you?*
Dove abiti?	*Where do you live?*
Quale è l'indirizzo?	*What is the address?*

Language practice 4

1 Complete the following sentences with the appropriate question word.

a .... abiti? – Io abito a Roma.
b .... è il tuo indirizzo? – Via Garibaldi 10.
c .... è Venezia? – In Italia.
d .... si scrive? – I-T-A-L-I-A.

00.11

2 Now play Conversation 1 again, but this time play Cristian's role. Say your address. Say where Annalisa is from. Substitute Cristian's number with yours or any number. Speak in the pauses provided. Try not to refer to the text.

SKILL BUILDER

1 Decide if the following parts of conversation are formal (F) or informal (I).

a Buongiorno, professoressa! F I
b Arrivederci, Signor Rossi! F I
c Ma tu sei italiano? F I
d Lei è di Napoli? F I
e Io abito a Venezia e tu? F I
f Qual è il tuo numero di telefono? F I
g Come stai? F I
h Come sta? F I
i Bene, grazie, e Lei? F I

2 Complete the sentences with sei, è, or sono.

a Cristian, tu .... studente?
b Io .... studente di italiano.
c Io sono di Roma, e Lei .... di Milano?
d .... italiano.
e L'appartamento .... a Venezia.

00.12

3 Write the phone numbers you hear.

a ....
b ....
c ....
d ....
e ....

TEST YOURSELF

Correct the mistakes in the sentences.

a Io abito in Roma.

....

b Io abito a via Garibaldi 7.

....

c Dove è il tuo numero di telefono?

....

d Ciao, signora Rossi!

....

e Io abito di piazza Ferretto.

....

f Lei sei italiano?

....

Before you move on to Unit 1, assess your progress using the **My review** section on page xviii, and reflect on your learning experience with the **My takeaway** section available online.

1

In this unit you will learn how to:

» Talk about where you are from and the languages you speak.
» Say how old you are using the verb **avere**.
» Briefly introduce someone you know.

Amici

My study plan

I plan to work with Unit 1

○ Every day
○ Twice a week
○ Other ___________

I plan to study for

○ 5–15 minutes
○ 15–30 minutes
○ 30–45+ minutes

My progress tracker

Day / Date	Listening	Speaking	Reading	Writing	Conversation
	○	○	○	○	○
	○	○	○	○	○
	○	○	○	○	○
	○	○	○	○	○
	○	○	○	○	○
	○	○	○	○	○
	○	○	○	○	○

My goals

What do you want to be able to do or say in Italian when you complete this unit?

		Done
1	....	○
2	....	○
3	....	○

My review

SELF CHECK

	I can ...
●	... say my nationalit(ies) and the language(s) I speak.
●	... say how old I am and ask someone for their age.
●	... briefly introduce someone and say where they are from.
●	... briefly introduce someone and say where they live and work.
●	... ask simple questions regarding people's basic biographical information.

CULTURE POINT 1

Lingue e dialetti d'Italia *Languages and dialects of Italy*

Italian is the lingua nazionale (*national language*) of Italy, San Marino, The Vatican City, and Switzerland, as well as a lingua ufficiale (*official language*) of some parts of Slovenia and Croatia. There are also other languages spoken within Italy: tedesco (*German*), francese (*French*), and sloveno (*Slovenian*), to name a few. Moreover, Italian has a great variety of dialetti (*dialects*), making it one of the richest countries in Europe in terms of linguistic diversity. These dialetti were widely spoken until the end of the nineteenth century, when Italy was unified politically and the Tuscan dialetto was chosen as the lingua nazionale: Italian. These dialects are still spoken today, and they are very different from each other. For example, the word bambino (*child*) is nennillo in Neapolitan dialect and toseto in Venetian dialect. Due to the influence dialetti have on how Italian is pronounced locally, it is possible to pinpoint the origin of an Italian speaker with a precision of a 50 km radius!

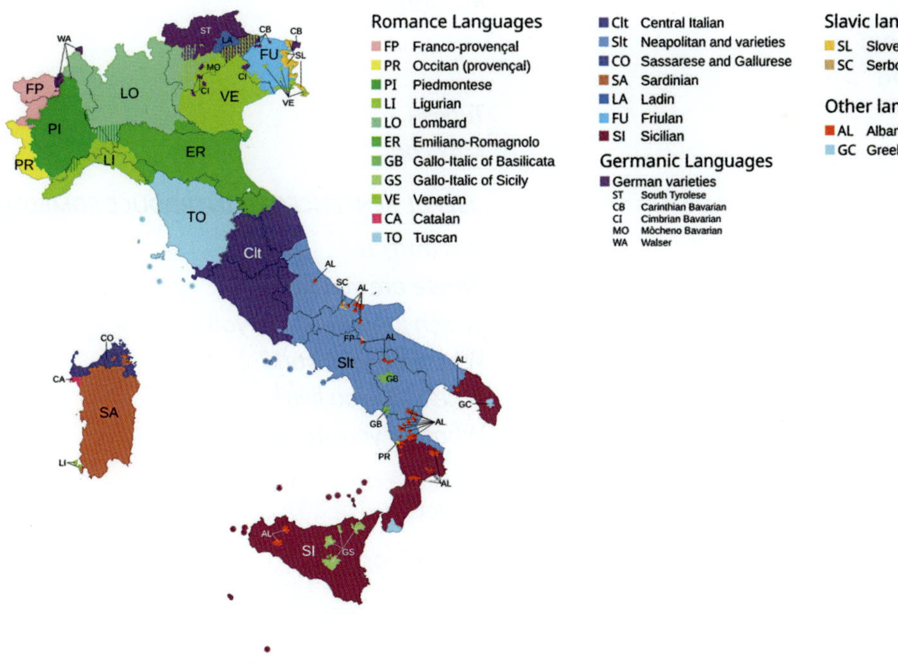

Look at the map and find the following information:

a three minority languages spoken in Italy

b where francese (*French*) is spoken

c where greco (*Greek*) is spoken

Learn more about Italian dialects by scanning the QR code.

VOCABULARY BUILDER 1

01.01

Look at the words and phrases and complete the missing English words and expressions. Then listen and try to imitate the pronunciation of the speakers.

NAZIONALITÀ E LINGUE	*NATIONALITIES AND LANGUAGES*
statunitense	*from the United States*
argentino/a	*Argentinian*
brasiliano/a	*Brazilian*
cinese	*Chinese*
francese	....
giapponese	*Japanese*
britannico/a / inglese	*British/English*
marocchino/a	*Moroccan*
portoghese	*Portuguese*
russo/russa	*Russian*
spagnolo/a	....
tedesco/a	....
turco/a	*Turkish*
messicano/a	*Mexican*

FRASI UTILI PER PRESENTARE UNA PERSONA	*USEFUL SENTENCES TO INTRODUCE SOMEONE*
questo/a è...	*this (m/f) is ...*
Di dove sei?	*Where are you from?*
Quali lingue parli?	*Which languages do you speak?*
Dove lavori?	*Where do you work?*
Dove abiti?	*Where do you live?*
Cosa studi?	*What do you study?*
studente/studentessa	.... *(m/f)*
università	*university*

For more nationalities, see the dedicated table in the Glossary.

Vocabulary practice 1

1 Give the nationality corresponding to the città capitale.

a Lisbona
b Berlino
c Londra
d Mosca
e Washington, D.C.
f Tokyo
g Lima
h Camberra
i Istanbul
j Atene
k Toronto
l Città del Messico

2 And you? Where are you from? What language do you speak?

Pronunciation practice

01.02

1 Listen to the following words. Note how the underlined syllables are pronounced.

argentino	portoghese	giapponese	ghepardo
leggere	spaghetti	gelato	funghi

G + I is pronounced like English *jig*. G + H + I is pronounced like English *gig*.

G + E is pronounced like English *gem*. G + H + E is pronounced like English *gherkin*.

2 Practice pronouncing the following words.

a giraffa	**d** leghe	**g** aghi
b ginnastica	**e** angelo	**h** formaggio
c geometria	**f** ghiro	**i** ghetto

CONVERSATION 1

Fotografia di gruppo *Group photograph*

01.03

1 Listen to the conversation without looking at the text. How much can you understand? Play it a few times and see whether you can make out a few new words and phrases each time. Then listen to the conversation again and follow along in the text.

Cristian is getting settled in the apartment. As he is passionate about storia dell'arte (*art history*) he is putting up posters of famous paintings, as well as fotografie (*photos*) of his amici (*friends*). Annalisa knocks on his door to check if he needs help. She sees the pictures and is a little curious about a picture with a very diverse (= vario) group of young people. Let's hear some bits of their conversation. Pay attention to how Cristian introduces his friends. Also pay attention to where each of the friends is from and where they currently live.

Annalisa Sono amici dell'università?

Cristian Sì, questa è la foto di gruppo dell'università.

Annalisa Ah!

Cristian Questo è Matteo, lui vive a Mestre. Questa è Martina, è tedesca, di Bonn, ma abita a Madrid. E questo è Ahmed, è marocchino ma vive e lavora in Italia.

Annalisa È un gruppo molto vario!

Cristian Sì, siamo di nazionalità differenti. Questo è James, lui è inglese, ma ora studia a New York. Ah, e questa è Hongfen, lei è cinese. Parla quattro lingue: cinese, italiano, inglese, francese. E legge anche il greco!

Annalisa Fenomenale! Senti, ma tu studi o lavori?

Cristian Io lavoro. Insegno storia dell'arte.

2 True or false? Vero o falso?

a	Cristian è studente.	vero	falso
b	Martina è spagnola.	vero	falso
c	James è studente.	vero	falso
d	Hongfen è poliglotta.	vero	falso

LANGUAGE BUILDER 1

Language discovery 1

Look at the conversation and complete the endings of the words. What do you notice? Why is the ending different? What ending do we use with a female or a male person?

a Quest .... è Matteo. Lui vive a Mestre.
b Quest.................... è Martina, lei è tedesc...
c Quest .... è James, lui è ingles...
d Quest .... è Hongfen, lei è cines...

Italian words have a gender!

Did you figure out when to use questo or questa? When we indicate someone or something that is nearby, we use the word questo/a (this). Unlike in English, Italian words (nouns and adjectives) take a gender: they can be either feminine or masculine. As a general rule, masculine nouns and adjectives end in -o and feminine in -a: italiano/italiana.

Adjectives ending in -e can be either masculine or feminine: James è inglese. Amy è inglese. For nouns ending in -e, it's best to learn the gender together with the noun.

There is an ongoing debate in Italian society concerning what to use when someone's gender is nonbinary, or when we do not want to specify the gender. Many ideas have been put forward. For written language, people replace the last vowel with an *. Example: messican*. In spoken language, there still isn't a consensus on whether to use the vowel u or add a new vowel, the schwa **= ə**. -*/u/ə

Masculine	Feminine	Nonbinary
-o (italiano)	-a (italiana)	-*/ u/ ə
-e (inglese)	-e (inglese)	

Language practice 1

Complete the sentences with the correct form of questo. Then add the nationality and remember that it should agree in gender with the person it describes.

a Quest .... è Pablo. È ...., di Madrid. (use neutral gender ending)
b Quest .... è Yuko. Lei è di Tokyo. Lei è ....
c Quest .... è Magali. Lei è ...., di Parigi.
d Quest .... è Hans. Lui è di Berlino. Lui è ....
e Quest .... è Kathleen. Lei è ...., di Toronto.
f Quest .... è David. Lui è ...., di New York.
g Quest .... è Aicha. Lei è ...., di Marrakesh.

LANGUAGE BUILDER 2

Language discovery 2

01.04

Listen to the conversation again and repeat each line in the pauses. Try to imitate the phrasing and intonation you hear. Then look at the phrases from the conversation. Notice the verb endings and how they change with the subject. Can you identify a pattern?

Matteo vive a Mestre.
Martina abita a Madrid.
Ahmed vive e lavora in Italia.
Tu studi o lavori?
Io insegno storia dell'arte.
Hongfen parla 4 lingue.

Actions in the present: regular verbs

Verbs contain many pieces of information. They tell what is happening, when it is happening, and who is doing it. Compare: she lives in Venice with I live in Naples. English verbs don't change very much to show who is performing the action, so the subject needs to be specified. In Italian, however, the verb itself can tell you just about everything you need to know, so typically the subject pronoun is not even needed.

Regular Italian verbs fall into three groups determined by the ending of the infinitive (the basic form of the verb, such as *to hide, to run, to think*): -are, -ere, or -ire. To change the form according to the subject, drop the -are, -ere or -ire ending and replace it with a personal ending: parlare → parl- → io parlo.

Each group has its own rules, but the first two are very similar.

lavorare (*to work*) and vivere (*to live*)

	Lavorare	Vivere		Lavorare	Vivere
io	lavor-**o**	viv-**o**	noi	lavor-**iamo**	viv-**iamo**
tu	lavor-**i**	viv-**i**	voi	lavor-**ate**	viv-**ete**
lui/lei	lavor-**a**	viv-**e**	loro	lavor-**ano**	viv-**ono**

Some common regular -are and -ere verbs are:

vivere	*to live*	parlare	*to speak*
leggere	*to read*	insegnare	*to teach*
studiare	*to study*		

Language practice 2

1 Complete these sets of sentences. Say the verbs out loud.

a IO

1 Io parl .... inglese e tedesco
2 Io mi chiam .... Mary.
3 Io viv .... a Venezia
4 Io legg .... un'e-mail.
5 Io abit .... in via Garibaldi 10.
6 Io studi .... a New York.

b TU

1 Tu lavor .... all'università?
2 Tu parl .... inglese?
3 Tu abit .... in piazza Ferretto?
4 Tu viv .... a Roma?
5 Tu legg .... l'e-mail?

c VOI

1 Voi parl .... inglese?
2 Voi lavor .... ?
3 Voi abit .... a Mestre?

d LUI/LEI

1 Yuko parl .... giapponese.
2 James lavor .... a Londra.
3 Matteo viv .... a Mestre.
4 Hongfen legg .... il greco.
5 Martina abit .... a Madrid.
6 Pablo studi .... storia dell'arte.

e NOI

1 Noi lavor ....
2 Noi parl .... inglese.
3 Noi abit .... in piazza Ferretto.
4 Noi viv .... in Italia.
5 Noi legg .... un'email.

f LORO

1 Loro parl .... Italiano.
2 Loro viv .... a Londra.
3 Yuko e James lavor .... a New York.

01.05

2 Now play Conversation 1 again, but this time you will play Cristian's role. Speak in the pauses provided. Introduce some people you know (or fictional) from various countries.

CULTURE POINT 2

Arte e antiquariato in Italia *Arts and antiques in Italy*

Italy has the largest number of UNESCO sites in the world: cinquantotto (*fifty-eight*). Italy's natural and cultural wealth is immeasurable, including archeological sites and unique monuments. Indeed, in 2018, sessantadue (*sixty-two*) million tourists visited Italy—more than Italy's total population of cinquantanove (*fifty-nine*) million.

Most artistic treasures such as quadri (*paintings*) or sculture (*sculptures*) are on display, but many are also stored in the basements of galleries and museums (as there just isn't enough space!) or they lay undiscovered in old mansions or people's soffitte (*attics*). Therefore, if you visit one of the mercati dell'antiquariato (*antiques markets*) taking place weekly in almost all Italian cities, and you are lucky, you can go home with a valuable piece of art or antique furniture.

Napoli

Look at the list of UNESCO sites in Italy and answer the questions.

a Annalisa è di Napoli. Which UNESCO sites did she grow up next to?
b Which mountains are the UNESCO area that Cristian comes from?
c Which cities have a historical center that is part of UNESCO?

VOCABULARY BUILDER 2

01.06

Look at the words and phrases and listen, then try to imitate the pronunciation of the speakers.

NUMERI DA 11 A 100	*NUMBERS FROM 11 TO 100*
11 undici	*eleven*
12 dodici	*twelve*
13 tredici	*thirteen*
14 quattordici	*fourteen*
15 quindici	*fifteen*
16 sedici	*sixteen*
17 diciassette	*seventeen*
18 diciotto	*eighteen*
19 diciannove	*nineteen*
20 venti	*twenty*
30 trenta	*thirty*
40 quaranta	*forty*
50 cinquanta	*fifty*
60 sessanta	*sixty*
70 settanta	*seventy*
80 ottanta	*eighty*
90 novanta	*ninety*
100 cento	*hundred*

DESCRIVERE QUALCOSA/QUALCUNO	*DESCRIBING SOMETHING/SOMEONE*
avere	*to have*
Quanti anni hai?	*How old are you?* (lit. *How many years do you have?*)
Io ho.... anni.	*I'm ... years old.* (lit. *I have ... years*)
Quanto costa?	*How much does it cost?*

Vocabulary practice 2

01.07

Listen and mark the number you hear.

a 24 75 44
b 56 97 18
c 17 61 89
d 16 19 32
e 38 41 28
f 58 71 12

01.08

Now play the audio and repeat the numbers. To say a specific two-digit number, just add the unit, as you would do in English. For example: 62 = sessanta + due = sessantadue.

Notice that when the first digit ends in a vowel and the second one begins with a vowel, you drop the first vowel: 88 = ottanta + otto = ottantotto

CONVERSATION 2

La misteriosa donna in soffitta *The mysterious woman in the attic*

01.09

1 Here are some words and phrases to help you understand the conversation.

quadro	*painting*	stile	*style*
antico	*ancient*	secondo me	*in my opinion*
sguardo	*look*		

01.10

2 Listen to the conversation without looking at the text. How much can you understand? Play it a few times and see whether you can make out a few new words and phrases each time. Then listen to the conversation again and follow along in the text. Pay attention to how the characters ask someone's age and say how old they are.

Always the passionate art historian, Cristian has discovered a quadro in soffitta (*painting* in the *attic*). Hiding behind a pile of old suitcases, it is the portrait of a woman with an undefinable sguardo (*look*), painted in barocco (*Baroque*) style. Now he is very curious to discover the identity of the woman portrayed. First, he asks Annalisa. Vediamo (*Let's take a look*)!

Cristian	Chi è la signora nel quadro in soffitta?
Annalisa	Quale quadro? Non ho idea!
Cristian	È un quadro antico. Ha uno stile barocco. La signora è spagnola, o italiana.
Annalisa	Sono curiosa! Vediamo!
	They go up to the attic.
Annalisa	È probabilmente una signora veneziana. Quanti anni ha?
Cristian	Mm, secondo me ha venti o trenta anni.
Annalisa	Sì, anche secondo me. Ha uno sguardo misterioso, enigmatico...
Cristian	Sì, come la Monnalisa di Leonardo.
Annalisa	Sì. E... tu quanti anni hai?
Cristian	Io ho 29 anni. E tu?
Annalisa	Io ho 33 anni.

3 Complete the summary of the conversation with the missing words.

La signora del quadro è probabilmente spagnola o **a** .... o veneziana. Come la Monnalisa di Leonardo, la signora ha uno sguardo **b** .... ed enigmatico. Secondo Annalisa e Cristian la signora ha **c** .... o trenta anni.

Look at the woman in the painting. Help Annalisa and Cristian solve the mystery of her identity. At the end of each unit you will have a question to answer. The first letter of the solution will give you one letter in the name of the woman in the attic. Each time you find the answer you're looking for, note the first letter on page 296.

LANGUAGE BUILDER 3

Language discovery 3

Find the three phrases in the conversation that are used to give your age. What do you notice about the verb? Is it essere?

a .... **b** .... **c** ....

Saying how old you are with the verb avere (*to have*)

In English, to say someone's age, the verb *to be* is used: *I am 35 years old.* In Italian, however, people *have* so many years: io ho 35 anni—*I "have" 35 years.*

The verb avere (*to have*), like essere, is irregular and it is a case of simply memorizing the forms. The good news is that, like essere, it is used quite often, and there is plenty of opportunity for practice! For the moment, say the verbs out loud. Remember that the h is silent in Italian.

avere (*to have*)

io	(non) ho	noi	(non) abbiamo
tu	(non) hai	noi	(non) avete
lui/lei/Lei	(non) ha	lloro	(non) hanno

Of course, avere can be used to talk about other things, not just age:

Cristian ha un amico a Mestre.	*Cristian has a friend in Mestre.*
Annalisa ha un computer.	*Annalisa has a computer.*

Language practice 3

Complete the following sentences with the correct form of the verb avere.

a Scusi, signora, Lei quanti anni ....?

b Senti, tu quanti anni .... ?

c L'Italia .... cinquantotto siti UNESCO.

d Noi .... un quadro antico in soffitta.

e Voi non .... idea.

f La signora .... quarantadue anni.

g Annalisa e Cristian .... trentatre e ventinove anni, rispettivamente.

h Ogni anno (every year), l'Italia .... circa sessantadue milioni di turisti.

To make a negative statement in Italian, simply put non before the verb: Io non ho idea.

LANGUAGE BUILDER 4

Language discovery 4

01.11

Listen to the conversation again and repeat each line in the pauses provided. Try to imitate the phrasing and intonation you hear. Then complete the sentences.

a È .... quadro antico.

b È probabilmente .... signora veneziana.

c Ha .... stile barocco.

d Ha .... sguardo misterioso, enigmatico.

What form of un do we use with feminine words? What about masculine words?

Indefinite articles (un, una)

The indefinite article (*a/an*) is used to talk about things in a general way: *a book*, *an apple*. In Italian, articles, like nouns and adjectives, have a gender, and they agree with the noun:

Ho un amico a Mestre.	*I have a (male) friend in Mestre.*
Ho una coinquilina di Napoli.	*I have a (female) roommate from Naples.*

When the following word starts with a vowel, una takes an apostrophe: un'italiana. Likewise, before a consonant combination starting with s or p (or with an x, y, ps or gn), un becomes uno to make pronunciation easier: uno sguardo.

un	masculine words starting with vowel or simple consonant: un abito, un italiano	**una**	feminine words starting with consonant: una signora
uno	masculine words starting with s + consonant, p + consonant, x, y, gn, ps: uno stile, uno gnu, uno yogurt	**un'**	feminine words starting with a vowel: un'italiana

Language practice 4

Look at the words. Say what you have or you don't have for each item listed, following the model.

Example: amico americano → *Io (non) ho un amico americano.*

a macchina (car, fem.)
b computer (masc.)
c studio (study room, masc.)
d quadro (masc.)
e appartamento (masc.)
f sguardo (masc.)
g Coinquilino (masc.)
h fotografia di abor (fem.)

SKILL BUILDER

1 In the sentences below there is something missing: either a word .... or the ending of a word .... Complete them.

a Maria è portoghes ....
b .... anni hai?
c Quest .... è Chiara, una studentessa italiana.
d Jenny .... inglese e francese.
e Noi abit .... in Italia.
f Io ho .... computer Apple.
g Carlos lavor... a Madrid.
h Yuko .... giapponese.
i Matteo e Giorgio viv .... a Mestre.
j Secondo me, Elisa .... 25 anni.

2 Complete the questions with the question words from the box. You can use some more than once.

quanti	chi	dove	quali

a .... è l'appartamento?
b .... anni hai?
c .... abiti?
d .... è Yuko? Yuko è un'amica giapponese.
e Di .... sei? Io sono di Roma.
f .... lingue parli? Io parlo inglese e italiano.

01.12

3 Listen to these people talking and complete the sentences.

a Buongiorno, io sono Pablo e ho .... anni.
b Pablo è .... studente spagnolo.
c Scusi, Lei quanti anni ....?
d Io ho .... amica portoghese.

TEST YOURSELF

1 **Read the social media profiles and decide if the statements are true (vero) or false (falso).**

Habib ...

Ciao amic*! Io mi chiamo Habib e sono nigeriano. Ho ventisei anni e sono uno studente all'università.

Sylvia ...

Io sono Sylvia e sono di Marrakech ma vivo a Roma. Ho trentaquattro anni e ho un ristorante.

Alejandra ...

Buongiorno! Mi chiamo Alejandra e sono messicana. Abito a Venezia con un'amica.

Shuangyu ...

Ciao, mi chiamo Shuangyu. Ho quarantadue anni. Ho molti amici italiani. Sono professore.

a	Habib lavora.	vero	falso
b	Sylvia è marocchina.	vero	falso
c	Alejandra abita da sola.	vero	falso
d	Shuangyu lavora.	vero	falso

2 **Look at the picture below and describe the people you see. Make up their names and nationalities, e.g. Questa è Maria. Lei è italiana.**

3 **Introduce a famous person that you admire in Italian. Use this template:**

This is ... He/she is + nationality, city of origin. He/she lives in + city of residence. Invent an address. Say how old they are.

La misteriosa donna in soffitta *The mysterious woman in the attic*

Look again at the list of UNESCO heritage sites in Italy using the QR code in Culture Point 1.

What is the name of the volcano/mountain that is included in the list? The first letter will begin forming the name of the woman in the attic on page 12.

Before you move on to the next unit, assess your progress using the **My review** section on the first page of the unit, and reflect on your learning experience with the **My takeaway** section available online.

In this unit you will learn how to:

» Tell others what you do for a living and where you work.
» Name jobs and professions.
» Talk about your hobbies and free time.

2

Lavoro e passioni

My study plan

I plan to work with Unit 2

○ Every day
○ Twice a week
○ Other ___________

I plan to study for

○ 5–15 minutes
○ 15–30 minutes
○ 30–45+ minutes

My progress tracker

Day / Date	Listening	Speaking	Reading	Writing	Conversation
	○	○	○	○	○
	○	○	○	○	○
	○	○	○	○	○
	○	○	○	○	○
	○	○	○	○	○
	○	○	○	○	○
	○	○	○	○	○

My goals

What do you want to be able to do or say in Italian when you complete this unit?

		Done
1	....	○
2	....	○
3	....	○

My review

SELF CHECK

	I can ...
●	... say what my job is and ask others about their jobs.
●	... tell people where I work.
●	... describe what other people do for a living and where they work.
●	... say what I do in my free time.
●	... briefly describe someone else's hobbies and activities in their free time.

CULTURE POINT 1

Bonus cultura per i giovani *Culture bonus for young people*

Italians are passionate about hobbies that reflect their vibrant culture and love for socializing. Cucinare (*cooking*) and enjoying meals with family and friends are central to Italian life, with many embracing the art of preparing traditional dishes. Calcio (*soccer*) is another major pastime, whether playing or cheering for local and national teams. Italians also have a deep appreciation for arte (*art*), storia (*history*), and architettura (*architecture*), often spending weekends exploring museums, historical sites, or nearby countryside.

To further nurture this cultural engagement, especially among the younger generation, the Italian government has introduced an exciting initiative. The Bonus Cultura (*culture bonus*) is a voucher of 500 euros that Italian teenagers can receive once they turn eighteen years old. They can spend the voucher on several attività culturali (*cultural activities*) listed on the initiative's website "18app.italia.it." These attività include biglietti (*tickets*) for cinema (*cinemas*), teatri (*theatres*), musei (*museums*), concerti (*concerts*), and many other cultural events. With the voucher you can also purchase libri (*books*), giornali (*newspapers*), and musica (*music*).

Check out the official *Bonus Cultura* website. They have listed various activities and events you can book with the voucher. You might already recognize some of them. If you had the 500 euros of the *Bonus Cultura*, which ones would you like to book?

VOCABULARY BUILDER 1

Look at the words and phrases and complete the missing English words and expressions. Then listen and try to imitate the pronunciation of the speakers.

COSA FAI NEL TEMPO LIBERO?	*WHAT DO YOU DO IN YOUR FREE TIME?*
ballare	....
dormire	*to sleep*
fare una passeggiata	*to go for a walk*
fare sport	....
giocare a...	*to play (a sport or games)*
guardare un film/una serie	*to watch a film/a series*
leggere	*to read*
suonare	*to play (an instrument)*
riposare	*to rest*
fare scrolling sui social	....
uscire	*to go out*
amare	*to love*
capire	*to understand*
preferire	....

OGGETTI PER IL TEMPO LIBERO	*ITEMS FOR YOUR FREE TIME*
il cinema	....
il concerto	....
la galleria	....
il libro	*book*
la musica	....
il teatro	....
la passeggiata	*walk/stroll*
la pallavolo	*volleyball*
il calcio	*football/soccer*
i videogiochi	*video games*
lo scrolling	*scrolling*

Vocabulary practice 1

Select the correct verb to complete the sentence.

a Costanza mangia / dorme / legge un libro.

b Lucia e Paola suonano / ballano / giocano a calcio.

c Lui dorme / mangia / legge un panino.

d Noi balliamo / riposiamo / guardiamo un film

e Facciamo / suoniamo / capiamo una passeggiata?

CONVERSATION 1

Hai piani? *Do you have plans?*

02.02

1 Here are a few words and expressions to help you understand the following conversation. Note their meanings.

noioso	*boring*	abbastanza	*enough*
qualcosa	*something*	altro	*other things*
C'è una festa anni '80.	*There is an '80s party night.*	forse	*maybe*

02.03

2 Listen to the conversation without looking at the text. How much can you understand? Play it a few times and see whether you can make out a few new words and phrases each time. Then listen again and read the text.

Annalisa's friend Aicha is in town and they are getting ready for il fine settimana (*the weekend*). Cristian is in his room trying to decipher more information about the mysterious painting he found in the attic. Suddenly the girls knock at his door and try to get him engaged with their piani (*plans*). Listen to how they talk about free time, interests, and activities.

Annalisa Cristian, hai piani per questo fine settimana?

Cristian No, studio e lavoro. Forse gioco a Dungeons & Dragons con Matteo...

Annalisa Noioso! Noi giochiamo a pallavolo e poi... discoteca! C'è una festa anni '80.

Cristian Mmmm, io non amo ballare, preferisco i libri e le gallerie d'arte.

Annalisa Aicha! Incredibile, Cristian preferisce i libri alla musica!

Cristian No... amo la musica, ovviamente, ma preferisco altro.

Annalisa Certo, capisco. Forse un aperitivo dopo la pallavolo? È abbastanza intellettuale? (ride – *laughs*)

Cristian Ok va bene. Finisco di preparare le lezioni e arrivo.

3 Based on the conversation you have just listened to, what are Annalisa, Aicha, and Cristian doing this weekend?

Annalisa ....

Aicha ....

Cristian ....

LANGUAGE BUILDER 1

Language discovery 1

Look at the conversation again and complete the table with the correct plural form, including the articles, that you can find in the conversation.

Singolare	Plurale
il libro	
la galleria	
la lezione	

Can you see a rule to form the plural of masculine and feminine words?

Plural of nouns

In English, we usually form the plural by adding -s; in Italian the final letter of the word is changed. For masculine words ending in -o the new ending will be an -i (libro-libri). Feminine words ending in -a take the letter -e (galleria-gallerie). Both feminine and masculine words ending in -e change the final letter into -i (il cane-i cani or la lezione-le lezioni).

	Singular	Plural
Masculine	-o	-i
Feminine	-e	-i
	-a	-e

Foreign nouns (*film, cinema*) and nouns with a stress on the final letter (città, caffè) do not change their ending from singular to plural.

Language practice 1

Give the plural of the following words.

a teatro ....

b galleria ....

c concerto ....

d social ....

e passeggiata ....

f televisore ....

g stazione ....

h libro ....

i scrolling ....

LANGUAGE BUILDER 2

Language discovery 2

Listen to the conversation again and repeat each line in the pauses provided. Try to imitate the phrasing and intonation you hear. Then complete the sentences.

a Non amo ballare, ... i libri.

b Cristian .... i libri.

c Certo, ...

It seems we have a new group of verbs! Can you tell the ending of the infinitive?

Verb conjugation, verbs ending in -ire

You're already familiar with regular verbs ending in -are (like amare) and -ere (like vedere). The third group of regular verbs ends in -ire. Good news: verbs ending in -ire are very similar to the verbs in -ere! Only the voi form is different. Try to complete the table based on what you know about -ere verbs.

dormire (*to sleep*)

io	dorm........................	noi	dorm........................
tu	dorm........................	voi	dormi**te**
lui/lei/Lei	dorm........................	loro	dorm........................

Some -ire verbs are a bit special–they insert -isc- between the stem and the endings. The endings are the same as for verbs like dormire, but they have that extra -isc- added in all the singular and the loro forms. The noi and voi forms are regular, with no -isc-. Notice the pattern:

preferire (*to prefer*)

io	prefer**isco**	noi	preferiamo
tu	prefer**isci**	voi	preferite
lui/lei/Lei	prefer**isce**	loro	prefer**iscono**

Verbs like preferire, capire, and finire behave like this.

Certo, capisco. *Of course, I understand.* Finisco le lezioni. *I'll finish the lessons.*

Now that you have seen all three group of verbs in the present tense, have you noticed how the subjects io, tu, and noi have the same endings (-o, -i, -iamo), no matter the group? This might be very handy if you need to use these forms but you don't remember which group the verb belongs to!

Language practice 2

Match the beginning of each sentence with the correct ending in the right column.

1 Pietro e Barbara	**a** dormo sempre la domenica mattina.
2 Io	**b** preferiscono ballare.
3 Clarissa	**c** finiamo gli esercizi di italiano.
4 Tu	**d** capisce bene lo spagnolo.
5 Io e Daniela	**e** capisci l'italiano?

Speaking practice

02.05

Now play Conversation 1 again, but this time play Cristian's role. Speak in the pauses provided and for an extra challenge, tell Aicha and Annalisa your own plans for the weekend instead of Cristian's.

CULTURE POINT 2

L'arte dell'aperitivo *The art of aperitivo*

In Italy, aperitivo (*aperitif*) is that blissful moment between the end of work and dinner. It is a time to catch up with friends and enjoy a nice cocktail while eating some stuzzichini (*nibbles*), like olive (*olives*), patatine (*chips*) or noccioline (*peanuts*). Aperitivo is usually available from about 6 p.m. to 8 p.m., in almost any bar (*café*) in Italy. Some places offer a wider range of food, and the whole experience is then called apericena (*aperi-dinner*). The key to the perfect aperitivo can also be the location itself: perhaps on a balcony overlooking the rooftops of Rome, or along a canal at sunset in Venice. Not bad, right? Nowadays, one of the most popular cocktails for *aperitivo* is (Aperol) Spritz.

Learn how to make the iconic Aperol Spritz and answer the questions.

a How many ingredients do you need to make an Aperol Spritz?
b In which città (*city*) was the drink created?

VOCABULARY BUILDER 2

02.06

Look at the words and phrases and complete the missing English words and expressions. Then listen and try to imitate the pronunciation of the speakers.

PROFESSIONI	***PROFESSIONS***
l'architetto/a	*architect*
l'attore/attrice	....
l'avvocato/a	*lawyer*
il/la cameriere/a	*waiter*
il/la commesso/a	*shop assistant*
il/la dentista	*dentist (m/f)*
il/la dottore/dottoressa	....
il/la fotografo/a	*photographer*
l'ingegnere/a	*engineer*
l'insegnante	*teacher (m/f)*
il/la meccanico/a	....
il/la parrucchiere/a	*hairdresser*
il/la programmatore/programmatrice	*programmer*
lo/la scrittore/scrittrice	*writer*

POSTI DI LAVORO	***JOB PLACES***
il negozio	*shop*
l'officina	*workshop/garage*
l'ospedale	....
il ristorante	....
la scuola	....
lo studio	*study/atelier*
l'ufficio	*office*
lavoro da casa	*remote working*

CHE LAVORO FAI?	***WHAT JOB DO YOU DO?***
faccio il meccanico	*I am a mechanic*
faccio la dentista	*I am a dentist* (f)

Nouns indicating professions might sometimes be irregular with their endings. Some simply end in -o or -e in the masculine and -a in the feminine form, e.g., cuoco, cuoca (cook). Those that end -tore in the masculine usually end in -trice in the feminine (programmatore, programmatrice) and some nouns have the same form for both masculine and feminine (dentista, insegnante). For relatively new professions there is no translation and the English form is used (blogger, content creator, influencer). The best tip is to focus on the professions that you might need more often, like yours and those of your friends and family. With time the other ones will stick, too!

Vocabulary practice 2

Match the professions with the places where people work.

1 Lavora in una scuola.
2 Lavora in un ristorante.
3 Lavora in un'officina.
4 Lavora in un ufficio.
5 Lavora in un negozio.
6 Lavora in uno studio.

a È cameriere/a.
b È insegnante.
c È meccanico/a.
d È commesso/a.
e È programmatore/a.
f È fotografo/a.

Pronunciation practice

02.07

1 Listen to the following words, paying attention to how the underlined syllables are pronounced.

a architetto
b influencer
c programmatrice
d ingegnere
e cameriere
f parrucchiere
g fotografo
h blogger

The Italian *r* sound is rolled on the tongue. This *r* sound is the same sound as the *t* in *water* or *better* pronounced in standard American English. A tip to roll your *r* could be to start from the letter *l* or *d*, placing the top part of your tongue against the palate, and morph it into a rolled *r* by blowing and giving out a sound.

2 Practice pronouncing the following words:

a rosso
b carro
c Andrea
d Trapani
e greco
f giornalista
g carne
h ingrato
i prudenza

Do you feel confident? Why don't you try the following Italian tongue twister?

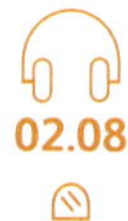
02.08

Trentatré trentini entrarono a Trento tutti e trentatré trotterellando.

Thirty-three Trentonians [people from Trento, an Italian city] came into Trento, all thirty-three trotting.

CONVERSATION 2

E tu, che lavoro fai? *And you, what do you do for work?*

02.09

1 Here are a few words and expressions to help you understand the following conversation. Note their meanings.

bello	*beautiful*	Che vista spettacolare!	*What an amazing view!*
allora	*so …*	anche	*also*
ecco	*here it is/there are*	Facciamo un brindisi!	*Let's make a toast!*

02.10

2 Listen to the conversation without looking at the text. How much can you understand? Play it a few times and see whether you can make out a few new words and phrases each time. Then listen to the conversation again and follow along in the text.

Cristian, Annalisa, and Aicha have decided to have an aperitivo in one of the newest places on the canal, where they can sip un aperitivo while watching the gondole (*gondolas*, typical Venetian boats) pass by. Cristian invited his friend Matteo to join them and while they are waiting for le bevande (*drinks*) to arrive, they start talking about what they do for a living. Pay attention to how they say what they do and where.

Matteo Bello questo bar!

Aicha Sì, che vista spettacolare!

Matteo Allora, Annalisa, che lavoro fai?

Annalisa Faccio l'ingegnera.

Matteo Interessante! Dove lavori?

Annalisa L'ufficio è a Venezia. E tu?

Matteo Io faccio il meccanico, ma l'officina è a Mestre. Sai, i meccanici non lavorano molto a Venezia: loro hanno le gondole! E tu Aicha, studi o lavori?

Aicha Lavoro, faccio la fotografa. Ho lo studio a Milano. E tu Cristian?

Matteo Cristian fa l'insegnante di arte in una scuola. Ha molto talento.

Cristian Grazie! Ecco le bevande, facciamo un brindisi!

3 Match the person with the correct profession.

1 Annalisa	**a** insegnante
2 Aicha	**b** ingegnera
3 Matteo	**c** meccanico
4 Cristian	**d** fotografa

4 Why is Matteo working in Mestre and not in Venice?

LANGUAGE BUILDER 3

Language discovery 3

How do Matteo and Aicha say what they do? What is the word after faccio and before their profession? Why are those words different?

Faccio .... ingegnera. Lavoro, faccio .... fotografa.

Definite articles

You already know the indefinite articles un and una (meaning "a/an"). Italian also has a definite article ("the") which agrees with the noun in gender and number:

	Singular	Plural
Masculine	il	i
Feminine	la	le

Just like in English, it is used when referring to something specific or something that was previously mentioned:

L'ufficio è a Venezia. *The office is in Venice.*

Here, l'ufficio refers specifically to Annalisa's office, not just any office. However, the definite article is used much more often in Italian than in English. Compare:

Loro hanno le gondole. *They have gondolas.*

Ho lo studio a Milano. *My studio is in Milan.*

I parrucchieri non lavorano la domenica. *Hairdressers do not work on Sundays.*

Italian grammar requires the use of definite articles in many situations where English might not need them, for example with general statements such as I parrucchieri non lavorano la domenica. Little by little, you will discover the correct usage in the next units.

Definite articles also change based on the sound of the word that follows.
When the following word starts with a vowel, il and la change to l' (l'insegnante, l'ingegnera); i changes to gli (gli amici). When the following word starts with an s + consonant, or an x, y, z, ps or gn: il changes to lo (lo studio, lo psicologo) and i changes to gli (gli scrittori, gli gnocchi).

Articles are important, since they show the gender of a noun when it is not clear. Think of nouns in -e that can be both masculine and feminine: il cantante, la cantante.

Language practice 3

Insert the proper definite article into the following sentences.

a .... ufficio di Antonio è moderno.

b Noi studiamo in una scuola americana. .... scuola è a Roma.

c .... gatti sono animali indipendenti.

d .... galleria lavora con .... fotografie di Aicha.

e Noi siamo .... attori per questo film.

LANGUAGE BUILDER 4

Language discovery 4

02.11

Listen to the conversation again and repeat each line in the pauses provided. Try to imitate the phrasing and intonation you hear. Then choose the correct form of the verb to complete the sentence.

faccio fa fai

Matteo Allora, Annalisa, che lavoro .... ?

Annalisa .... l'ingegnera.

Matteo Cristian .... l 'insegnante

The verb fare *(to do, to make)*

One of the most important verbs in Italian is the verb fare (*to do, to make*). As seen in the conversation, it's used to state what you do: faccio l'ingenere. Fare is also used in many other very useful idiomatic expressions, which will appear in later units. The verb fare is irregular.

fare (*to do, to make*)

io	faccio	noi	facciamo
tu	fai	voi	fate
lui/lei/Lei	fa	loro	fanno

Notice that in English you also ask *What do you do?* and you "do" a job, but you state your profession with *I am* ... In Italian you can either say faccio la fotografa or sono fotografa.

Language practice 4

Complete the sentences with the correct form of fare.

a Antonio e Luisa, voi che lavoro ....?
b Luca .... il dottore e io .... l'architetta.
c Loro .... un lavoro creativo. Marta .... la content creator e Gianluca .... lo scrittore.
d Andrea, tu .... il cuoco? – No, ... il cameriere.
e (noi) .... un brindisi?
f Che lavoro .... Federico e Fabio?
g Tu e Chiara .... un lavoro bellissimo!
h Ragazzi, (noi) .... un aperitivo?
i No, Ilaria non .... la programmatrice.

Speaking practice

02.12

Now play Conversation 2 again, but this time you will play Annalisa's role. Speak in the pauses provided. Try not to refer to the text and also try to state your own profession and where you work instead of Annalisa's.

SKILL BUILDER

1 You have just registered on an Italian website for language exchange. Create your profile, including basic information about yourself and your hobbies and interests.

....

....

....

02.13

2 Listen to how Cristian describes Matteo and complete with the missing words in the gaps. Then listen again and check if your choices were correct.

MATTEO

Matteo è un ragazzo simpatico. È italiano, di Mestre e **a** .... il meccanico. Siamo **b** .... dall'università, ma oggi lui lavora in **c** .... a Mestre. Matteo parla due lingue, italiano e inglese, ma **d** .... anche **e** .... spagnolo. Matteo ama giocare a D&D con **f** .... amici, suonare la chitarra e guardare Netflix. Quando finisce **g** .... lavoro, nuota, **h** .... una passeggiata o sta sui social. Nel fine settimana non fa molte attività, perché la domenica **i** ....

3 Vero o falso? ***True or false?*** **What have you learned about Matteo from his profile? Read each statement about Matteo, then choose** vero **if it's *true* and** falso **if it's *false*.**

a Matteo fa il meccanico.	vero	falso
b Non parla spagnolo.	vero	falso
c Dopo il lavoro, sta sui social.	vero	falso
d Lavora la domenica.	vero	falso

TEST YOURSELF

1 Change the sentences to the plural (all the elements—verbs, articles, nouns).

Example: Io amo la pizza. *Noi amiamo le pizze.*

1 Io leggo il libro	**a** Noi ....
2 Tu fai l'influencer?	**b** Voi ....
3 Lei preferisce l'ufficio	**c** Loro ....
4 Lui capisce lo spagnolo	**d** Loro ....

2 Find the odd one out.

1 il	**a** libro	**b** parrucchiere	**c** attrice	**d** programmatore
2 lo	**a** autista	**b** studio	**c** psicologo	**d** yogurt
3 la	**a** galleria	**b** lezione	**c** cameriere	**d** blogger
4 l'	**a** amica	**b** commessa	**c** officina	**d** architetta
5 i	**a** francesi	**b** teatro	**c** libri	**d** ristorante
6 gli	**a** fotografi	**b** svizzeri	**c** zuccheri	**d** influencer

La misteriosa donna in soffitta *The mysterious woman in the attic*

Now, go back to the conversation between Annalisa and Cristian. She tells Aicha that he prefers ... something to dancing. The first letter of those items will continue forming the name of the woman in the portrait on page 294.

Before you move on to the next unit, assess your progress using the **My review** section on the first page of the unit, and reflect on your learning experience with the **My takeaway** section available online.

3

In this unit you will learn how to:

» Talk about family using possessive adjectives.

» Describe someone's physical appearance and personality.

» Use the verb **andare**.

Mamma mia!

My study plan

I plan to work with Unit 3

○ Every day

○ Twice a week

○ Other ________

I plan to study for

○ 5–15 minutes

○ 15–30 minutes

○ 30–45+ minutes

My progress tracker

Day / Date	Listening	Speaking	Reading	Writing	Conversation
	○	○	○	○	○
	○	○	○	○	○
	○	○	○	○	○
	○	○	○	○	○
	○	○	○	○	○
	○	○	○	○	○
	○	○	○	○	○

My goals

What do you want to be able to do or say in Italian when you complete this unit?

		Done
1	....	○
2	....	○
3	....	○

My review

SELF CHECK

	I can ...
●	... talk about family relations.
●	... describe people's appearance and personality in a simple manner.
●	... describe what other people do for a living and where they work.
●	... use possessive adjectives.
●	... use the verb andare.

CULTURE POINT 1

Mamma mia! Famiglie in Italia *Families in Italy*

The Swedish band ABBA can be credited for singing "Mamma mia!" (*mother of mine*) to the world, but in Italy it is a very common expression which can be used to express surprise, fear, appreciation, disappointment, and many feelings often having nothing to do with la mamma or la famiglia (*family*).

Italians are traditionally portrayed as having famiglie grandi (*big families*) but this is no longer true, as nowadays Italy has one of the lowest birth rates in the world. With an average of one figlio/a (*child*) per family, and one of the longest life expectancies in Europe, there are more nonni (*grandparents*) than nipoti (*grandchildren*). Even if it is no longer common for grandparents to live with their children and grandchildren, family is still very important, and family members traditionally gather to celebrate vacanze (*holidays*), compleanni (*birthdays*), and other festive occasions, or for il pranzo della domenica (*Sunday lunch*).

E tu? Hai una famiglia grande (*big*) o piccola (*small*)? Hai un nonno? Hai un figlio/a/*?

VOCABULARY BUILDER 1

03.01

Look at the words and phrases and complete the missing English words and expressions. Then listen and try to imitate the pronunciation of the speakers.

LA FAMIGLIA	*THE FAMILY*
i genitori	*parents*
il padre (papà)	*father (dad)*
la madre (mamma)	....
il figlio/la figlia	........./.........
il fratello	*brother*
la sorella	*sister*
i fratelli	*siblings*
il nonno/la nonna	*grandfather/grandmother*
il/la nipote	*grandchild/grandson/granddaughter (also nephew/niece)*
lo zia/la zia	*uncle/aunt*
il marito	*husband*
la moglie	*wife*
il compagno/la compagna	*partner*
la coppia	....
il cognato/la cognata	*brother-in-law/sister-in-law*
il matrimonio	*marriage*
sposato/a	*married*
divorziato/a	....
il cugino/la cugina	*cousin*
il figlio/la figlia unico/a	*only child*
maggiore (grande)	*older/elder*
minore (piccolo/a)	*younger*

ESPRESSIONI UTILI	*USEFUL EXPRESSIONS*
Ti presento i miei.	*Let me introduce you to my parents.*
Hai fratelli o sorelle?	*Do you have siblings?*

The Italian word for parents is genitori. The word parenti is a false friend, as it indicates one's *relatives*, but not *parents*:

I miei genitori vivono a Napoli ma ho molti parenti a Roma. — *My parents live in Naples but I have many relatives in Rome.*

Notice also that the word for *siblings* is the plural of fratello (*brother*). The Italian national anthem is called Fratelli d'Italia *(Brothers of Italy)* but here it means *siblings*, so everyone is included.

Vocabulary practice 1

Try to guess the relations in Annalisa's and Cristian's families.

a Niccolò è il figlio del fratello di Annalisa. Niccolò e il .... di Annalisa.

b Angela è la madre di Annalisa e Giuseppe è il padre di Annalisa. Loro sono i .... di Annalisa.

c La madre di Cristian ha una figlia, Petra. Petra è la .... di Cristian.

d Il fratello di Annalisa è sposato con Carlotta. Carlotta è la .... di Annalisa.

e Petra non è sposata ma vive con Clara. Clara è la .... di Petra.

f Niccolò è il figlio del fratello di Annalisa. Annalisa è la .... di Niccolò.

g Carlotta è sposata con Giovanni. Carlotta è la .... di Giovanni e Giovanni è il .... di Carlotta.

Pronunciation practice

03.02

Listen to the words and notice how the speaker pronounces the underlined sound gli (+ vowel). Repeat each word after the speaker.

a moglie
b figlio
c famiglia
d aglio (*garlic*)
e maglietta (*t-shirt*)
f miglio (*mile*)
g gli
h luglio (*July*)
i millefoglie (*millefeuille*)

The sound gli/glie/glia/glio/gliu is one of the trickiest in Italian. Even some Italians cannot pronounce it properly. It is similar to the Spanish sound ll in llamo. Arch your tongue against your palate and try pronouncing this sound many times. Or say "l-y" very quickly, until it sounds like gli. With a little practice, you will succeed!

CONVERSATION 1

La mia famiglia *My family*

03.03

1 Here are a few words and expressions to help you understand the following conversation. Note their meaning.

lontano da / vicino a	*far from/close to*
qui/lì	*here/there*
oggi/domani	*today/tomorrow*
Quando?	*When?*

03.04

2 Listen to the conversation without looking at the text. Play it a few times and try to make out a few new words and phrases each time. Then listen to the conversation again and read the text.

Annalisa told Cristian that her family would be visiting from Napoli. Cristian is a bit worried: he has a stereotypical image of Neapolitan families as being loud and fond of cooking and eating until late at night, and he needs his peace and quiet while he prepares for a very difficult application for a job. However, he does not want to upset Annalisa with his assumptions, so he's tactfully trying to find out about the upcoming visit.

Cristian Quando arriva la tua famiglia?

Annalisa I miei genitori arrivano oggi. Vanno all'hotel Panorama. Mio fratello, sua moglie e il loro figlio arrivano domani.

Cristian Hai solo un nipote?

Annalisa Sì, Niccolò è figlio unico. Io ho solo un fratello maggiore, Giovanni, ma abbiamo due cugini a Napoli e anche i nostri nonni vivono lì. Mio nonno ha 95 anni!

Cristian Mamma mia! Vivono con i vostri genitori?

Annalisa No, però abitano vicino.

Cristian E... anche tuo fratello, tua cognata e tuo nipote vanno all'hotel Panorama?

Annalisa No, il loro hotel non è lontano da qui.

3 Decide if the statements are vero (*true*) or falso (*false*).

a La famiglia di Annalisa arriva a casa di Annalisa e Cristian. vero falso
b Niccolò è il figlio di Giovanni. vero falso
c I nonni di Annalisa abitano con Giovanni. vero falso
d Niccolò ha due fratelli. vero falso
e Giovanni arriva domani. vero falso

LANGUAGE BUILDER 1

Language discovery 1

How does Cristian ask about Annalisa's family and how does she describe it? Find the phrases meaning "your family," "their hotel," "our grandparents," and "your parents." Put them next to the subject you think they relate to.

a Tu ....
b Noi ....
c Voi ....
d Loro ....

Possessive adjectives

To indicate possession, English uses the adjectives *my, your, her, his, our, your, their.* These are called possessive adjectives, and they exist in Italian, too. As you know by now, in Italian adjectives agree with the noun they refer to in gender and number. Therefore, each possessive adjective in Italian has four options: masculine singular or plural and feminine singular or plural. Loro is an exception, as it conveniently never changes.

03.05

Listen to the speaker going over the adjectives and repeat, paying special attention to the plural ones.

	Masculine singular	Feminine singular	Masculine plural	Feminine plural
io	(il) mio	(la) mia	(i) miei	(le) mie
tu	(il) tuo	(la) tua	(i) tuoi	(le) tue
lui/lei/Lei	(il) suo	(la) sua	(i) suoi	(le) sue
noi	(il) nostro	(la) nostra	(i) nostri	(le) nostre)
voi	(il) vostro	(la) vostra	(i) vostri	(le) vostre)
loro	(il) loro	(la) loro	(i) loro	(le) loro

Quando arriva la tua famiglia? *When does your family arrive?*

Dov'è il loro hotel? *Where is their hotel?*

Note that, unlike in English, in Italian it is not possible to know whether the "owner" of an object is masculine or feminine as the adjective agrees with the object and not the owner: il suo computer, la sua famiglia, i suoi genitori, le sue sorelle: suo/a/i/e can mean *his/her*. The context usually makes it clear who the possessive pronoun refers to.

Language practice 1

Ecco is one of the most useful words you'll learn in Italian—you can use it whenever you want to point something out: Here it is! Change the sentences as in the example using the correct possessive adjectives.

Example: Io ho una famiglia. *Ecco la mia famiglia!*

a Noi abbiamo una macchina. ....

b Annalisa ha una famiglia piccola. ....

c Clara e Petra hanno un B&B a Bolzano. ....

d Tu hai un computer nuovo. ....

e Voi avete un'amica fotografa. ....

f Giovanni ha una casa grande. ....

g Annalisa e Cristian hanno un quadro in soffitta. ....

h Aicha ha un piano. ....

LANGUAGE BUILDER 2

Language discovery 2

03.06 **Listen to the conversation again and repeat each line in the pauses provided. Try to imitate the phrasing and intonation you hear. Then read the following summary of Annalisa's family. Note that some possessive adjectives are preceded by the definite articles and some are not. What do the words that don't need a definite aritcle have in common?**

Mio fratello, sua moglie e suo figlio arrivano domani. Il loro hotel è vicino a noi.

Mio nipote è figlio unico.

Noi abbiamo due cugini a Napoli e anche i miei nonni abitano a Napoli.

Mio nonno ha 95 anni.

Mamma mia! Singular family nouns need no article!

As Language Builder 1 shows, Italian possessive adjectives are usually preceded by definite articles. However, there is a specific subset of words for which the article is not needed: singular nouns indicating family members—mio nonno, tuo nipote, sua moglie, nostra madre, vostra figlia. But there is an exception even to this subset: loro is always preceded by the definite article:

Il loro figlio si chiama Massimo. *Their son's name is Massimo.*

Strangely enough, the word famiglia is not considered a family noun, so it needs a possessive with article: la mia famiglia. And words like compagno/a (*partner*) are also not considered family nouns: il mio compagno. Pets are also not family, but of course only for grammar purposes!

Language practice 2

03.07 **1 Listen to Cristian as he describes his family, then answer the questions below.**

Example: Dove abita la zia di Cristian? *Lei abita a Bolzano.*

a Di dove è il padre di Cristian?

b Dove vive sua madre?

c Quanti fratelli ha Cristian?

d Cosa fanno i suoi cugini?

2 Answer these questions about your family.

a Dove abita la tua famiglia?

b Hai fratelli? Se sì, quanti anni hanno?

c Hai i nonni? Se sì, quanti anni hanno e dove vivono?

CULTURE POINT 2

La faccia più famosa dell'arte *The most famous face in the arts*

The Medici family was one of the wealthiest and most powerful dynasties of Italy, ruling Florence for centuries. They started as bankers and soon became signori (*lords*) of Florence and patrons of artisti (*artists*) and poeti (*poets*). The pittore (*painter*) Sandro Botticelli worked for the Medici and in many of his quadri (*paintings*) he depicted Simonetta Vespucci, a noble lady at the Medici court. You can admire Simonetta's bella faccia (*beautiful face*) and flowing capelli (*hair*) in *The Birth of Venus* and *Primavera*, among other quadri in the Galleria degli Uffizi in Florence. Her immagine (*image*) has become a symbol of Italy, so that in 2023 the government chose it for the tourism campaign "Open to meraviglia" (*wonder*), where Venus/Simonetta poses as an influencer and invites people to visit her beautiful country.

Go to the Uffizi website on the page devoted to Botticelli:

a In how many paintings can you recognize Simonetta's faccia?

b Look at the painting *Primavera*. How many people can you count? Say the number in Italian. Quanti anni hanno, in your opinion?

VOCABULARY BUILDER 2

03.08

Look at the words and phrases and complete the missing English words and expressions. Then listen and try to imitate the pronunciation of the speakers.

DESCRIVERE L'ASPETTO E LA PERSONALITÀ	*DESCRIBING ONE'S LOOKS AND PERSONALITY*
Com'è?	*What is he/she like?*
l'aspetto fisico	*physical appearance*
avere i capelli biondi/neri	*to have blond/black hair*
castani/rossi	*brown/red*
bianchi/grigi	*white/grey*
ricci/lisci	*curly/straight*
corti/lunghi	*short/long*
avere gli occhi marroni	*to have brown eyes*
azzurri/verdi	*blue/grey*
essere alto/a	*to be tall*
essere basso/a	*to be short*

LA PERSONALITÀ	*PERSONALITY*
introverso/a	....
simpatico/a	*nice/friendly*
calmo/a	....
nervoso/a	*nervous*
serio/a	*serious*
avere la faccia triste/allegra	*to have a sad/cheerful face*

Vocabulary practice 2

Look at the pictures and complete the descriptions with the missing words.

a Ha i capelli .... e neri.

b Ha i capelli ....

c Ha gli .... marroni.

CONVERSATION 2

Ha una faccia seria… *(She) has a serious face …*

03.09

1 Here are a few words and expressions to help you understand the following conversation. Note their meanings.

andiamo d'accordo	*we get along well*	dopo	*later*
ossessionato da	*obsessed by*	studioso	*studious*
Murano	*island suburb of Venice known for artistic glass making*		

03.10

2 Listen to the conversation without looking at the text. Play it a few times and try to make out a few new words and phrases each time. Then listen to the conversation again and read the text.

Annalisa is showing the apartment to her family while Cristian is via (*away*). They want to know what Cristian looks like (com'è fisicamente) and about his personality. Annalisa's young nephew, Niccolò, wants to see the painting of the woman in the attic. Let's listen to their conversation. Pay attention to how Annalisa describes Cristian.

Annalisa Bella Venezia, vero? Dove andate oggi?

Mamma Oggi io, Carlotta e Giovanni andiamo in gondola, ma papà va a Murano.

Annalisa Perfetto! Dopo andiamo a casa? Cristian, il mio coinquilino, è via.

Carlotta Cristian… com'è?

Annalisa È di Bolzano. È un po' introverso e studioso. Andiamo d'accordo.

Mamma E com'è fisicamente?

Annalisa Ha 29 anni, è alto, ha i capelli castani e gli occhi azzurri. È ossessionato da un quadro in soffitta…

They go up to the attic.

Mamma Che bella signora! Ha i capelli neri e ricci e ha una faccia seria, triste…

Niccolò Ma è la zia Ginaaaaaa!!!

3 Match the sentence halves to create sentences describing the conversation.

1 La famiglia di Annalisa	**a** non è a casa.
2 Cristian	**b** è curiosa.
3 La donna misteriosa	**c** è la zia di Niccolò.
4 Gina	**d** ha i capelli neri.

LANGUAGE BUILDER 3

Language discovery 3

Look at the conversation again. Do you notice a pattern in the endings of the nouns and adjectives that describe the people?

Venezia è una città bella.

Carlotta è curiosa.

Cristian ha i capelli marroni.

La donna del quadro ha una faccia seria e triste.

Adjective and noun agreement (gender and number)

Adjectives are words that describe things.

Venezia è bella. *Venice is beautiful.* (la città is feminine)

Unlike in English, most adjectives in Italian follow the noun they describe.

Ha una faccia seria. *[She] has a serious face.*

Adjectives agree with the noun in gender and number. For example, feminine singular nouns must be accompanied by a feminine singular adjective: città bella. Notice that the endings are the same as for nouns.

	Singular	Plural
Masc.	**-o** (alto)	**-i** (alti)
Fem.	**-a** (alta)	**-e** (alte)

Some adjectives have only singular and plural forms, which are the same for masculine and feminine. The endings are: -e for the singular and -i for the plural.

	Singular	Plural
Masc. / Fem.	**-e** (intelligente)	**-i** (intelligenti)

Often the endings are the same, so it is easy to match adjective and noun: la faccia seria. But sometimes, the adjective and noun have different endings: la faccia triste.

Language practice 3

Pick one noun from the first column, then match it with an adjective in the second column. Then write a combination in the third. Note the adjectives need to be changed. Several combinations are possible.

un appartamento una famiglia una faccia gli amici le amiche	piccolo/a intelligente grande turco/a serio/a	Un appartamento piccolo

LANGUAGE BUILDER 4

Language discovery 4

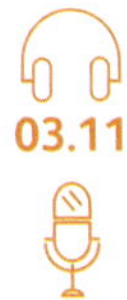

Listen to the conversation again and repeat each line in the pauses provided. Try to imitate the phrasing and intonation you hear. Then look at these sentences from the conversation. Can you guess the pattern of the verb andare? What does it mean?

Dove andate oggi?
Dopo andiamo a casa?
This is now in English in the conversation.
Oggi andiamo in gondola
Papà va a Murano.

The verb **andare**

Andare (*to go*) is a very useful verb, and it's irregular in the present tense.

andare (*to go*)

io	vado	noi	andiamo
tu	vai	voi	andate
lui/lei/Lei	va	loro	vanno

Vado all'hotel. — *I'm going to the hotel.*
Vanno a scuola. — *They're going to school.*

Notice that a combines with a definite article to form a single word:
a + il = al
a + la = alla (all' before a vowel)
a + I = ai
a + le = alle
Andiamo alla Basilica di San Marco. — *We're going to St. Mark's Basilica.*

When talking about going to a city versus to a country or region, andare is followed by different prepositions: a with the name of the city and in followed by the country, state, or region:

Papà va a Murano. — *Dad is going to Murano.*
I turisti vanno in Italia. — *Tourists go to Italy.*

Andare is also used in idiomatic expressions, such as andare d'accordo (*to get along*):
andiamo d'accordo — *we get along.*

Language practice 4

1 Complete the following text with the missing verbs by choosing from the list.

vanno (x2)	va (x3)	vai	vado

Annalisa è di Napoli ma vive a Venezia. La sua famiglia **a** .... a Venezia per una visita. Loro **b** .... all'hotel Panorama. Loro visitano la bella città di Venezia: **c** .... in gondola e in piazza San Marco. Il padre di Annalisa adora il vetro artigianale (handcrafted glass) e **d** .... a Murano. Niccolò **e** .... in gondola con sua nonna e i suoi genitori. E tu, dove **f** .... in vacanza? Io **g** ....

03.12

2 Listen to the questions related to the conversation and answer them in the pauses provided. Try to create full sentences using the verbs required.

Example: Io sono di Napoli e tu? *Io sono di Istanbul.*

SKILL BUILDER

Read this short text about the Medici family, then answer the questions in Italian. Make full sentences with the subject and verb.

La famiglia Medici è una famiglia influente del Rinascimento in Italia, a Firenze. Sono banchieri e patroni di artisti e poeti. Vivono a Firenze e governano la città. Artisti come Michelangelo e Leonardo da Vinci lavorano per i Medici e creano molte opere d'arte importanti e famose. Hanno una grande biblioteca e supportano la scienza e la letteratura. La loro eredità artistica è ancora visibile oggi. Molti turisti vanno a Firenze per ammirare le sculture di Donatello e i quadri di Sandro Botticelli. Simonetta Vespucci, una nobile signora alla corte dei Medici, è la protagonista dei quadri di Botticelli. Ha una faccia regolare, con occhi azzurri e lunghi capelli biondi. L'immagine di Simonetta in *Primavera* e la *Nascita di Venere* è un simbolo dell'Italia e del Rinascimento di Firenze.

a Da dove vengono i Medici?
b Cosa fanno i Medici? (qual è la loro professione?)
c Quali artisti lavorano per i Medici?
d Chi (*who*) è Simonetta Vespucci?
e Com'è Simonetta fisicamente?

TEST YOURSELF

1 Complete the sentences with the correct form of the given adjective.

a Firenze è una città (artistico/a) ....
b Michelangelo è un pittore e scultore (famoso/a) ....
c I Medici supportano artisti (importante) .... come Botticelli e Leonardo.
d Donatello, Michelangelo e Botticelli creano opere (bello/a) .... e (immortale) ....

e La Primavera ha una faccia (sereno/a) ....

f I capelli di Simonetta Vespucci sono (biondo/a) ....

2 Cristian is describing his family. Complete with the correct possessive adjectives, with or without the articles.

a .... famiglia è piccola. **b** .... padre è di Bolzano e lavora in posta. **c** .... madre è di Salzburg in Austria ma vive a Bolzano. Lei fa la dentista. **d** .... genitori sono divorziati. Ho una sorella maggiore, Petra. **e** .... sorella e **f** .... compagna hanno un B&B sulle Dolomiti. Sono una coppia molto contenta. **g** .... B&B è molto bello e accogliente (*welcoming*). Ho una zia a Bolzano **h** .... figli, **i** .... cugini, studiano all'università di Trento.

3 Andare, stare o fare? Complete the sentences with the correct form of these three irregular verbs. Sometimes more than one solution is possible.

a L'autobus .... a Milano.

b Come .... tua madre? Bene, grazie.

c Matteo .... il meccanico.

d Cosa [noi] .... oggi? .... in gondola.

e Io .... a New York.

f I miei genitori .... a Londra.

La misteriosa donna in soffitta *The mysterious woman in the attic*

Time for your riddle! We talk about personality traits, and by now you know that Cristian is introverso. Annalisa is the opposite: she is .... The first letter of this adjective will be the next clue in guessing the name of the woman in the painting!

Before you move on to the next unit, assess your progress using the **My review** section on the first page of the unit, and reflect on your learning experience with the **My takeaway** section available online.

4

In this unit you will learn how to:

» Talk about your daily routine.
» Ask and give information about shops' opening hours.
» Say how often you do something.

Il tran-tran quotidiano

My study plan

I plan to work with Unit 4

○ Every day
○ Twice a week
○ Other ____________

I plan to study for

○ 5–15 minutes
○ 15–30 minutes
○ 30–45+ minutes

My progress tracker

Day / Date	Listening	Speaking	Reading	Writing	Conversation
	○	○	○	○	○
	○	○	○	○	○
	○	○	○	○	○
	○	○	○	○	○
	○	○	○	○	○
	○	○	○	○	○
	○	○	○	○	○

My goals

What do you want to be able to do or say in Italian when you complete this unit?

		Done
1	....	○
2	....	○
3	....	○

My review

SELF CHECK

	I can ...
●	... talk about my daily routine.
●	... describe people or things I know or I don't know with the correct verb.
●	... tell the date and time.
●	... talk about shops' opening and closing hours.
●	... describe how often I do something.

CULTURE POINT 1

La dolce vita?

The iconic expression la dolce vita (***the sweet life***) emerged from the legendary film of the same name, which captured the vibrant essence of 1950s' Rome. In an era when Italy flourished amidst an economic boom, life was painted as a mix of leisure and self-indulgence. Is that still so? In the modern Italian lifestyle, it seems the joy of life still revolves around food. A 2023 study showcases Italy's deep culinary connection, revealing that il pranzo (*lunch*), embraced by 75.7 percent at home, shines as the day's centerpiece. Yet habits are changing to keep up with the pace of modern life. City life in Italy is quite similar to city life across the world. Nowadays people work long hours and often opt for a brief pausa pranzo (*lunchbreak*) near their workplace instead of enjoying a leisurely lunch at home. However, la colazione (*breakfast*), a comforting ritual, is reported to still be practiced by 81.5 percent of Italians each day. The Italian colazione is usually dolce (*sweet*), often consisting of biscotti (*cookies/biscuits*), pane (*bread*) / fette biscottate (*a type of crunchy biscuit*) con burro (*with butter*) e marmellata (*and jam*), or cereali (*cereals*). Cornetto (*croissants*) and cappuccino al bar (*at the café*) is a treat to be had occasionally.

E tu? Do you go a casa (*home*) for la pausa pranzo?

Fai colazione (*Do you eat breakfast*)?

Preferisci una colazione dolce (*sweet*) o salata (*savory*)?

Look at the IMDb page for *La Dolce Vita* and watch a trailer released by the BFI (British Film Institute). Do you know the name of the iconic fountain where Marcello Mastroianni and Anita Ekberg take a midnight dip?

VOCABULARY BUILDER 1

Look at the words and phrases and complete the missing English words and expressions. Then listen and try to imitate the pronunciation of the speakers.

PARTI DEL GIORNO	*PARTS OF THE DAY*
la mattina	....
la notte	....
il pomeriggio	*afternoon*
la sera	*evening*
la colazione (fare colazione)	*breakfast (to have breakfast)*
il pranzo (pranzare)	*lunch (to have lunch)*
la cena (cenare)	....
GIORNI DELLA SETTIMANA	***DAYS OF THE WEEK***
lunedì	*Monday*
martedì	*Tuesday*
mercoledì	*Wednesday*
giovedì	*Thursday*
venerdì	*Friday*
sabato	*Saturday*
domenica	*Sunday*
ROUTINE GIORNALIERA	***DAILY ROUTINE***
Sono esausto/a!	*I am tired!*
ogni giorno	*every day*
mi alzo / mi faccio la doccia / mi preparo	*I get up/I shower/ I get ready*
sempre	*always*
alzarsi	*to get up*
arrabbiarsi	*to get angry*
divertirsi	*to have fun*
farsi la barba	*to shave*
farsi la doccia	*to shower*
prepararsi	....
riposarsi	*to rest*
svegliarsi	*to wake up*
vestirsi	*to get dressed*
VERBI UTILI	***USEFUL VERBS***
conoscere	*to know, to be familiar with (something/someone)*
sapere	*to know (how to do something)*

Vocabulary practice 1

Label the pictures with verbs used for daily routines. What time of day would most people normally do these things?

a

b

c

d

Pronunciation practice

04.02

Listen to the following words, paying attention to how the underlined syllables are pronounced.

a conosco
b pesca
c sciare
d pesce
e scuola
f maschile

The cluster sc can have two different sounds in Italian. Notice that this is very similar to English: compare scar and scout with science and scene. Sc takes a hard sound or a soft sound depending on the vowel that follows. Sc is pronounced as a soft sound when it is followed by the vowels e or i. The soft sound of sc is the same as the sh sound you have in English in the words she, short, or sheer. Sc is pronounced as a hard sound when it is followed by the vowels a, o, u, or the letter h. The hard sound of sc is the same as the sk sound you have in English in the words skin, skate, or skill.

Practice pronouncing the conjugation of the verb conoscere (*to know*):

conoscere (*to know*)

io conosco	noi conisicamo
tu conosci	voi conoscete
lui/lei/Lei consce	loro conoscono

CONVERSATION 1

Una capa terribile *A terrible boss*

04.03

1 Here are a few words and expressions to help you understand the following conversation. Note their meanings.

Rispondere male.	*to snap at* (lit. *to answer badly*)
Non so perché.	*I don't know why.*
sembra	*seems*
così	*so*
Usciamo!	*Let's go out!*

04.04

2 Listen to the conversation a few times without looking at the text. Then listen to the conversation again and read the text.

Annalisa has just gotten home from work exhausted, like she does every day. La sua capa (*her boss*) is quite esigente (*demanding*) and it seems they are not getting along very well. Thankfully, Aicha calls her and when she finds out her friend had a bad day, she immediately comes up with a plan to make Annalisa forget about work. As Italians love to say: non di solo pane vive l'uomo (*man does not live by bread alone*).

Aicha Allora, il nuovo lavoro?

Annalisa Non so… Terribile.

Aicha Perché?

Annalisa Ogni giorno mi alzo, mi preparo e vado a lavoro con entusiasmo… ma la mia capa è molto esigente, non ascolta le mie idee, risponde male. È lunedì e sono esausta. Quando arriva venerdì?!

Aicha Wow, la tua capa sembra un po' nervosa.

Annalisa Esatto, si arrabbia sempre e non so perché.

Aicha Sai cosa facciamo? Usciamo! Così ti diverti e non pensi al lavoro. Conosci Sandra? Andiamo al pub con lei.

Annalisa Fantastico! Mi faccio una doccia e arrivo.

3 Answer the questions.

a On what day does the conversation take place?
b What word does Aicha use to describe Annalisa's boss? What does it mean?
c What is Annalisa doing before heading to the pub?

LANGUAGE BUILDER 1

Language discovery 1

Without looking back at the conversation, complete the sentences from the conversation with the words below. Notice the verbs they go with. What do these verbs have in common?

mi (x2) ti si

Annalisa	Ogni giorno	**a** .... alzo, **b** .... preparo.
Annalisa	La mia capa	**c** .... arrabbia.
Aicha	Così (tu)	**d** .... diverti e non pensi al lavoro.

Reflexive verbs

Many Italian verbs that describe routine, daily actions are reflexive—the subject and the object of the action are the same, e.g., *to enjoy oneself*.

Ogni giorno mi alzo. *Every day I get (myself) up.*

Mi faccio una doccia e arrivo. *I'll shower (myself) and I'll be there.*

You can recognize reflexive verbs because they are always accompanied by a reflexive pronoun. The base form of reflexive verbs ends in the pronoun si (alzarsi, lavarsi, farsi una doccia). The pronoun, of course, must agree with the subject:

mi	myself	ci	ourselves
ti	yourself	vi	yourselves
si	himself/herself/yourself formal	si	themselves

See how it works with a very useful verb: divertirsi.

divertirsi (*to have fun*)

io	mi diverto	noi	ci divertiamo
tu	ti diverti	voi	vi divertite
lui/lei/Lei	si diverte	loro	si divertono

Note that English has very few reflexive verbs (i.e., *to enjoy oneself*, *to hurt oneself*), and often uses "get" where Italian uses a reflexive verb: arrabbiarsi (*to get angry*), prepararsi (*to get ready*), vestirsi (*to get dressed*).

Language practice 1

04.05

Listen to the audio and decide which sentences include a reflexive verb. Then try to work out the base form of the underlined reflexive verbs.

a	Nel fine settimana Andrea si riposa.	Base form: ....
b	Faccio colazione con un cappuccino.	Base form: ....
c	Chiara, ti fai la doccia la mattina o la sera?	Base form: ....
d	Oggi Antonio e Marco si sposano.	Base form: ....
e	Quando andiamo al parco?	Base form: ....
f	Io e Omar ci divertiamo insieme.	Base form: ....

LANGUAGE BUILDER 2

Language discovery 2

04.06

Listen to the conversation again and repeat each line in the pauses provided. Try to imitate the phrasing and intonation you hear.

Look at Aicha's proposal to Annalisa. What do you think the verbs sai and conosci mean? What is the main difference between the two?

Aicha Sai cosa facciamo? Usciamo! Così ti diverti e non pensi al lavoro. Conosci Sandra? Andiamo al pub con lei.

To know: **sapere** and **conoscere**

Italian uses two different verbs for knowing a fact or how to do something versus knowing a person or a place.

Sai cosa facciamo?	*Do you know what we are going to do?*
Sanno suonare il piano.	*They know how to play the piano.*
Conosci Sandra?	*Do you know Sandra?*
Conosco bene Tokyo.	*I know Tokyo well.*

Conoscere is a regular verb (but be careful with the pronunciation of -sc-). It conveys the sense "to be familiar with" or "to know of."

Sapere is irregular, but it follows a similar pattern to avere. Try to complete the table based on the conversation and what you already know.

sapere (*to know a fact*)

io	**a**	noi	sappiamo
tu	**b**	voi	sapete
lui/lei/Lei	sa	loro	sanno

Language practice 2

1 Choose the correct verb to complete the sentences.

- **a** Non conosciamo / sappiamo a che ora parte il treno
- **b** Martina conosce / sa suonare la chitarra
- **c** Conoscete / Sapete la mia amica Izumi?
- **d** Dario e Felipe conoscono / sanno dov'è un ristorante italiano.
- **e** Ana e Paula conoscono / sanno un ristorante italiano.
- **f** Conosco / so molto bene l'Italia.
- **g** Conosci / sai cucinare indiano?

04.07

2 Now play Conversation 1 again, but this time you will play Annalisa's role. Speak in the pauses provided. Try not to refer to the text.

CULTURE POINT 2

Aperto o chiuso? *Open or closed?*

Look at the inside of a typical shop in Murano, a picturesque village near Venice. What would you say is their popular local product? What would you like to buy in this shop?

In Italy, shop opening hours can vary slightly depending on the regions and cities. In smaller towns, di solito (*usually*), i negozi (*shops*) aprono (*open*) in the morning verso (*around*) 9 a.m. or 10 a.m. and chiudono (*close*) for the pausa pranzo (*lunch break*) at 12 p.m. or 1 p.m. During this period, many shops might remain closed for a couple of hours. But fear not! The afternoon breathes new life, with doors reopening at 3:30 p.m. or 4 p.m., and the streets come alive again, buzzing with activity until the evening, spesso (*often*) until 7 p.m. or 8 p.m. I supermercati (*supermarkets*) aprono earlier, around 8 a.m. and follow orario continuato (*non-stop opening hours*) until 8 p.m. or 9 p.m., and so do i negozi in bigger cities. Depending on the season and the region, some negozi might be closed on Sundays.

Are opening hours in Italy like the ones in your country? What is similar and what is different?

VOCABULARY BUILDER 2

Look at the words and phrases and complete the missing English words and expressions. Then listen and try to imitate the pronunciation of the speakers.

AVVERBI DI FREQUENZA	*FREQUENCY ADVERBS*
di solito	*usually*
sempre/mai	*always/never*
spesso/raramente	*often/*....................
qualche volta	*sometimes*

I MESI E LE STAGIONI	*MONTHS AND SEASONS OF THE YEAR*
gennaio	*January*
febbraio	....
marzo	*March*
aprile	*April*
maggio	*May*
giugno	*June*
luglio	*July*
agosto	....
settembre	*September*
ottobre	....
novembre	....
dicembre	*December*
l'inverno/l'estate	*winter/summer*
la primavera/l'autunno	*spring/*....................

Remember, in Italian, months and days of the week aren't capitalized.

Vocabulary practice 2

1 Arrange the words below from lowest to highest frequency.

spesso	raramente	mai	sempre	qualche volta	di solito

0 **mai** 1 ..... 2 ..... 3 ..... 4 ..... 5 .....

2 Answer the questions.

- **a** Quanto spesso vai al cinema?
- **b** In quali mesi è primavera?
- **c** In quali mesi è autunno?
- **d** Quando è il tuo compleanno (*birthday*)?
- **e** Qual è la tua stagione preferita (*favorite season*)? Perché?

Sempre (*always*) must *always* go immediately after the verb. Mai (*never*) also goes immediately after the verb, with non before the verb. The other adverbs can be placed before or after the verb.

CONVERSATION 2

Il tempo vola! *Time flies!*

04.09

1 Listen to the conversation a few times without looking at the text. Then listen to the conversation again and read the text.

It's now dark outside and while Annalisa is ready to leave the house to meet Aicha and Sandra, Cristian is still working in his room. He found a good post advertised in a famous art gallery in New York and he is trying his best to obtain la posizione (*position*) before la scadenza (*deadline*). Before leaving the house, Annalisa checks on Cristian. It is during their conversation that he suddenly realizes the time has literally flown by.

Annalisa Cristian, vado al pub. Tutto bene?

Cristian Sì, preparo il CV per una posizione in una galleria di New York. La scadenza è il 15 maggio, ho poco tempo.

Annalisa Lavori sempre, anche la sera! Perché non esci qualche volta?

Cristian Lo so, ma è davvero importante. Ah, esco anche io per comprare delle cose. A che ora chiude il supermercato?

Annalisa È chiuso. Apre domani mattina alle otto.

Cristian Chiuso? Ma che ore sono?!

Annalisa Sono le nove e venti.

Cristian Veramente?! Il tempo vola!

Annalisa (*laughs*) Eh, sì. Quando ti diverti... il tempo vola.

2 Answer the questions.

a Would you be able to tell what time the supermarket opens?
b What other time is mentioned in the dialogue?

The verb uscire (*to leave/go out*) is another irregular one:

io esco	noi usciamo
tu esci	voi uscite
lui/lei/Lei esce	loro escono

Watch out for the pronunciation of the sc sound!

LANGUAGE BUILDER 3

Language discovery 3

1 Read the conversation and complete these sentences.

a Vado .... pub.

b Esco per comprare .... cose.

c Apre domattina .... otto.

2 These words are each a combination of two words. Can you identify them?

Combined prepositions

Prepositions are small but important words—they tell us about the relationship between things. When a preposition (di (*of, from*), a (*to, at*), da (*from, by*), in (*in, at*), and su (*on, about*)) comes before the definite article (il, lo, la, l', i, gli, la, le), they are combined into a single word. This happens very frequently in Italian, for example when going somewhere:

Vado al (a + il) pub.	*I am going to the pub.*
Andiamo a correre nel (in + il) parco!	*Let's go running in the park!*
Vanno alla (a + la) stazione.	*They are going to the station.*

The preposition di in combination with the definite article can express simple ownership but can also mean "some."

Il pranzo della domenica.	*Sunday lunch (i.e. the lunch of Sunday).*
Esco anche io per comprare delle cose.	*I am also going out to buy some things.*

In English, ownership can be shown by adding 's or s' added to a noun—for example, "the teacher's name" or "my parents' house." In Italian, di is used to translate this sort of phrase and the noun comes first: il nome dell'insegnante, la casa dei miei genitori.

Study the combined prepositions in the table below, but you don't have to memorize all of them. Notice that the combinations follow a predictable pattern, and they make pronunciation easier.

	il	l'	lo	i	gli	la	le
a	al	all'	allo	ai	agli	alla	alle
da	dal	dall'	dallo	dai	dagli	dalla	dalle
su	sul	sull'	sullo	sui	sugli	sulla	sulle
in	nel	nell'	nello	nei	negli	nella	nelle
di	del	dell'	dello	dei	degli	della	delle

Language practice 3

Complete the sentences by combining the prepositions with their correct article.

a Il cinema apre (a + le) .... sette.

b Stasera esco con (di + gli) .... amici.

c Oggi Jasmin va (a + la) .... lezione di yoga.

d Non faccio mai una passeggiata (in + il) .... parco.

e La colazione è (su + il) .... tavolo.

f Ben arriva (da + gli) .... Stati Uniti.

g Questa è la casa (di + gli) .... zii.

h Le mie sorelle vanno (a + il) .... ristorante.

LANGUAGE BUILDER 4

Language discovery 4

04.10

Listen to the conversation again and repeat each line in the pauses provided. Try to imitate the phrasing and intonation you hear. What questions do the speakers ask for the answers below? What do they specifically ask about?

Q: a ....? A: È chiuso. Apre domani mattina alle otto.

Q: b ....? A: Sono le nove e venti.

Telling time

In Italian to ask for the time say Che ora è?/Che ore sono? To give the time, use Sono le followed by the hour, and then add the minutes introduced by e (*and*).

Sono le undici e dieci.	*It's eleven (and) ten.*
Sono le nove e venti.	*It's twenty past nine.*

Have you noticed that the verb is plural—sono? That's because the number of hours is plural. If it's one o'clock, noon, or midnight, you use è.

È l'una.	*It's one o'clock.*
È mezzogiorno.	*It's noon.*
È mezzanotte.	*It's midnight.*

To express half an hour, say trenta or mezza (*half*). Likewise, for a quarter of an hour, say quindici or un quarto.

Sono le nove e mezza.	*It's half past nine.*
Sono le cinque e un quarto.	*It's five fifteen.*

When it is closer to the coming hour, the minutes can be subtracted from the coming hour using meno (*minus*).

Sono le sei meno dieci.	*It's ten to six.* (lit. *It's six minus ten.*)

> Note that although Italians usually write the time in the 24-hour clock format, they prefer to use the 12-hour clock format when speaking.

To find out at what time something happens, ask A che ora...? (*At what time ... ?*) and the answer should start with the combined prepositions alle (plural number of hours) or all' (if it's one) followed by the time. If it's mezzogiorno o mezzanotte, just use a.

Apre domani mattina alle otto.	*It opens tomorrow morning at eight.*
Chiude all'una.	*It closes at one.*
Chiude a mezzanotte.	*It closes at midnight.*

Language practice 4

1 Write out the following times presented in numerals and answer the question: A che ora...?

- **a** A che ora apre il teatro? (17:50) ....
- **b** A che ora pranzi? (12:00) ....
- **c** A che ora chiude la scuola? (16:30) ....
- **d** A che ora finisce la lezione? (21:05) ....
- **e** A che ora ceni? (20:20) ....
- **f** A che ora fai colazione? (07:15) ....

04.11

2 Listen to the audio and note the time and date.

- **a** Time: .... Date: ....
- **b** Time: .... Date: ....
- **c** Time: .... Date: ....
- **d** Time: .... Date: ....

04.12

3 Now play Conversation 2 again, but this time you will play Annalisa's role. Speak in the pauses provided. Try not to refer to the text and speak about the schedule of the supermarkets in your city.

SKILL BUILDER

1 Let's get to know Aicha better. Listen to how Annalisa describes her and complete with the missing words.

Aicha è una mia cara amica, molto simpatica ed estroversa. Fa la fotografa a Milano e lavora per uno studio molto importante. La sua giornata è molto intensa: **a** .... fa colazione alle **b** .... , **c** .... velocemente e va in ufficio in bicicletta. Lavora dalle **d** .... alle **e** .... ma **f** .... fa shooting anche nel fine settimana. È una fotografa con molto talento! **g** .... dopo cena **h** .... e guarda una serie. Il **i** .... giochiamo insieme a pallavolo, perché amiamo molto lo sport. Nel weekend usciamo **j** ....: amiamo ballare **k** .... molto!

2 Riflessivo o no? Choose the correct form.

- **a** Mi faccio / Faccio la doccia prima di uscire.
- **b** Marco si mangia / mangia la pizza con gusto.
- **c** Anna e Petra si ballano / ballano sempre in discoteca.
- **d** Ti alzi / Alzi presto per andare al lavoro?
- **e** Io mi studio / studio molto per gli esami.
- **f** Voi vi divertite / divertite sempre alle feste.

3 A role play. You are making plans with Annalisa to meet for an aperitivo after work. Complete the dialogue and read your part out loud.

finisco	finisce	A che ora?	conosco	perfetto!

Annalisa	Dove preferisci andare?
You	**a** .... un bar carino. Si chiama "Floral"
Annalisa	Lo conosco. Perfetto!
You	**b** ....
Annalisa	Non so, io finisco di lavorare alle 6:30 pm. Tu?
You	**c** .... alle 6pm. Faccio una doccia e esco di casa alle 6:45pm.
Annalisa	Bene. Chiamiamo Aicha?
You	Non so a che ora **d** ...., perché ha una sessione fotografica.
Annalisa	Va bene, non importa. Alle 7pm al "Floral"?
You	**e** ....

TEST YOURSELF

1 Now it's your turn. Say aloud what time it is:

a	14:15	**e**	09:30
b	11:45	**f**	15:40
c	18:20	**g**	16:50
d	13:00	**h**	12:30

2 Write a diary for a typical day of yours, including timings and relevant reflexive verbs.

07:00 Di solito mi sveglio alle sette, ...

07:10 ....

....

....

....

....

....

....

La misteriosa donna in soffitta *The mysterious woman in the attic*

Here's a new riddle for you: During which month is All Saints' Day celebrated in Italy? The initial letter of this particular month will combine with other letters to unveil the name of the enigmatic lady in the attic.

Remember to use **My review** and **My takeaway** to assess your progress and reflect on your learning experience.

5

In this unit you will learn how to:

» Identify food and drink items.
» Talk about quantities using direct object pronouns and **ne**.
» Order at a café or a restaurant using **volere**.
» Express your preferences with **mi piace/mi piacciono**.

Un cappuccino, per favore!

My study plan

I plan to work with Unit 5

○ Every day
○ Twice a week
○ Other ________

I plan to study for

○ 5–15 minutes
○ 15–30 minutes
○ 30–45+ minutes

My progress tracker

Day / Date	Listening	Speaking	Reading	Writing	Conversation
	○	○	○	○	○
	○	○	○	○	○
	○	○	○	○	○
	○	○	○	○	○
	○	○	○	○	○
	○	○	○	○	○
	○	○	○	○	○

My goals

What do you want to be able to do or say in Italian when you complete this unit?

		Done
1	....	○
2	....	○
3	....	○

My review

SELF CHECK

	I can ...
●	... talk about food.
●	... say what I like.
●	... discuss quantities of food.
●	... say what I want.
●	... order at a restaurant or café.

CULTURE POINT 1

Il bar italiano *The Italian café*

The word bar in Italy has a much broader meaning than, for instance, in the UK and the U.S. Italian bars are more like cafés. In fact, the bar is sometimes called caffé. Some of the most ancient and renowned bars are l'Antico Caffè Greco in Rome and the Caffè Florian in Venice.

The bar is the center of social life, perhaps the most beloved place in every Italian town. You may visit your favorite bar several times a day: in the morning for a colazione (*breakfast*) with an espresso or a cappuccino paired with a cornetto (*croissant*), and in the early evening for aperitivo. You can also stop by in the afternoon for a merenda (*snack*), such as a tramezzino (*sandwich*) or a pizzetta (*small square pizza*).

Typically, Italians consume their espresso in piedi (*standing*) at the bancone (*counter*), but they also sit at a table if they have more time, to enjoy quattro chiacchiere (*a chat*) with friends. It is unusual to see people bring their laptops and work at the bar, but this trend is becoming popular in university towns.

In Italy if you order a caffè, by default you will receive an espresso. If you want any other type of coffee, you need to specify, for example un caffè americano, which is a filtered coffee. If you ask for a caffè macchiato (caldo/freddo), you will receive an espresso with a shot of hot or cold milk. A decaf espresso is called il caffè decaffeinato. At home, Italians often make coffee using a stovetop coffee maker called la moka. A latte does not exist in Italy, but you can order un bicchiere di latte and ask the barista to add a shot of espresso.

At the restaurant, the order of courses is fixed. You can choose to skip il secondo or il primo if you prefer a light meal, but you usually wouldn't order a contorno at the same time with a primo, or an antipasto with a secondo.

Explore the website of Caffè Pedrocchi in Padua, one of the most iconic bars in Italy.

Look at the menu: quanti tipi di caffè conosci?

VOCABULARY BUILDER 1

05.01

Look at the words and phrases and complete the missing English words and expressions. Then listen and try to imitate the pronunciation of the speakers.

VERBI E FRASI UTILI	*VERBS AND USEFUL PHRASES*
vorrei...	*I would like ...*
volere	*to want*
per favore	*please*
mi piace/mi piacciono	*I like*
bere	*to drink*
mangiare	*to eat*
hai fame!	*you are hungry*
AL BAR	***AT THE CAFÉ***
il caffè/l'espresso	*coffee/espresso*
il cornetto/la brioche	....
il tramezzino	....
il bicchiere di latte	....
il bicchiere d'acqua naturale/gassata	*glass of still/sparkling water*
la spremuta d'arancia	*freshly squeezed orange juice*
il succo di frutta	*fruit juice*
seduti al tavolo	*sitting at the table*
in piedi	....
la merenda	*afternoon snack*
il tost al formaggio/prosciutto	*toasted sandwich with cheese and/or ham*
la tazza	*cup*
dolce/salato	*sweet/savory*
nutriente	*nutritious*
vegetariano/a	*vegetarian*
AL RISTORANTE	***AT THE RESTAURANT***
l'antipasto	*appetizer*
il primo	*first course* (usually pasta/rice/soup)
il secondo	*second course* (meat/fish/vegetarian)
il contorno	*side dish* (usually vegetables or potatoes)
il dolce/il dessert	*dessert*
il pane	*bread*

Vocabulary practice 1

Find the odd one out.

a primo – tramezzino – secondo – spremuta
b spremuta – espresso – cappuccino – macchiato
c dolce – cornetto – brioche – tramezzino
d succo di frutta – latte – primo – espresso

Pronunciation practice

05.02

Listen to how the speaker pronounces the words below, paying particular attention to the underlined parts, then repeat.

1 latte **2** espresso **3** tazza **4** macchiato **5** succo **6** cornetto

Double consonants

In Italian, all consonants except *h* can be doubled. Double consonants are pronounced much more forcefully than single consonants. With double *f*, *l*, *m*, *n*, *r*, *s*, and *v*, the sound is prolonged; with double *b*, *c*, *d*, *g*, *p*, and *t*, the voice must rest on the vowel that precedes the consonants a bit longer than usual. It can be difficult at first to differentiate between single and double consonants, but with practice you will succeed. Start by exaggerating the double consonants until you fully master the difference.

05.03

Practice with the following pairs:

1 note (*notes*) / notte (*night*)
2 pane (*bread*) / panne (*broken*)
3 rosa (*rose*) / rossa (*red*)
4 polo (*pole*) / pollo (*chicken*)
5 capa (*boss*) / cappa (*cloak*)
6 caro (*dear*) / carro (*carriage*)

CONVERSATION 1

La colazione al bar *Breakfast at the café*

05.04

1 Listen to the conversation a few times. Then listen again and read the text. Pay attention to how Matteo and Cristian order at the bar and how they say what they like and do not like.

Cristian and Matteo meet al bar, la mattina before work. Both have a long day ahead and need a forte (*strong*) shot of espresso. Matteo fa colazione al bar but Cristian is a firm believer in a colazione nutriente e proteica *(nutritious and protein-based)* a casa.

Barista	Cosa volete?
Matteo	Vorrei un cappuccino e un cornetto alla marmellata, per favore. E tu Cristian, cosa vuoi?
Cristian	Io vorrei un caffè.
Matteo	Non ti piacciono i cornetti?
Cristian	Sì, ma non mi piace fare la colazione dolce. Vado al bar perché mi piace l'espresso.
Matteo	Anche io il mattino voglio bere un caffè forte come l'espresso del bar.
Cristian	Normalmente faccio colazione con muesli e yogurt, o pane e formaggio, la colazione salata tipica delle Alpi!
Matteo	Sì, la colazione dolce non è molto nutriente...
Cristian	Fare una colazione nutriente e proteica è molto importante.
Matteo	Vero! Scusi, barista, vorrei anche un tramezzino e un tost al formaggio!
Cristian	Mamma mia! Hai fame!!

2 What do Cristian and Matteo have to drink and eat? The table with items from the conversation.

Cristian	Matteo

E tu cosa mangi per colazione? Cosa bevi? Dove fai colazione?

LANGUAGE BUILDER 1

Language discovery 1

Look at the sentences from the conversation. Find the Italian sentence corresponding to the English phrases. How do you say *you guys want*, *you want*, *I want* in Italian?

a What do you guys want?
b And you, Cristian, what do you want?
c I also want to drink a strong coffee.

Expressing wants with the verb **volere**

The verb volere is used to express what a person wants. It can be followed by an object or an action (a verb in the infinitive, base form):

Io voglio un cornetto.	*I want a croissant.*
Io voglio bere un caffé forte.	*I want to drink a strong coffee.*
Io voglio mangiare un cornetto.	*I want to eat a croissant.*

The verb volere is irregular. Notice the pattern of the verb.

volere (*to want*)

io	voglio	noi	vogliamo
tu	vuoi	voi	volete
lui/lei/Lei	vuole	loro	vogliono

To express what someone wants more politely, as when asking for something or ordering at a café or restaurant, use vorrei (*I would like*). Vorrei un cappuccino, per favore. (*I'd like a cappuccino, please.*) This is the conditional tense of volere, which you will learn about in future units. For now, just remember the polite form vorrei.

Speaking of irregular verbs ... notice how the verb bere, to drink, has regular verb forms but an irregular stem. The infinitive is bere, but the stem is bev-: io bevo, tu bevi, lui/lei/Lei beve, noi beviamo, voi bevete, loro bevono.

Language practice 1

Complete the conversation among a cameriere (*server*) and customers at a restaurant. Use the correct form of the verb volere or vorrei.

Cameriere Buonasera, signori, cosa **a** .... ?

Signore Io **b** .... un antipasto, la bruschetta. E tu, Maria, **c** .... un antipasto?

Signora Per me no, grazie. Io **d** .... un primo, le lasagne.

Cameriere Bene. **e** .... un secondo?

Signore Io sì. **f** .... un secondo vegetariano, l'omelette ai funghi.

Signora Per me no, non **g** .... mangiare molto.

Cameriere Allora, una bruschetta, le lasagne e un'omelette ai funghi. E da bere?

Signore Mmm, Maria, tu **h** .... il vino?

Signora No, per me acqua gassata.

Signore Anche io non **i** .... bere vino. Scusi, cameriere, **j** .... una Coca Cola Zero.

LANGUAGE BUILDER 2

Language discovery 2

Listen to the conversation again and repeat in the pauses provided. Then look at the following sentences from the conversation. When is mi piace used and when is mi piacciono used?

Non ti piacciono i cornetti?
Non mi piace fare una colazione dolce.
Mi piace l'espresso.
Mi piacciono i biscotti.

Say what you like: mi piace/mi piacciono

In Italian, when one says "I like," they literally say that something is pleasing to them: Il cappuccino mi piace. *(I like cappuccino,* literally: *cappuccino is pleasing to me*). If what they like is plural, then they use the form piacciono: Mi piacciono i cornetti. (*I like croissants,* literally: *croissants are pleasing to me*).

When you like doing something, use piace and a verb in the infinitive:

Mi piace andare al bar. *I like going to the café.*

To say you like, use ti piace/piacciono (informal) or Le piace/piacciono (polite):

Ti piace questa colazione nutriente?	*Do you like this nutritious breakfast?*
Non ti piacciono le bruschette?	*Don't you like bruschette?*
Le piace cenare al ristorante?	*Do you like eating out at a restaurant?*

	Singular object	Activity (verb)	Plural object
io	(non) mi piace	(non) mi piace	(non) mi piacciono
tu	(non) ti piace	(non) ti piace	(non) ti piacciono
lei	(non) le piace	(non) le piace	(non) le piacciono

How do you agree or disagree with someone expressing their preferences? If someone says Mi piace il caffé (*I like coffee*) and you agree, say: anche a me (*me too*). To disagree, say: a me no (*I don't*). If somebody says Non mi piace il caffé (*I don't like coffee*) and you agree, say: Neanche a me (*neither do I*). If you disagree, say: a me sì (*I do*).

Language practice 2

1 Look at the list of objects and decide whether to use piace or piacciono.

- l'aperitivo
- la bruschetta
- gli spaghetti
- andare al ristorante
- la colazione dolce
- i biscotti
- il pane
- la spremuta d'arancia
- le lasagne
- fare colazione al bar
- i cereali
- lo yogurt
- l'omelette
- i funghi
- studiare l'italiano
- il latte

05.06

2 Listen to the speaker say what they like. Repeat and then agree or disagree with them using the expressions: Anche a me! – A me no. – Neanche a me! – A me sì.

05.07

3 Now play Conversation 1 again, but this time you will play Cristian's role. Speak in the pauses provided. Try not to refer to the text.

CULTURE POINT 2

Cucina italiana o cucina regionale? *Italian cuisine or regional cuisine?*

Italy is famous for its cibo (*food*), with restaurants offering Italian cucina (*cuisine*) in every corner of the world. However, when people travel to Italy, they soon discover that there is no such thing as typical Italian food: every province of Italy has its own piatti (*dishes*), inspired by local traditions. If you want to know more, join actor Stanley Tucci in his series *Searching for Italy*, in which he explores the unique culinary tradition of every region of Italy.

Roughly 130 years before Tucci's series, another man was inspired by Italy's gastronomic richness: Pellegrino Artusi. This wealthy businessman is best known as the author of the bestselling cookbook *Science in the Kitchen and the Art of Eating Well*, published in 1891. The book contains over 3000 ricette (*recipes*) celebrating Italy's multicultural cuisine, from Sicilian couscous to Tuscan ribollita (*bread soup*), Northern Italian risotto, and Austrian-inspired frittata dolce con ribes (*sweet omelet with currants*). But it is so much more than a book of recipes—it also makes for great literature, offering a collection of amusing anecdotes about Italian history and traditions.

a Quali piatti italiani conosci? Di dove sono?

b Quali piatti italiani ti piacciono?

Stanley Tucci's love for Italian cuisine is well known. Stanley is of Italian descent, and he loves to explore the food of the country of his ancestors. Watch the trailer for his show, *Stanley Tucci: Searching for Italy*. Can you name any of the dishes you see?

VOCABULARY BUILDER 2

05.08

Look at the words and phrases and complete the missing English words and expressions. Then listen and try to imitate the pronunciation of the speakers. For more food items, see the dedicated table in the Glossary.

IL CIBO	*FOOD*
la carne	*meat*
il pollo/il manzo	*chicken/beef*
il pesce	*fish*
la frutta	....
la fragola	*strawberry*
la mela	*apple*
l'arancia	*orange*
le uova (sing. un uovo)	*eggs*
la verdura	*vegetables*
l'insalata	*salad*
la patata	....
il peperone	*pepper*
il pomodoro	*tomato*
la cipolla	*onion*
lo zucchero	*sugar*
l'olio d'oliva	....
il riso	*rice*
il sale/il pepe	*salt/pepper*
LE QUANTITÀ	***QUANTITIES***
un etto/100 grammi	*100 grams*
un chilo/1000 grammi	*1 kg*
un litro	*1 liter*
un pezzo/un pacco	*a piece/a packet*
un cucchiaio/cucchiaino	*tablespoon/teaspoon*
ESPRESSIONI UTILI	***USEFUL EXPRESSIONS***
ci vuole/ci vogliono	*it takes/it is necessary/you need*

An especially useful expression with the verb volere is ci vuole / ci vogliono. It is used to talk about what or how much of something is needed to accomplish a certain goal. Per fare il tiramisù ci vuole il caffé / ci vogliono due bicchieri di caffè. (To make tiramisu you need coffee/you need two glasses of coffee.). Like with mi piace/mi piacciono, ci vuole is followed by a singular object, ci vogliono is followed by a plural object.

Vocabulary practice 2

Facciamo una ricetta! Cosa ci vuole? Look at three famous Italian dishes and try to identify the ingredients you need to make them. Write each ingredient below the dish it is needed for. For each ingredient, use either ci vuole or ci vogliono, as in the example. If necessary, look up the le ricette on the Internet.

- la mozzarella
- 15 biscotti
- 1 bicchiere di caffè
- 2 etti di riso
- un cucchiaino di zafferano (*saffron*)
- una cipolla
- 750 grammi di mascarpone (*creamy cheese*)
- 1 etto di zucchero
- il basilico (*basil*)
- il pomodoro
- un cucchiaio di olio d'oliva
- 1 cucchiaio di burro
- 5 uova
- 500 grammi di farina (*flour*)
- l'acqua
- 5 grammi di lievito (*yeast*)
- 1 litro di brodo vegetale (*vegetable stock/broth*)
- il sale

La pizza napoletana	Il tiramisù	Il risotto alla milanese
ci vogliono 5 grammi di lievito		

CONVERSATION 2

Una ricetta napoletana: *A Neapolitan recipe*

05.09

1 Here are a few words and expressions to help you understand the following conversation. Note their meanings.

pronto/a/i/e	*ready*
cuocere	*to cook, as in "to turn from raw to cooked"*
mettere	*to put*
la consegna a casa	*home delivery*

05.10

2 Listen to the conversation a few times. Then listen to the conversation again and read the text.

Aicha and Annalisa are in Aicha's kitchen. Some friends are coming over, and Annalisa is trying to replicate a signature recipe suo padre makes: pasta con patate. Il padre di Annalisa does not specify the exact quantities of the recipe: un pizzico (*pinch*) of this, un po' (*a bit*) of that. Annalisa, however, thinks that cucinare (*to prepare food*) is an exact science, and she needs to be sicura (*sure*) of everything. Listen to how Annalisa and Aicha discuss their culinary attempt, paying attention to how they ask each other about ingredients and quantities.

Aicha	Le patate sono pronte. Metti il sale? E le cipolle?
Annalisa	Sì, lo metto. Le cipolle le preparo dopo.
Aicha	Sì, ma quante?
Annalisa	Mio padre ne mette... un po'! Una, due...
Aicha	E la pasta?
Annalisa	La cuociamo separatamente... penso...
Aicha	Sei sicura? Come pasta usiamo i maccheroni?
Annalisa	Sì, li preferisco. E secondo te quanta pasta mettiamo?
Aicha	Mmmm, non so. Siamo in dieci, ne mettiamo un chilo? Ne facciamo un etto per persona, secondo me va bene.
	The pasta is almost ready and their friends are arriving ...
Aicha	Serviamo la pasta?
Annalisa	No, non la serviamo, non è buona! Telefoniamo al ristorante Mamma Mia, fanno la consegna a casa...

3 Based on the conversation, complete the ricetta for pasta con patate with the necessary ingredients.

Per fare questa ricetta, ci vogliono le **a** .... e la pasta, preferibilmente i **b** .... Per dieci persone ci vuole un **c** .... di pasta e ci vogliono due **d** .... Ovviamente ci vuole anche il **e** ....

There are about 350 types of pasta in Italy, and Italians are very particular about which sauce goes with each kind. There is pasta fresca all'uovo (*fresh egg pasta*), such as lasagne (always plural in Italian) or cannelloni, or pasta secca (*dry pasta*): spaghetti, penne, maccheroni or pasta di grano duro (*durum wheat pasta*) such as orecchiette, which means "little ears."

LANGUAGE BUILDER 3

Language discovery 3

Look at these questions and find the answers in the conversation. Which word in the answer stands for a word used in the question? What is the relationship between the word in the question and its substitute?

a Metti il sale? ....

b Prepari le cipolle? ....

c Usiamo i maccheroni? ....

d Serviamo la pasta? ....

Direct object pronouns

A direct object directly receives the action of the verb: Metti il sale? *Add the salt?* Il sale is the direct object. To avoid repeating words, a pronoun can be used instead: Sì, lo metto. *Yes, I'm adding it.* Lo is the direct object pronoun, and it stands for il sale. Mangi la frutta? Sì, mangio la frutta = Sì, la mangio.

In Italian, the pronoun must reflect the gender and number of the nouns it stands for:

	Masculine	**Feminine**
Singular	lo	la
Plural	li	le

Notice that, unlike in English, the pronoun always goes before the verb:

Usiamo i maccheroni? — *Are we going to use macaroni?*
Sì, li preferisco. — *Yes, I prefer it* (lit. *them*).

If the sentence is negative, the pronoun goes between non and the verb:

Mangi la carne? – No, non la mangio. — *Do you eat meat ?—No, I don't eat it.*

These direct object pronouns can refer to people, as well as things. Like any masculine word, lui is replaced by lo, lei is replaced by la, and loro can be replaced by either li or le, depending on whether loro is a group of males or females. In Italian, the generic plural for a mixed group is li, but nowadays, in writing, people tend to use the * or the schwa **ə**: **l*/l ə**.

There are also pronouns to replace the words io, tu, noi, and voi: io = mi, tu = ti, noi = ci, voi = vi. So now you can say *I love you* in Italian: Io ti amo! Find out more about pronouns in Unit 8 and the Grammar summary.

Language practice 3

Complete the sentences with the correct pronoun replacing the underlined words.

- **a** Non mi piace la cipolla e non .... mangio.
- **b** Vuoi un caffè? No grazie, non .... voglio.
- **c** Prepariamo le lasagne e .... cuociamo.
- **d** Mangi i peperoni? Sì, ... mangio.
- **e** Chiamo i miei amici e .... invito a casa.
- **f** Bevi il latte? Sono allergico e non .... bevo.
- **g** Inviti Sandra? Sì, ... invito.
- **h** Fai la colazione? Sì .... faccio al bar.
- **i** Conosci Mary e Lena? Sì, ... conosco.
- **j** Vuoi un antipasto? Sì, ... voglio.
- **k** E Cristian? .... invitiamo?
- **l** Le fragole? Io .... adoro!

LANGUAGE BUILDER 4

Language discovery 4

05.11

Listen to the conversation again and repeat each line in the pauses provided. Try to imitate the phrasing and intonation you hear. Then read the text and find the following questions in the conversation and complete the responses. What does ne refer to? Why do you think it was used instead of the direct object pronouns? Also, based on what you know about agreement, complete quanto/a/e/e with the appropriate vowel.

- **a** Quant .... cipolle (mettiamo)? ....
- **b** Quant .... pasta mettiamo ? ....

Ne: the pronoun of quantity

To ask about the quantity of something in Italian, use the question word quanto/a/i/e (which agrees with the gender and number of the word that follows):

Quanta pasta mangi?	*How much pasta do you eat?*
Quante cipolle ci vogliono?	*How many onions do we need?*

To avoid repeating the item, use ne:

Quanta pasta mangi? – Io mangio un etto di pasta. = Io ne mangio un etto.

How much pasta do you eat?—I eat 100 grams of it.

Ne replaces di + object. Like all pronouns, it is placed before the verb. If the sentence is negative, ne goes between non and the verb.

Quanto zucchero metti nel caffé? – Non ne metto.

How much sugar do you put in [your] coffee?—I don't put any (of it).

Language practice 4

1 Match a question in the left column with an answer in the right column, creating a full sentence.

Example: Quanto zucchero vuoi? *Ne voglio un cucchiaino.*

1 Quanta acqua bevi?	**a** Un bicchiere, con un po' di caffè.
2 Quanto latte bevi?	**b** Normalmente solo uno, il mattino.
3 Quanto sale metti?	**c** Quattro o cinque, con il tè.
4 Quante patate cuociamo?	**d** Un litro al giorno.
5 Quanto burro metti in questa ricetta?	**e** Un pizzico. Non mi piacciono i cibi salati.
6 Quanti biscotti mangi a colazione?	**f** 2 etti. È una ricetta molto calorica.
7 Quanti caffé bevi al giorno?	**g** Tre ma grandi.

05.12

2 Listen to the speaker asking questions about your daily dietary habits. Answer using ne and the appropriate quantity.

Example: Quanta acqua bevi? *Ne bevo due litri*.

05.13

3 Now play Conversation 2 again, but this time you will play Aicha's role. Speak in the pauses provided. Try not to refer to the text.

SKILL BUILDER

1 **Look at the menu of the Neapolitan restaurant Mamma Mia. Read and complete the dialogue below with the missing words. You can look up i piatti tipici on the Internet.**

MENU

ANTIPASTI

Insalata caprese di mozzarella e pomodoro

Pizza fritta

Prosciutto e melone

Bruschetta

PRIMI

Spaghetti al pomodoro e basilico

Pasta con patate

Tagliatelle al ragù napoletano

SECONDI

Baccalà alla napoletana

Pesce alla griglia del giorno

Fritto misto

Scaloppine alla pizzaiola

CONTORNI

Zucchine alla griglia

Patate napoletane

DESSERT

Pastiera napoletana

Tiramisù

Espresso

Annalisa Buonasera, vorrei ordinare con consegna a casa.

Cameriere Bene, cosa desidera?

Annalisa Come antipasto, vorrei un po' di bruschette.

Cameriere **a** .... bruschette?

Annalisa **b** .... vorrei 10. Poi vorrei la pasta con patate per dieci persone. Mettete anche il formaggio nella pasta?

Cameriere Sì, **c** .... mettiamo, ma se una persona è allergica, allora **d** .... mettiamo a parte (*on the side*).

Annalisa E le zucchine alla griglia sono fresche?

Cameriere Sì, **e** .... prepariamo fresche tutti i giorni.

Annalisa Va bene, allora **f** .... prendo per cinque persone. E cinque fritti misti.

Cameriere Vuole i dessert? La pastiera è deliziosa.

Annalisa Va bene, **g** .... prendo.

TEST YOURSELF

1 Complete the following sentences with either piace or piacciono.

- **a** Non mi .... cucinare: preferisco mangiare!
- **b** Ti .... i cannelloni con la mozzarella?
- **c** Non mi .... i cornetti: preferisco muesli e yogurt.
- **d** Sono vegetarian* quindi non mi .... la carne.
- **e** Ti .... il cibo italiano?

2 Answer the questions using direct object pronouns or ne.

- **a** Prepari le lasagne?
- **b** Quanti caffè bevi al giorno?
- **c** Metti il pepe?
- **d** Quanti cucchiaini di zucchero metti nel caffè?
- **e** Mangi gli spaghetti?
- **f** Compri il pane per favore?

3 Cosa mangi normalmente? Cosa bevi? Keep a diary of what you eat and drink every day of the week. Include quantities, if applicable.

4 A friend of yours is visiting Italy and staying with an Italian family. Tell them what they should expect in terms of breakfast.

La misteriosa donna in soffitta *The mysterious woman in the attic*

You learned the word for oil, olio. But what about vinegar? Italy is famous for its balsamic vinegar, a DOP (Denominazione d'Origine Protetta) product from the Northern city of Modena. The first letter of the word for vinegar will give you the last letter in the name of the woman in the painting!

Remember to use **My review** and **My takeaway** to assess your progress and reflect on your learning experience.

6

In this unit you will learn how to:

» Describe a city.
» Locate monuments and buildings.
» Ask for and follow directions.
» Express obligation, possibility, and permission.

Vita in città

My study plan

I plan to work with Unit 6

○ Every day
○ Twice a week
○ Other ___________

I plan to study for

○ 5–15 minutes
○ 15–30 minutes
○ 30–45+ minutes

My progress tracker

Day / Date	Listening	Speaking	Reading	Writing	Conversation
	○	○	○	○	○
	○	○	○	○	○
	○	○	○	○	○
	○	○	○	○	○
	○	○	○	○	○
	○	○	○	○	○
	○	○	○	○	○

My goals

What do you want to be able to do or say in Italian when you complete this unit?

		Done
1	....	○
2	....	○
3	....	○

My review

SELF CHECK

	I can ...
●	... describe what to find in a city.
●	... give or listen to directions to reach a specific location.
●	... identify and describe the position of objects in a physical space.
●	... tell what I must/must not do.
●	... tell what I can/cannot do.

CULTURE POINT 1

Venezia è un pesce: la città sull'acqua *Venice is a fish: the city on water*

Very few cities in the world can boast the same fame as Venezia, the "Floating City"—a mesmerizing destination built on a cluster of isole (*islands*) connected by canals and picturesque ponti (*bridges*). The Canal Grande (*Grand Canal*) winds through the city leading to scenic piazze (*squares*). Although a bit expensive, gondola rides are a must, allowing visitors to immerse themselves in Venezia's enchanting ambiance. The city's cultural scene shines with the renowned Biennale di Venezia and the vibrant Carnevale, where masks and costumes create a festive atmosphere.

High tides continue to pose challenges for Venice, often causing acqua alta (*exceptional tide peaks*) that inundate the city and its islands. Fortunately, there is a solution called MOSE, an engineering system featuring rows of mobile gates that can temporarily separate the lagoon from the sea. Despite challenges from rising sea levels and tourism, Venezia continues to captivate with its charm and remains a testament to human creativity and the enchanting power of a city shaped by water.

Palazzo Ducale is one of the most famous edifici (*buildings*) in Venezia, standing as a masterpiece of Venetian Gothic architecture. Within its walls, visitors can explore the palace's various sale (*chambers*) and breathtaking artwork, including Tintoretto's monumental painting *Il Paradiso*, one of the largest oil paintings in the world.

Explore Palazzo Ducale's website and find out:

a the opening hours and days

b what exhibitions are on at the moment

c in what sala (*hall*) you can spot Tintoretto's masterpiece *Il Paradiso*

VOCABULARY BUILDER 1

06.01

Look at the words and phrases and complete the missing English words and expressions. Then listen and try to imitate the pronunciation of the speakers.

LA CITTÀ	***CITY***
l'albero	*tree*
la biblioteca	*library*
l'edificio	*building*
la fontana	....
l'incrocio	*intersection*
la libreria	*bookshop*
il mercato	....
il monumento	....
il negozio	*shop*
il ponte	*bridge*
il semaforo	*traffic light*
la strada	*street*
LE INDICAZIONI	***DIRECTIONS***
a destra (di)	*to the right (of)*
a sinistra (di)	....
accanto a	*next to*
davanti, di fronte a	*in front of, opposite to*
dietro a	*behind*
dritto	*straight*
lontano da	*far from*
sopra	*above*
sotto	*under/underneath*
vicino a	*close to*
VERBI	***VERBS***
attraversare	*to cross*
girare	*to turn*
passare	*to pass/pass through/spend*

Vocabulary practice 1

Choose the odd one out.

a strada, piazza, lontano, via

b ponte, fontana, scuola, monumento

c a sinistra, dritto, dietro, semaforo

d attraversare, andare, mangiare, girare

e dritto, ristorante, libreria, negozio

f davanti, museo, di fronte, vicino

CONVERSATION 1

Dov'è il tuo ufficio? *Where is your office?*

06.02

1 Here are a few words and expressions to help you understand the following conversation. Note their meanings.

Dimmi!	*Tell me!*	Mi sono perso!	*I am lost!*
volentieri	*with pleasure*	ancora	*again*
un favore	*a favor*		

06.03

2 Listen to the conversation a few times without looking at the text. Then listen to the conversation again and read the text.

Annalisa is just about to head out for work when Cristian asks for un favore (*a favor*). Out of curiosity, he starts inquiring about the location of her office in Venice. It is worth noting that Venezia, unlike other cities in Italy, does not have vie (*streets*) or piazze, but calli and campi. The only via is via Garibaldi, where Annalisa and Cristian live. Listen to their conversation to see how Annalisa provides him with le indicazioni (*directions*) to find her workplace.

Cristian Annalisa, passi dal supermercato? Devo comprare il latte, ma non ho tempo.

Annalisa Sì, va bene. Ho un supermercato vicino al mio ufficio.

Cristian Fantastico, grazie! E, dimmi, dov'è esattamente il tuo ufficio?

Annalisa Conosci la libreria "Acqua Alta"?

Cristian Certo, la dobbiamo visitare!

Annalisa Volentieri! Ecco, quando esci dalla libreria, giri a sinistra e arrivi in una strada lunga. Se continui per venti metri, davanti al negozio di artigianato, giri a sinistra e poi a destra. L'ufficio è in Ramo dei Orbi, dietro alla fontana.

Cristian Ehm, mi sono perso! Google Maps?

Annalisa Cristian, abiti a Venezia da mesi! Devi imparare la geografia della città!

3 List the itinerary described by Annalisa from Libreria Acqua Alta to Ramo dei Orbi.

....

....

....

....

In Venice, where water serves as the roads, maintaining a collection of books might seem risky, yet the Libreria Acqua Alta faces no such peril. This self-proclaimed "most beautiful bookstore in the world" has safeguarded its titles by storing them in waterproof basins, bathtubs, and even a gondola. With rooms brimming with books, magazines, and maps, the store's cozy charm is a must-see for any booklovers!

LANGUAGE BUILDER 1

Language discovery 1

Read the conversation and complete the sentences. How do the speakers express a need or a duty?

a .... comprare il latte.

b La .... visitare.

c .... imparare la geografia della città!

Expressing needs and duties with the verb **dovere**

The verb dovere is extensively used in Italian and can be translated as "to have to," "to be obligated to," and "must." Depending on the form used, it also covers the meanings of "need to," "should," and "be supposed to" (these last two will be detailed in the upcoming units). One crucial rule to remember is that dovere is always followed by an infinitive.

Devo comprare il latte.	*I have to/I need to buy some biscuits.*
Devi imparare la geografia della città!	*You must learn the geography of the city!*

Dovere is an irregular verb in the present tense, so it is important to remember all its forms. Try it yourself: complete the table with the forms you found in the conversation.

io	**a**	noi	**c** ....
tu	**b**	voi	dovete
lui/lei/Lei	deve	loro	devono

Language practice 1

Look at Cristian's list of chores for the week. The ones with a check (✓) are already done. Some of the chores are meant to be done by or with other people. Write what he/they still have to do or don't have to do.

- Comprare il latte
- Preparare le lezioni ✓
- Preparare i costumi per il cosplay (con Matteo)
- Pagare l'affitto (con Annalisa) ✓
- Scoprire il nome della signora nel quadro (con Annalisa)
- Chiamare Petra
- Scrivere email per candidatura ✓
- Organizzare riunione amici università (con Matteo) ✓

Example: Cristian deve comprare il latte. / Cristian e Annalisa non devono pagare l'affitto.

LANGUAGE BUILDER 2

Language discovery 2

06.04

Listen to the conversation again and repeat each line in the pauses provided. What words do the speakers use to describe locations and proximity? Choose the correct option.

a il supermercato è vicino / accanto all'ufficio.

b L'ufficio è davanti / dietro alla fontana.

Locating items and places

Review le indicazioni (directions) in the vocabulary builder.

Adverbs of place are used to tell where something happens, the position of something in space, and how far something or someone is from the speaker or listener. Unlike adjectives, they don't change to agree with what they describe. They are usually followed by a preposition, either a (*to*), di (*of, from*), or da (*from*).

Davanti al negozio di artigianato.	*In front of the craft shop.*
Lontano dal supermercato.	*Far from the supermarket.*
A sinistra del museo.	*To the left of the museum.*

As you might have noticed, the preposition used is not always directly translatable with the English equivalent (e.g. davanti a but *in front of*), so be careful!

Language practice 2

06.05

1 Listen to the audio track and sketch Annalisa's location in relation to the fountain.

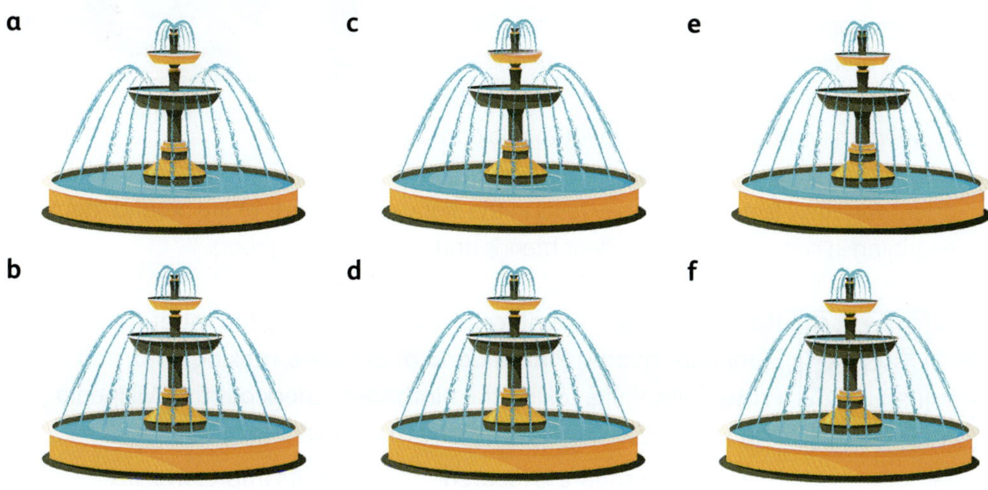

2 **You are approached by a passante (*passenger*) whose phone is out of battery and who needs to get to the station. Complete the dialogue and read your part aloud.**

Passante	Scusi, ho una domanda. È lontana la stazione?
You	(Say it's close) **a** ....
Passante	Grazie. Dov'è esattamente?
You	(Say they have to cross the bridge and turn right. At the big fountain they have to turn left and go straight.) **b** ....
Passante	Perfetto. È accanto al mercato?
You	(Say yes, it's next to the market and in front of the library) **c** ....
Passante	Grazie mille, arrivederci!

06.06

3 **Now play Conversation 1 again, but this time you will play Annalisa's role. Speak in the pauses provided. Try not to refer to the text.**

CULTURE POINT 2

La piazza, una finestra sull'italia *The piazza, a window on Italy*

Piazza Navona, Rome

All cities in Italy, however small, have a piazza—a public square with streets branching out from its center. It is the beating heart of each community, typically embraced by a beautiful chiesa (*church*), il municipio (*town hall*), and an array of inviting negozi, bar, edicole (*newsstands*), and farmacie (*pharmacies*). As you immerse yourself in the Italian experience, you will realize that the piazza truly embodies the town's spirit, its rhythm, and its vibrant essence. It is the place where people gather before heading together toward their destinations, or where they simply find a moment to relax on the church's steps or a cozy panchina (*bench*), basking in the warm glow of the late afternoon sun. Here is where they revel in the sights and sounds of life around them, engaging in conversations with dear friends and cherished neighbors.

Italy boasts two magnificent jewels in the top ten list of the largest European squares: **Piazza Carlo di Borbone**, ranking third, and **Prato della Valle**, taking the ninth spot. Check out the Wikipedia page for Piazza Carlo di Borbone to discover:

a where the square is located **b** its impressive size!

VOCABULARY BUILDER 2

Look at the words and phrases and complete the missing English words and expressions. Then listen and try to imitate the pronunciation of the speakers.

LA CITTÀ	*CITY*
la fermata dell'autobus	*the bus stop*
il fruttivendolo	*the greengrocer*
la gelateria	....
il locale	*bar, club*
l'ospedale	....
la palestra	*gym*
il parco	....
la panetteria	*bakery*
la piscina	*swimming pool*
la pizzeria	....
la stazione	....

When visiting a place, the verb andare is followed by either the preposition a, da, or in. Here are a couple of helpful tips: for all names ending in -ia, use the preposition in (e.g. in pizzeria, in farmacia, in gelateria); for all places where a professional is involved in the name, use da (dal fruttivendolo, dal barbiere).

MEZZI DI TRASPORTO	*TRANSPORTATION*
l'aereo	*plane*
l'autobus	....
il biglietto	*ticket*
la bicicletta	....
la macchina	*car*
la nave	*boat, ship*
il taxi	....
il traghetto	*ferry*
il treno	....

VERBI	*VERBS*
guidare	*to drive*
timbrare il biglietto	*to stamp your ticket*
prendere	*to take*

Vocabulary practice 2

Match the questions with the correct locations.

1	Dove mangi una pizza?	**a**	in piscina
2	Dove compri la frutta?	**b**	alla stazione
3	Dove fai esercizio fisico?	**c**	in pizzeria
4	Dove nuoti?	**d**	dal fruttivendolo
5	Dove prendi un gelato?	**e**	in palestra
6	Dove prendi il treno?	**f**	in gelateria

CONVERSATION 2

Un giro in gondola *A gondola tour*

06.08

1 Here are a few words and expressions to help you understand the following conversation. Note their meanings.

Prima di andare a casa.	*Before we go home.*	È il mio sogno!	*It's my dream!*
Andiamo!	*Let's go!*	interrompere	*to interrupt*

06.09

2 Listen to the conversation without looking at the text. Then listen to the conversation again and read the text. Try to identify the buildings and businesses they mention.

Petra, Cristian's sister, and her partner, Clara, decide to surprise Cristian with a spontaneous visit. They meet up at la stazione (*station*) Venezia Santa Lucia. When the girls express their desire to fare un giro in gondola (*take a gondola tour*) Cristian offers to be their guida (*city guide*). However, he quickly realizes that the girls do not seem very interested in the architecture.

Cristian Benvenute a Venezia!

Clara Grazie Cristian! Prima di andare a casa, facciamo un giro in gondola? È il mio sogno!

Cristian Certamente. Possiamo vedere la città con calma e posso fare da guida.

In góndola...

Cristian Davanti a voi c'è il ponte di Rialto.

Clara Che bello! Ci sono sempre molti turisti?

Cristian Sì è normale. A sinistra ci sono due palazzi importanti: Palazzo Grimani e Palazzo Moretta.

Petra Cristian, cos'è questo edificio a destra?

Cristian È solo una farmacia. Accanto...

Petra E questo invece?

Cristian Petra, non mi puoi interrompere sempre! È una gelateria.

Petra Davvero? Beh, è il momento perfetto per un gelato, no?

3 Which one of the businesses pictured below do Cristian, Clara, and Petra not come across during their gondola ride? What is its name in Italian?

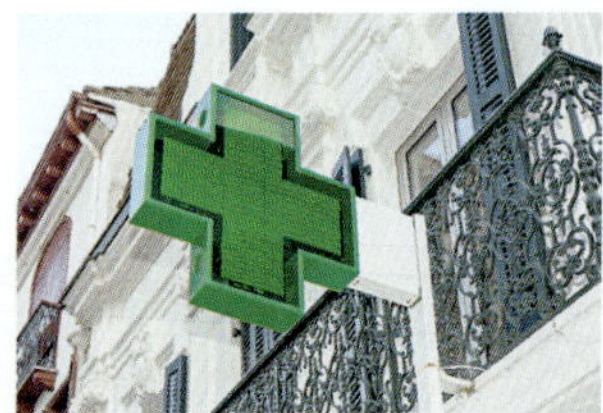
a

b

c

LANGUAGE BUILDER 3

Language discovery 3

In these lines from the conversation, what do the forms c'è and ci sono express? When do we use one or the other? Is there a discernible pattern?

Davanti a voi c'è il ponte di Rialto.
Ci sono sempre molti turisti?
Ci sono due palazzi importanti.

There is/there are: c'è and ci sono

C'è is the short form of ci è (*there is*) and it's used with singular nouns, while ci sono (*there are*) is the plural form. Both state the presence or existence of someone or something.

Davanti a voi c'è il ponte di Rialto.	*In front of you there is the Rialto bridge.*
C'è una gelateria qui vicino?	*Is there an ice-cream shop near here?*
Ci sono due palazzi importanti.	*There are two important palaces.*
Non ci sono molti turisti in questa zona.	*There aren't a lot of tourists in this area.*

Language practice 3

1 Complete the sentences with c'è or ci sono.

a .... una chiesa
b .... delle persone
c .... delle biciclette
d .... una fontana
e .... un municipio
f .... degli alberi
g .... una piazza
h .... i turisti
i .... degli edifici
j .... una strada
k .... un monumento
l .... dei bambini

2 Describe your hometown, using c'è and ci sono.

....

....

....

....

....

LANGUAGE BUILDER 4

Language discovery 4

06.10

Listen to the conversation again and repeat each line in the pauses provided. Then look at these sentences. What do you think this new verb expresses?

Possiamo vedere la città.

Posso fare da guida.

Non mi puoi interrompere sempre!

How would you translate these sentences?

Expressing possibility and asking for permission with potere

Potere is used where English would use forms like "can," "may," or "to be able to." This verb is used in questions to ask for permission to do something, to state that someone can or is able to do something, and in its negative form to express an impediment or a prohibition.

Posso fare da guida.	*I can be your guide.*
Non mi puoi interrompere sempre!	*You cannot always interrupt me!*
Possiamo prendere un gelato?	*May we have (lit. take) ice cream?*

Just like dovere, potere is irregular in the present tense and is always followed by another verb in the infinitive. Look at the table and complete it with the irregular forms.

potere (*to be able*)

io	**a**	noi	**b** ....
tu	**c**	voi	potete
lui/lei/Lei	può	loro	possono

In Italian, potere expresses possibility. To express the ability to do something in Italian, use the verb sapere, which in such contexts would mean ***to know how to***. For example, posso suonare il piano would translate to ***I can play the piano***, indicating that I can play the piano in this room, but it doesn't necessarily mean I know how to play it. On the other hand, so suonare il piano would mean ***I know how to play the piano***.

Language practice 4

1 Complete the sentences with the correct form of potere.

a Papà, oggi (noi) .... andare al parco?

b Fatima e Alessia non .... finire i compiti.

c Ragazzi, vi (io) .... aiutare a trovare la chiesa. Non è lontana!

d Jasmin non .... prendere il treno alle 16:00.

e (voi) .... comprare dei biscotti anche per me, se andate al supermercato?

2 **Now play Conversation 2 again, but this time you will play Cristian's role. Speak in the pauses provided. Try to describe part of your city and the important monuments or buildings you can find there.**

06.11

SKILL BUILDER

1 **Read the paragraph about some iconic Italian piazze. Have you ever visited one of these piazze? Which one do you prefer? Why? Then decide if these statements are true (vero) or false (falso).**

...

Piazza del Campo è la piazza principale di Siena, famosa per la sua bellezza e perché ospita il celebre Palio di Siena, una competizione che coinvolge tutta la città. La piazza ha la forma simile a una conchiglia ed è circondata dall'enorme Palazzo Pubblico, dal municipio e dalla sua torre da splendidi palazzi nobiliari.

...

Con i suoi 90.000 mq di superficie Prato della Valle a Padova è una delle più grandi piazze d'Europa. È un grande spazio di forma ellittica con al centro un'isola verde che è circondata da un canale con statue di personaggi storici. Gli abitanti di Padova vengono qui per passeggiare, andare in bicicletta e visitare il grande mercato del sabato mattina.

...

Gioiello del barocco dell'Italia del sud, la Piazza del Duomo di Lecce è una piazza chiusa, come un magnifico giardino con una sola entrata. Nella piazza ci sono raffinate sculture in pietra di santi e animali mitologici, scolpiti nella bellissima pietra leccese. Al suo interno c'è il duomo con un maestoso campanile e il palazzo del seminario.

a Piazza del Campo is one of the biggest squares in Europe. vero falso
b In Prato della Valle there is a big market every Saturday. vero falso
c In Piazza del Duomo di Lecce there are statues of historical characters. vero falso
d Piazza del Campo has the shape of a shell. vero falso
e Piazza del Duomo in Lecce has only one entrance. vero falso

06.12

2 **It's time to get to know Petra! Listen to Cristian's description and complete the text with the correct words.**

Mia sorella Petra è una grande amante (*lover*) della natura. Abita in montagna, nel nord Italia. Petra e la sua compagna Clara, non **a** .... vivere **b** .... dalle Dolomiti e hanno un B&B nella città di Dobbiaco, non **c** ...., ma **d** .... un parco naturale. Nel loro B&B **e** .... tutto per chi ama il benessere (*wellbeing*). Petra ama fare yoga e meditazione, va sempre **f** .... e fa lunghe passeggiate sui sentieri (*paths*) di montagna. Un suo difetto (*weakness*)? Non ama abbastanza l'arte e l'architettura... **g** .... fare un corso intensivo con me!

3 It's your turn! Petra wants to visit your city and asks for advice in an online forum. Would you be able to help her by describing your city and what you can do there?

TEST YOURSELF

1 Match the sentence halves.

1 In questa città non ci sono	**a** usare la tua macchina, domani?
2 Sara, possiamo	**b** una farmacia.
3 È tardi, devo	**c** cucinare molto bene.
4 Davanti alla fontana c'è	**d** andare.
5 Miriam sa	**e** ospedali.

2 Correct the wrong sentences.

a In piazza ci sono una banca.
b La stazione è dietro il parco.
c A Milano c'è la Pinacoteca di Brera.
d Alba non possiamo venire a teatro, stasera.
e Scusi, cerco la farmacia. Dove devono andare?

La misteriosa donna in soffitta *The mysterious woman in the attic*

Do you recall the location of Italy's largest square, Piazza Carlo di Borbone? The initial letter of that city's name will keep adding to the identity of our mysterious lady!

Remember to use **My review** and **My takeaway** to assess your progress and reflect on your learning experience.

7

In this unit you will learn how to:

- Recount events in the past using verbs in the **passato prossimo**.
- Discuss accommodation in a hotel.
- Talk about the weather.
- Use **molto**, **poco**, **troppo**.

In albergo

My study plan

I plan to work with Unit 7

- ○ Every day
- ○ Twice a week
- ○ Other ___________

I plan to study for

- ○ 5–15 minutes
- ○ 15–30 minutes
- ○ 30–45+ minutes

My progress tracker

Day / Date	Listen	Speak	Read	Write	Converse
	○	○	○	○	○
	○	○	○	○	○
	○	○	○	○	○
	○	○	○	○	○
	○	○	○	○	○
	○	○	○	○	○
	○	○	○	○	○

My goals

What do you want to be able to do or say in Italian when you complete this unit?

		Done
1	....	○
2	....	○
3	....	○

My review

SELF CHECK

	I can ...
●	... say what I can find in a hotel.
●	... talk about the weather.
●	... recount some events in the past tense.
●	... talk about holidays.
●	... use molto, poco, troppo.

CULTURE POINT 1

In agriturismo *Staying at a farm*

Italy is famous for its historical cities, but it also has incredible natural landscapes. In fact, many Italians choose to spend their vacanze (*vacations/holidays*) either in campagna (*in the countryside*), in montagna (*in the mountains*), or al mare (*at the seaside*). One of the best ways to enjoy la natura (*nature*) is to lodge at an agriturismo, a word that was officially coined to describe a farm stay. Since the 1950s, farmers have been adapting their fattorie (*farms*) to welcome ospiti (*guests*), providing the opportunity to participate in the life of the farm in rustic and cozy accommodation. One of the perks of agriturismo is il cibo fatto in casa (*home-made food*), often sourced and produced directly from the farm. Guests can pick fruit and vegetables, make cheese, and observe animals. Some of these agriturismi can be high end, featuring a piscina (*swimming pool*) and a spa, but most are simple and charming.

Explore the official website of agriturismi in Italy.

a Select a region. Quanti agriturismi ci sono?

b Click on posizione. What types of landscapes can you filter by? What do lago, collina, and pianura mean?

c Pick an agriturismo and explore its page. How much can you understand?

VOCABULARY BUILDER 1

07.01

Look at the words and phrases and complete the missing English words and expressions. Then listen and try to imitate the pronunciation of the speakers.

IN VACANZA IN HOTEL	*ON VACATION AT A HOTEL*
la camera/la stanza	*room*
il letto singolo/ il letto doppio	*single/double bed*
l'aria condizionata	*air conditioning*
la connessione Wi-Fi	*Wi-Fi*
la mezza pensione/pensione completa	*half/full board*
senza barriere	*barrier free*
accessibile	*accessible*
la piscina	....
il pernottamento	*overnight stay*
la spiaggia	*beach*
la campagna	....
il bosco	*wood*
la fattoria	....
la montagna	....
il mare	....
il sole	*sun*

ATTIVITÀ IN VACANZA	*HOLIDAY ACTIVITIES*
nuotare	*to swim*
visitare	....
andare in barca	*to sail on a boat*
partire	*to depart*
tornare	*to return*
prenotare	*to book*
passeggiare	*to stroll/to take a walk*

Vocabulary practice 1

Match the phrases with the symbols that they describe.

1 pernottamento
2 letto doppio
3 aria condizionata
4 connessione Internet
5 piscina
6 campagna

a 

b 

c 

d 

e 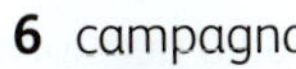

f 

CONVERSATION 1

Vacanza in agriturismo *Vacation in an agriturismo*

07.02

1 Listen to the conversation without looking at the text. Play it a few times and try to make out a few new words and phrases each time. Then listen to the conversation again and read the text.

It is summer and Annalisa is on vacation with Carlotta and two friends from her former volleyball team. Carlotta is from Puglia, a region in Southern Italy famous for its stunning spiagge and mare. They are spending a week in a masseria, a word that indicates an agriturismo in a typical farm from Puglia. Unfortunately, Aicha could not join them as she is busy with work, so her friends video call her to tell her about their trip.

Aicha	Ciao! Come va?
Annalisa e le sue amiche	Alla grande! Questa masseria è fenomenale! La nostra stanza ha l'aria condizionata e c'è la piscina. Pane fatto in casa per colazione...
Aicha	Fenomenale!
Annalisa	Ieri siamo andate al mare, abbiamo passeggiato sulla spiaggia, abbiamo dormito e abbiamo nuotato...
Aicha	E la sera dove siete andate?
Annalisa	Ieri sera abbiamo prenotato in un ristorante tipico, perché abbiamo la mezza pensione. Abbiamo mangiato pesce fresco, una delizia! Poi siamo andate a una festa in spiaggia e abbiamo ballato tutta la notte. Siamo tornate all'hotel alle quattro. E tu?
Aicha	Aha, e io... io ho lavorato in ufficio tutta la settimana!

2 Which one of these descriptions of agriturismi could be the masseria where Annalisa and her friends are staying?

a Gli Ulivi. Tipica fattoria della Puglia in un bosco di ulivi. Possibilità di fare il formaggio e l'olio d'oliva. Tre camere con letti doppi e singoli, aria condizionata e connessione Wi-Fi. Vicino a Bari.

b Il Fiore. A pochi chilometri dal mare, un agriturismo per le persone che amano il relax e la natura. Solo pensione completa. Perfetto per le famiglie. Corsi di cucina e possibilità di osservare gli animali. Non c'è la connessione Wi-Fi.

c Il Sole del Sud. Un agriturismo con tutti i comfort: piscina, aria, condizionata, Wi-Fi, camera con letti doppi o singoli. Vicino alla spiaggia. Colazione con prodotti locali e cibo fatto in casa.

LANGUAGE BUILDER 1

Language discovery 1

Match the phrases in the left column, which contain the past tense, with the corresponding verb in the infinitive in the right column. How many words does the past tense involve? What verb is the first word?

1 abbiamo passeggiato sulla spiaggia
2 abbiamo dormito
3 abbiamo nuotato
4 abbiamo mangiato
5 abbiamo ballato

a dormire
b mangiare
c ballare
d passeggiare
e nuotare

The past tense: passato prossimo (part 1)

In Italian the past tense is called passato prossimo and it involves two words: the first is called the helping verb, and in most cases this verb is avere. The second word is the main verb and is called the past participle. To form the participle, take the infinitive and replace -are with -ato, -ere with -uto, and -ire with -ito. For example: finire → finito. In passato prossimo, the helping verb changes to agree with the subject, but the past participle is the same.

	-are (ballare)	-ere (sapere)	-ire (dormire)
io	ho ballato	ho saputo	ho dormito
tu	hai ballato	hai saputo	hai dormito
lui/lei/Lei	ha ballato	ha saputo	ha dormito
noi	abbiamo ballato	abbiamo saputo	abbiamo dormito
voi	avete ballato	avete saputo	avete dormito
loro	hanno ballato	hanno saputo	hanno dormito

Tu hai mangiato. — *Did you eat?*
Io ho finito il mio lavoro. — *I finished my work.*
Abbiamo dormito fino a tardi. — *We slept late.*

Language practice 1

1 Complete the sentences with the passato prossimo of the verbs given.

a Ieri Annalisa .... (mangiare) un panino.
b Io non .... (dormire) bene.
c Noi .... (lavorare) tutto il weekend.
d Tu .... (preparare) il pranzo.
e Gli amici .... (telefonare).
f Voi .... (ballare) in discoteca.

2 Match one subject from the left column with one verb from the right column in order to create sentences in the passato prossimo that reflect the content of the conversation. Change avere in the middle column so that it agrees with the subject.

Aicha Annalisa e le sue amiche Loro Il proprietario dell'agriturismo Annalisa dice (says): Noi...	avere	preparare il pane fatto in casa dormire in spiaggia video-telefonare a Aicha lavorare tutta la settimana prenotare in un ristorante tipico

LANGUAGE BUILDER 2

Language discovery 2

Listen to the conversation again and complete these lines with the missing words. What verb is it? What do you notice in the participles following the verbs you inserted?

Aicha Ciaoo!!! Come va?

Annalisa e le sue amiche ... Ieri **a** .... andate al mare, abbiamo passeggiato sulla spiaggia, abbiamo dormito e abbiamo nuotato...

Aicha E la sera dove **b** .... andate?

Annalisa ... Poi **c** .... andate a una festa in spiaggia e abbiamo ballato tutta la notte. **d** .... tornate all'hotel alle quattro. E tu?

The past tense: passato prossimo (part 2)

When using the passato prossimo, there is a set of verbs that use essere instead of avere. They often indicate motion from point A to point B, such as andare, venire, tornare, partire, arrivare, entrare, and uscire. (See the Grammar Summary online for a full list.)

Annalisa è andata al mare. *Annalisa went to the seaside.*

Il treno è partito puntuale. *The train departed on time.*

Verbs that indicate a state of "being" in a particular place or "becoming" also use essere:

- **being:** stare, essere, rimanere = restare (*to remain*)
- **becoming:** nascere (*to be born*), morire (*to die*), diventare (*to become*)

Annalisa è diventata ingegnere. *Annalisa became an engineer.*

Io sono restata a casa. *I stayed at home.*

When paired with the verb essere, the past participle behaves like an adjective with four endings, so the last letter needs to agree with the subject in gender and number.

andare (*to go*)

io	sono andato/a/*	noi	siamo andati/e/*
tu	sei andato/a/*	voi	siete andati/e/*
Lui/lei/Lei/*	è andato/a/a/*	loro	Sono andati/e/*

Remember that the generic plural is always masculine (even for a mixed group). Nowadays, to make language more inclusive, people choose to replace the last vowel of the participle with * when addressing a mixed group, or to avoid reference to binary gender. This is done mainly in written language.

Language practice 2

1 The following story is recounted in the present tense. Change the verbs given in the present tense below to the past tense. Remember to change the last letter of the participle if necessary.

Oggi Annalisa e le sue amiche hanno una giornata molto intensa. La mattina vanno in barca per visitare una spiaggia lontana e particolarmente bella. Quando arrivano alla spiaggia, loro nuotano nel mare blu e cristallino. Alle 13 pranzano con focaccia e burrata, un tipo di mozzarella tipica della Puglia. Carlotta è vegana quindi non mangia la mozzarella ma prepara un panino con verdura. Il pomeriggio visitano un villaggio vicino. Qui Paola compra molti souvenir per la sua famiglia. Annalisa fotografa le case tipiche della Puglia e posta le fotografie sui social. Immediatamente arriva un messaggio di Aicha: "Dove andate???" E Annalisa risponde: "Visitiamo la Città Bianca." Le amiche tornano alla masseria alla sera ed escono ancora per andare al ristorante.

Ieri...

07.04

2 Listen to the questions and answer with full sentences using the passato prossimo.

a Cosa hai mangiato ieri?
b Cosa hai bevuto a colazione?
c Dove sei andato/a in vacanza recentemente (*recently*)?
d Quale città hai visitato recentemente?

07.05

3 Now play Conversation 1 again, but this time you will play Annalisa's role. Speak in the pauses provided. Try to describe your own day.

CULTURE POINT 2

Che tempo fa? *What's the weather like?*

From its northernmost point down to Sicily, Italy stretches across 12 degrees of latitude, including a great variety of climi (*climates*). As a peninsula, Italy has a 7900 km-long (4900 miles) costa (*coastline*), where il clima is Mediterranean: caldo (*warm*) and secco (*dry*). However, inland, the climate can be continental, with winters that are relatively freddi (*cold*) e umidi (*wet*) and summers that can be calde (*hot*) and umide (*humid*). Much territory is occupied by montagne: the Alpi in the North and the Appennini stretching vertically from north to south. In the mountains, il clima è fresco (*cool*) in the summer and molto freddo in the winter. In montagna la temperatura (*temperature*) can be as low as –20 °C (–4 °F), whereas in some parts of Italy it can be as hot as 45 °C (113 °F). Therefore, if you plan to travel around Italy, pack clothes for all kinds of tempo (*weather*)!

Lago di Braies in the Italian Alps

Look at the website of the previsioni del tempo (*weather forecasts*). Pick a city. Che tempo fa? Fa freddo (*cold*), fresco (*cool*), or caldo (*warm/hot*)?

VOCABULARY BUILDER 2

07.06

Look at the words and phrases and complete the missing English words and expressions. Then listen and try to imitate the pronunciation of the speakers.

IL TEMPO	*THE WEATHER*
Che tempo fa?	*What's the weather like?*
fa/è caldo	*it's* ....
fresco/freddo	*cool* ....
fa/è bello/brutto	*it's good weather/bad weather*
piove (verb piovere)	*it's raining*
c'è il vento	*it's windy*
c'è un temporale/una tempesta	*there's a storm*
c'è il sole	*it's* ....
è umido	....
è secco	*it's dry*
è nuvoloso	*it's cloudy*
la crema solare	*sunscreen*
nevica (verb nevicare)	*it's snowing*
la neve	*snow*
il ghiaccio	*ice*
il clima	....
temperato	*mild*

In Italian a word like tempo is multifunctional. It means both *time* and *weather.* It also means *rhythm* in music.

VERBI UTILI	*USEFUL VERBS*
dire	*to say*
prendere	*to take*
vedere	*to see*
spendere	*to spend*
scrivere	*to write*

Vocabulary practice 2

Che tempo fa? **Label the pictures with the appropriate description of the weather.**

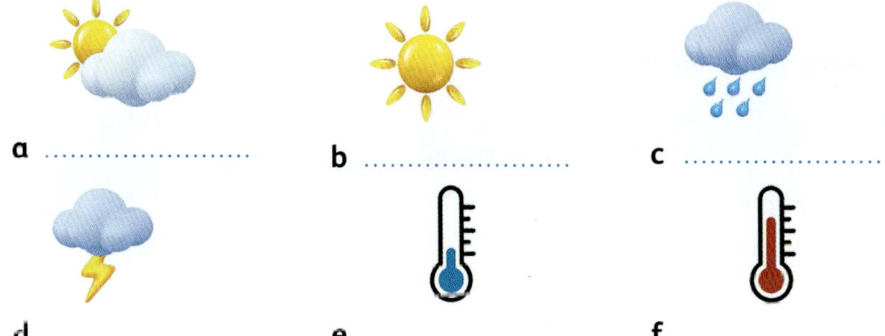

a .... **b** .... **c** ....

d .... **e** .... **f** ....

CONVERSATION 2

Vacanze romane *Roman holidays*

07.07

1 Here are a few words and expressions to help you understand the following conversation. Note their meanings.

costume da bagno *bathing suit* non ancora *not yet*

07.08

2 Listen to the conversation without looking at the text. Then listen to the conversation again and read the text. Pay attention to how the two people talk about actions in the past.

Cristian is in vacanza a Roma. He is going to a cosplay party based on a graphic novel set in Rome in the seventeenth century, *Angels and Devils*. He dressed the part and now he resembles a young signore, with his embroidered gilet, leather boots, and long-sleeved shirt. He even took a picture of the woman in the painting and put it into a collana (*necklace*). He did not take into account that a Roma fa molto caldo and now he's boiling in his costume (*costume*)! At the party, he's approached by a young woman with black hair who, for some reason, looks a bit like the mysterious painting ...

Donna in costume	Fa caldo a Roma, eh?
Cristian	Fa molto caldo!! Io sono di Bolzano e lì fa fresco, piove... non c'è sempre il sole!
Donna in costume	Aha! Hai messo la crema solare? E con questo costume...
Cristian	Ho speso molti soldi... e ora vorrei un costume da bagno!
Donna in costume	(*laughs*) Hai letto l'ultimo episodio di *Angels*?
Cristian	Non ancora. È bello?
Donna in costume	Bellissimo. L'autore ha scritto molte novels oltre a *Demons* e hanno fatto una serie TV di una, *The Michelangelo Code*.
Cristian	Non ho visto questa serie. Un amico mi ha detto che è interessante.
Donna in costume	Chi è la donna in questa collana?
Cristian	Non so...(*smiles*) sei tu?

3 Decide if the following statements are vero or falso.

a	A Roma fa fresco.	vero	falso
b	Cristian ha letto tutti gli episodi di *Angels and Devils*.	vero	falso
c	Cristian ha visto *The Michelangelo Code*.	vero	falso
d	A Bolzano non fa molto caldo.	vero	falso

LANGUAGE BUILDER 3

Language discovery 3

Look at the following sentences from the conversation and try to match the verbs in the passato prossimo with the corresponding infinitive. What do you notice in the participle? Does it follow the rule of -ato, -uto, -ito?

1 Hai messo la crema solare?	**a** mettere
2 Ho visto la serie TV.	**b** spendere
3 Hai letto l'ultimo libro?	**c** dire
4 Ho speso molti soldi.	**d** scrivere
5 L'autore ha scritto molte novels.	**e** leggere
6 Un amico mi ha detto che è bella	**f** fare
7 Netflix ha fatto una serie TV.	**g** vedere

The past tense: passato prossimo (part 3)

Some verbs in the passato prossimo have an irregular participle. This group includes some very common verbs such as fare, dire, essere, venire, prendere, etc., so you will encounter them very often. Notice that there is a pattern even among the irregular participles. Verbs that end in -endere in the infinitive often have a participle ending in -eso: spendere → speso, prendere → preso. Essere has a very different participle: stato.

For the verbs that require essere, the option of changing the participle is noted as o/a/i/e.

See a complete list of irregular participles in the Grammar Summary.

fare	fatto	**pendere**	preso
dire	detto	**spendere**	speso
leggere	letto	**mettere**	messo
scrivere	scritto	**promettere**	promesso
vedere	visto	**ammettere**	ammesso
essere	stato/a/e/i	**rimanere**	rimasto/a/e/i

C'è stato un temporale. *There was a storm.*

Io ho speso molti soldi. *I spent a lot of money.*

Abbiamo fatto un giro della città. *We did a tour of the city.*

Language practice 3

Complete the sentences with the passato prossimo, paying attention to the required helping verb and the participle.

a Ieri noi .... (fare) una passeggiata in campagna.

b Aicha, dove .... (essere)? In ufficio, ovviamente!

c La settimana scorsa il mio capo .... (scrivere) un'email a tutto lo staff.

d [Io] .... (dire) a Hans che a Roma in estate fa molto caldo.

e Ragazzi, [voi] .... (leggere) questo libro? È molto interessante!

f Cristian .... (rimanere) in hotel.

g Quanti soldi [tu] .... (spendere)?

h I miei genitori .... (prendere) il treno per Roma.

LANGUAGE BUILDER 4

Language discovery 4

07.09

Listen to the conversation again and repeat each line in the pauses provided. Try to imitate the phrasing and intonation you hear. Then look at these sentences from the conversation. When does molto/a/i/e mean "very" and when does it mean "many"? What do you notice in the word molto in the two cases?

a Fa molto caldo **b** L'autore ha scritto molte novels. **c** Ho speso molti soldi.

A little, a lot, too much: poco, molto, troppo...

In Italian molto means both *very* and *much/many*. However, it is used differently in each of these two cases. When molto means *very*, it usually comes before an adjective, reinforcing it:

Fa caldo? – Fa molto caldo! *Is it hot ?—It's very hot!*

In this case, molto is an adverb so it does not change, it does not agree with the adjective:

Venezia è molto bella. *Venice is very beautiful.*

Gli spaghetti sono molto buoni. *The spaghetti is very good.*

On the contrary, when molto is placed before a noun, it acts as an adjective, meaning *a lot*, *much* or *many*, and it agrees with the noun in gender and number: molto/a/i/e.

Bevo molta acqua. *I drink a lot of/much water.*

Ci sono molti turisti. *There are many tourists.*

The same rule applies to troppo: *too or too much/many.*

Questo gelato è troppo dolce. *This ice cream is too sweet.*

Ci sono troppe persone. *There are too many people.*

Poco works the same way, meaning *not very* or *little/few*:

Questo hotel è poco accessibile. *This hotel is not very accessible.*

Ho poco tempo. *I have little time.*

When you want to translate *a little/a few* in Italian you must say: un po'di or alcuni/e:

Ho alcuni amici. *I have a few friends.*

Ho un po' di tempo. *I have a little time.*

Molto + adjective can always be replaced with the -issimo form of the adjective: Fa molto caldo = fa caldissimo! Simply take the adjective, remove the last vowel, and substitute it with -issimo/a/e/i. It also works with adverbs such as bene and male: benissimo and malissimo.

Language practice 4

1 Complete the following sentences with the correct words in Italian.

a Non mi piace Venezia: ci sono (*too many*) .... gondole.

b Per pranzo mangiamo (*a little*) .... formaggio e frutta.

c Annalisa ha (*many*) .... amiche a Napoli.

d Cristian dice che in montagna in inverno è (*very*) .... freddo.

e Nel Sud Italia piove (*little*) ....

f Cosa fai stasera? Io esco con (*a few*) .... colleghi e vado al ristorante.

07.10

2 Now play Conversation 2 again, but this time you will play Cristian's role. Speak in the pauses provided. Try not to refer to the text.

SKILL BUILDER

07.11

1 Listen to the speaker ask questions and answer them by repeating the verb in the question.

Example: Cosa hai bevuto ieri? *Ieri ho bevuto una birra.*

07.12

2 Listen to the weather forecasts and complete the sentences with the missing information.

a A Milano oggi ci sono .... gradi. Molto caldo e umidità al 70%.

b Firenze: oggi molto .... con temperature attorno ai 24 °C.

c Per la settimana 1–7 luglio, le previsioni per Aosta dicono che .... e ci sono ....

d Previsioni per Bologna: caldo, tempo generalmente .... e temperature intorno ai 27 °C.

e Sulle Alpi ....

3 Read the following recensioni (*reviews*) of agriturismi in Italy. Then look at the reviews below and decide in which of them the information mentioned is present.

RECENSIONE 1. UN'ESPERIENZA BELLISSIMA ...

Ho passato una settimana meravigliosa all'agriturismo La Campagna Felice. Il proprietario è stato molto gentile e mi ha assegnato una stanza spaziosa e confortevole, con aria condizionata e vista sul panorama. Ho avuto l'opportunità di esplorare la campagna toscana, ho passeggiato nei boschi di ulivi e ho ammirato la natura. Ho anche partecipato a un corso di cucina toscana che è stato molto interessante.

RECENSIONE 2. QUASI PERFETTO! ...

Una cosa bella della mia vacanza all'agriturismo Il Sole di Maria è stata l'atmosfera familiare e cordiale di questo posto. Tutti i giorni Maria ha preparato la colazione con pane e marmellata fatti in casa. Ho fatto molte escursioni in barca e molte passeggiate sulla spiaggia. Unico difetto, nell'agriturismo non c'è la connessione Internet e sono andato con il mio computer in un bar del villaggio. Ma tutto il resto è perfetto!

RECENSIONE 3. TERRIBILE! ...

Ho passato un weekend terribile nell'agriturismo Stella Alpina. Il proprietario mi ha assegnato una camera piccola e fredda. Nel sito web ho letto che l'agriturismo ha la piscina ma non è vero, la piscina è chiusa. La mattina lo staff ha servito il caffè freddo e una colazione poco abbondante. Sono andato in treno ma ho visto che non è possibile fare escursioni perché l'agriturismo è molto lontano dalle montagne. Il tempo è stato brutto quindi sono rimasto tutto il weekend in camera al freddo.

a L'ospite ha avuto una stanza grande.

b L'ospite ha fatto un'esperienza gastronomica.

c L'ospite è andato al mare.

d L'ospite non ha mangiato bene.

4 Explain to a friend from your countr(ies) what an agriturismo is and what they can expect from a holiday there.

TEST YOURSELF

1 Correct the mistakes in the sentences. The mistakes are in the passato prossimo.

- **a** Cristian ha andato a Roma.
- **b** I turisti hanno visitati i monumenti e i musei.
- **c** A che ora ha partito il treno?
- **d** Hai veduto i quadri di Villa Borghese?
- **e** Aicha è rimasto in ufficio.
- **f** Avete mangiati i dolci tipici di questa regione?
- **g** Hai prenduto il biglietto dell'autobus?

2 Translate the following English sentences into Italian paying attention to the use of molto, poco, and troppo.

- **a** Venice is very beautiful.
- **b** I have many friends in Italy.
- **c** I drink little coffee but a lot of water.
- **d** In Venice there are too many tourists in summer.

La misteriosa donna in soffitta *The mysterious woman in the attic*

We are one step closer to forming the last name of the woman in the painting. There is a town in Puglia known for its white buildings, which is why its nickname is La Città Bianca, the white city. The first letter of the real name of this town will give you another clue toward discovering the identity of our mysterious character in the attic.

Remember to use **My review** and **My takeaway** to assess your progress and reflect on your learning experience.

8

In this unit you will learn how to:

- » Recognize and describe garments in Italian.
- » Talk about fashion and personal style.
- » Make informal direct requests and suggestions.

Una bella figura!

My study plan

I plan to work with Unit 8

- ○ Every day
- ○ Twice a week
- ○ Other ___________

I plan to study for

- ○ 5–15 minutes
- ○ 15–30 minutes
- ○ 30–45+ minutes

My progress tracker

Day / Date	Listening	Speaking	Reading	Writing	Conversation
	○	○	○	○	○
	○	○	○	○	○
	○	○	○	○	○
	○	○	○	○	○
	○	○	○	○	○
	○	○	○	○	○
	○	○	○	○	○

My goals

What do you want to be able to do or say in Italian when you complete this unit?

		Done
1	....	○
2	....	○
3	....	○

My review

SELF CHECK

	I can ...
●	... describe an outfit, including garments, colors, and materials.
●	... give advice and make informal requests using the imperative.
●	... properly use indirect object pronouns.
●	... properly use the adjectives bello and quello.

CULTURE POINT 1

Moda italiana *Italian fashion*

Italian moda (*fashion*) was revolutionized on February 12, 1951, when Italian businessman Giovanni Battista Giorgini orchestrated the first sfilata (*fashion show*) featuring exclusively Italian stilisti (*designers*). Before this event, all the attention was on Paris, but Giorgini recognized the potential of Italian stilisti and chose Florence as the location for his show. The combination of innovative design and high-quality tessuti (*fabrics*) gathered international attention. Unlike other countries, Italy's fabric and materials are still produced by traditional, local, often medium-sized companies. Stilisti such as Gucci, Versace, Valentino, and Armani contributed to a recognizable Italian style, often inspired by the Renaissance ideal of sprezzatura (*effortless grace*). Today, Italians often shop for abbigliamento (*clothing*) and accessori (*accessories*) online or in centri commerciali (*malls*). However, the cherished tradition of strolling in centro, admiring vetrine (*shop windows*), and enjoying seasonal saldi (*sales*) remains a beloved weekend activity for most Italians.

Take a look at the Italian version of the world's most famous rivista di moda (*fashion magazine*), *Vogue*. In the sfilate section, you will find a list of stilisti from all around the globe.

a Do you happen to know any Italian stilista?

b How and where do you prefer to shop for clothes?

VOCABULARY BUILDER 1

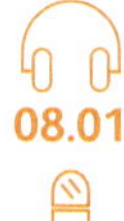
08.01

Look at the words and phrases and complete the missing English words and expressions. Then listen and try to imitate the pronunciation of the speakers.

ABBIGLIAMENTO	***CLOTHING***
la blusa	....
la borsa	*bag*
la borsetta	*purse*
il completo	*suit*
la giacca	....
i pantaloni	*pants/trousers*
i sandali	....
le scarpe	*shoes*
i tacchi	*heels*
il vestito	....
COLORI	***COLORS***
giallo/arancione	*yellow/orange*
bianco/nero	*white/black*
blu	....
rosso	....
rosa/viola	*pink/purple*
verde	*green*
STILE	***STYLE***
largo/a	....
aderente	*tight*
lungo/a	....
corto/a	*short*

Colors are adjectives and have four endings if they end in -o (rosso, a, i, e), or two endings if they end in -e (verde, i). However, the colors blu, rosa, and viola are exceptions and do not change.

Vocabulary practice 1

Look at the picture and complete the outfit description with the colors in the correct form.

Adriana ama i colori! Oggi, per esempio ha messo una blusa **a** .... e dei pantaloni **b** ...., insieme a una giacca **c** .... Anche la sua borsa è **d** ...., mentre i sandali sono **e** ....

CONVERSATION 1

Ti sta da Dio! *It looks awesome on you!*

1 Here are a few words and expressions to help you understand the following conversation. Note their meanings.

Non mi convince.	*It does not convince me.*	(non) ti sta bene	*it (does not) suits you*
il camerino	*fitting room*	mettere/mettersi	*to put on*
Ha ragione.	*He is right.*	provare	*to try*
Le sta da Dio!	*It looks awesome on her!*	scegliere	*to choose*

2 Listen to the conversation a few times without looking at the text. Then listen to the conversation again and read the text.

Tomorrow is Aicha's debut photo exhibition in Milan, and Annalisa is going along with Aicha and Filippo, Aicha's friend, to fare compere (*do some shopping*) for the occasion. They all know that Aicha has impeccable taste; she's a stilista nata (*born stylist*), so the two friends trust her advice and sense of style. After helping Filippo, it is now Annalisa's turn, and the two friends are putting all their efforts into finding the perfect outfit for her.

Annalisa Allora, come mi sta?

Filippo No, non mi convince. Troppo lungo.

Annalisa Ma posso mettere i tacchi, no?

Aicha È tutto il vestito che non ti sta bene, Filippo ha ragione. Prova questo.

Annalisa Mmm. Non è troppo aderente? Aicha non esagerare!

Filippo Secondo me è perfetto. Metti anche i sandali, così vediamo l'intero outfit. Aicha, tu come ti vesti?

Aicha Ho già deciso: un completo verde di Gucci con i tacchi rosa. Devo solo trovare una borsetta!

Filippo Divina! Annalisa, sei pronta? Apri il camerino, vogliamo vedere!

Annalisa Che dite? Vi piace?

Filippo Aicha, sei una stilista nata! Le sta da Dio!

3 Which one of the following pictures best represents Aicha's outfit for tomorrow night? Why?

a

b

LANGUAGE BUILDER 1

Language discovery 1

Throughout the conversation, the friends give some direct commands or instructions to each other. Can you tell which sentences present this type of expression and which one does not?

a Non mi convince.
b Prova questo.
c Non esagerare!
d Metti anche le scarpe.

Informal imperative

The Italian imperative, or imperativo, is used to give orders, instructions, or advice. The informal imperative, as seen in the conversation, is reserved for use with people you are familiar with, such as friends or family.

Prova questo. *Try this.* Apri il camerino. *Open the fitting room.*

The positive form of the informal imperative has the same ending (-i) as the present tense for verbs ending in -ere and -ire. For verbs ending in -are, the ending is -a.

	parlare	scrivere	aprire
positive imperative (tu)	parl**a**! (*speak!*)	scriv**i**! (*write!*)	apr**i**! (*open!*)

The negative imperative for tu in all verb groups is formed by placing non before the infinitive.

	parlare	scrivere	aprire
negative imperative (tu)	**non** parl**are**! (*don't speak!*)	**non** scriv**ere**! (*don't write*!)	**non** apr**ire**! (*don't open!*)

Language practice 1

1 Give some advice to Annalisa using the imperative form.

Example: Devo decidere cosa mettere. > (pensare al tipo di occasione)
Pensa al tipo di occasione!

a Non so dove andare a fare compere. > (scegliere una zona con molti negozi)

b L'evento è all'aperto > (comprare vestiti caldi)

c L'evento è formale > (vestire in modo elegante)

d Non posso spendere molto > (preparare un budget)

e Non posso spendere molto > (cercare negozi di seconda mano)

2 Now give your advice from 1 in the negative form.

Example: pensa al tipo di occasione > *Non pensare al tipo di occasione!*

LANGUAGE BUILDER 2

Language discovery 2

1 **Listen to the conversation again and repeat each line in the pauses provided. Then look at this phrase from the conversation. Who does the word le refer to in the sentence: Le sta da Dio!**

a Filippo **b** Annalisa **c** Aicha

2 **What other words precede the verb stare in the conversation?**

Indirect object pronouns

Italian indirect pronouns are words that replace the indirect object of a sentence. The indirect object is the person or thing that receives the action indirectly. To put it simply, they answer the question "to whom" or "for whom" something is done. Like direct object pronouns, they usually precede the verb.

Indirect object pronouns

mi	(to/for me)	ci	(to/for us)
ti	(to/for you)	vi	(to/for you plural)
gli	(to/for him)	gli	(to/for them)
le	(to/for her, to/for you formal)		

Le (*to her*) ho scritto una lettera. *I wrote her a letter.*

Gli (*to him*) ho chiesto un consiglio. *I asked him for advice.*

Some verbs are always used with indirect objects, such as piacere: mi piace, gli piace; stare bene/male: mi sta bene, le sta bene; mancare (*to miss*): mi manca, gli manca and interessare: mi interessa, le interessa.

Language practice 2

1 **Change the following sentences, replacing words in bold with indirect pronouns.**

Example: Ho suggerito a Filippo di mettere la giacca > *Gli ho suggerito di mettere la giacca*

a **A te** piacciono questi pantaloni ? > ....

b La commessa ha consigliato **a Stefano** queste scarpe > ....

c **A voi** sta molto bene il nero > ....

d Annalisa regala **a Aicha** una borsetta > ....

e Hanno detto **a noi** di mettere i tacchi > ....

f Aicha consiglia **a Filippo e Annalisa** l'outfit perfetto > ....

2 Help your friend Diego choose an outfit for a formal dinner.

Diego Ti piace questa giacca?

You **a** (Say no, it's too tight for him.)

Diego Ok. E questa?

You **b** (Say it's too short. Ask him if he likes the blue jacket next to white pants.)

Diego Sì, bella. Mi piace.

You **c** (Tell him to call the shop assistant and ask where the fitting room is.)

[...]

Diego Allora, come mi sta?

You **d** (Say it suits him. It's perfect.)

CULTURE POINT 2

Una questione di stile *A matter of style*

In Italy, festivities and special occasions are celebrated with joy and attention a vestirsi con stile (*to dress stylishly*). Dress codes vary, but l'eleganza (*elegance*) is always appreciated. I matrimoni (*weddings*) call for formal attire, with men in abito da cerimonia (*suits*) and women in vestiti eleganti (*chic dresses*). Religious celebrations require modesty, covering shoulders and knees. Festivals and carnivals, on the other hand, invite costumi colorati e maschere (*colorful costumes and masks*) for a lively atmosphere. Dinner parties and gatherings favor un abbigliamento formale, ma elegante (*smart but casual look*). Italians take pride in their appearance, embracing their unique sense of stile (*style*) with warmth and charm. Whatever the occasion, dressing with flair reflects the spirit of Italy's rich fashion heritage.

People wearing colorful costumes for Carnivale in Venezia

Head to the official website of Max Mara, a famous Italian fashion business. Check out the newest collection. If you were to attend an Italian evening wedding with the ceremony in a church, what outfit would you choose to wear?

VOCABULARY BUILDER 2

08.05

Look at the words and phrases and complete the missing English words and expressions. Then listen and try to imitate the pronunciation of the speakers.

ABBIGLIAMENTO	*CLOTHING*
i calzini	*socks*
il cappello	*hat*
il cappotto	*coat*
il costume	*swimsuit*
la gonna	*skirt*
i guanti	*gloves*
la maglietta/t-shirt	....
il maglione	*sweater*

la sciarpa	*scarf*
gli stivali	*boots*
lo zaino	*backpack*
STILE	***STYLE***
alla moda	*fashionable*
classico/a	....
elegante	....
fuori moda	*out of fashion*
giovanile	....
sportivo/a	*sporty*
MATERIALI	***MATERIALS***
il cotone	....
il cuoio/la pelle	*leather*
la lana	*wool*
il lino	....
la seta	*silk*
VERBI	***VERBS***
indossare	*to wear*

Vocabulary practice 2

In which season would you wear these clothes? Sort the words.

il costume	la maglietta
guanti	la sciarpa
i calzini di lana i sandali	la gonna di lino
il maglione	il cappotto

Cosa metto in...

ESTATE: ....

INVERNO: ....

CONVERSATION 2

Consigli di stile *Fashion tips*

08.06

1 Here are a few words and expressions to help you understand the following conversation. Note their meanings.

il tuo parere	*your opinion*
Mettilo lo stesso!	*Wear it anyway!*

08.07

2 Listen to the conversation a few times and try to make out a few new words and phrases each time.

Cristian is preparing for a wedding in his hometown next week, and he really wants to fare una bella figura (*make a good impression*). However, he is having some trouble finding the perfect outfit, so he turns to Annalisa for her advice. Listen to the changes Annalisa suggests and how they mention the garments in general.

Cristian Dammi il tuo parere: sono abbastanza elegante per il matrimonio? Voglio fare bella figura.

Annalisa Scherzi?! Per un matrimonio indossi quei pantaloni e quella giacca?

Cristian Sono troppo sportivi?

Annalisa No, ma sono due materiali e due blu differenti, guardali!

Cristian Hai ragione. Ho solo un completo, ma è di lana. Fa troppo caldo!

Annalisa Ma no, mettilo lo stesso, il matrimonio è sulle Dolomiti!

Cristian E le scarpe? Il completo è nero e non ho scarpe nere eleganti.

Annalisa Chiedile a Matteo! Ho visto che ne ha un bel paio: alla moda, di pelle nera...

Cristian Bella idea! Abbiamo anche lo stesso numero.

3 Decide if the following statements are vero (*true*) or falso (*false*).

a	Cristian è troppo elegante per il matrimonio.	vero	falso
b	Annalisa non vuole aiutare **Cristian**	vero	falso
c	Cristian ha un completo **blu**	vero	falso
d	Cristian non ha delle scarpe **nere**	vero	falso
e	Le scarpe di Matteo sono fuori **moda**	vero	falso

LANGUAGE BUILDER 3

Language discovery 3

How many forms of imperative can you spot in the conversation? Look at these two:

Dammi il tuo parere. Guardali!

How do pronouns connect to the main form of the verb? Do you see any pattern? Is there anything new you can notice?

Imperative with pronouns

At times, the imperative is used with direct or indirect object pronouns. In such instances, the pronoun gets tacked onto the end of the imperative form.

Guardali! *Look at them!* Mettilo lo stesso! *Wear it anyway!*

In the negative form (non + infinitive), add the pronoun to the end of the infinitive, but first drop the final -e.

Non metterlo! *Don't wear it!* Non guardarli! *Don't look at them!*

Verbs like dire, dare, and fare have an irregular imperative form, and when combined with pronouns they double the first letter of the pronoun, with the exception of the pronoun gli.

Fammi un favore. *Do me a favor*

Dammi il tuo parere. *Give me your opinion.* Digli la verità. *Tell him/them the truth.*

Language practice 3

Cristian is almost ready to leave Venice for the wedding and is on the phone with Petra. Put the verbs in the imperative form and use pronouns where needed.

Petra (Ascoltare – me) **a** .... Cristian, (non – dimenticare) **b** .... di portare anche un cappotto.

Cristian Un cappotto? Ma è settembre!

Petra (Guardare) **c** .... che fa freddo a Dobbiaco in questi giorni. Hai chiamato Sandro per confermare?

Cristian Beh no, ho dato la conferma online.

Petra (chiamare - lui) **d** .... lo stesso, forse non ricorda!

Cristian Va bene. Hai detto a mamma e papà che arrivo venerdì?

Petra No, non ancora.

Cristian (chiamare – loro) **e** .... per favore. Non amano le sorprese. (sentire) **f** ...., porto anche un ombrello?

Petra	Sì, (portare – l'ombrello) **g** ...., il tempo è molto variabile. E ovviamente (ricordarsi) **h** .... il regalo!
Cristian	Certo, certo. È già in valigia. Ci vediamo domani.
Petra	Perfetto, (telefonare – a me) **i** .... quando arrivi in stazione!

LANGUAGE BUILDER 4

Language discovery 4

08.08

Listen to the conversation again and repeat each line in the pauses provided. What words can you hear in the conversation before the following?

a .... figura

b .... pantaloni

c .... giacca

d .... paio

Can you tell why these forms change before each word and how? Would you be able to transform the following couples from singular to plural or vice versa?

e .... pantalone

f .... giacche

Quello and bello

Unlike most adjectives in Italian, bello (*beautiful*, *nice*, *fine*) and quello (*that*) usually come before the nouns they describe.

Che bei maglioni! — *What nice sweaters!*

Quel vestito è di seta. — *That dress is made of silk.*

Their forms are quite similar to those of the definite article and depend both on the gender and number of the noun, as well as its spelling.

Masculine

Singular	Plural	
bello/quello	begli/quegli	before s + consonant or z, y, ps, pn
bel/quel	bei/quei	before other consonants
bell'/quell'	begli/quegli	before vowels

Feminine

Singular	Plural	
bella/quella	belle/quelle	before all consonants
bell'/quell'	belle/quelle	before vowels

Also note that the adjective bello can be used to convey the intensity of a situation.

Questo è un bel problema! — *This is a big problem!*

Language practice 4

1 Match each adjective with the appropriate noun.

1 quel	**a** sport
2 bell'	**b** gonna
3 quello	**c** calzini
4 bella	**d** abbigliamento
5 quell'	**e** stivali
6 bei	**f** scarpe
7 quegli	**g** vestito
8 belle	**h** arancione

08.09

2 Now play Conversation 2 again, but this time you will play Annalisa's role. Speak in the pauses provided. Try to give Cristian your own advice.

SKILL BUILDER

1 A friend is texting you to ask for some advice on what to wear for a wedding in Italy in June. Text them back with some ideas, using the imperative form.

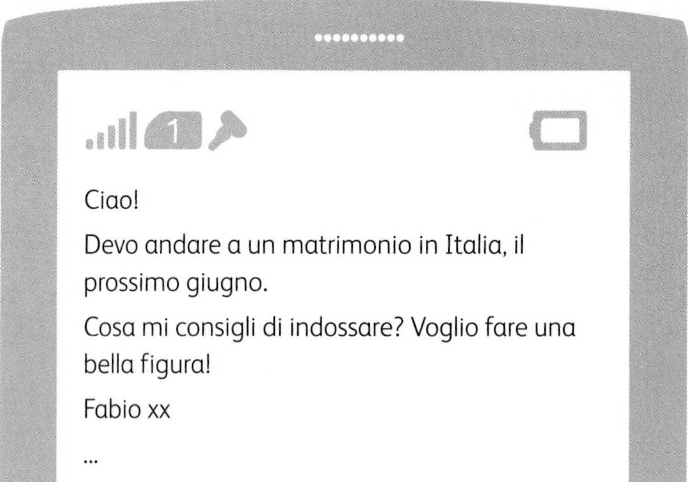

08.10

2 Listen to Cristian's description of Annalisa and complete the text with the words you hear.

mi	le	quel	divertiti	bel

Annalisa è la mia coinquilina qui a Venezia. È simpatica e molto socievole, la sua vita è piena di amici. Fa l'ingegnera e lavora per un **a** .... progetto: il MOSE di Venezia. **b** .... progetto è molto importante nella sua vita: anche se le sue amiche **c** .... dicono sempre "Annalisa, sei giovane: **d** ....!", per lei il lavoro è al primo posto. In passato ha giocato a pallavolo come professionista e adesso continua a giocare, per passione, insieme alla sua amica Aicha. Annalisa **e** .... piace, perché ha molte passioni: lo sport, la musica, gli amici ma non **f** .... piace molto cucinare. Sono molto contento di vivere insieme a lei.

3 Look at the picture and describe their outfits in as much detail as possible (garments, colors, materials).

....

....

....

....

....

TEST YOURSELF

1 Complete the sentences with the correct indirect object pronoun.

a Elena porta solo gonne. Dice che (a lei) .... stanno bene.

b Pilar, chiedi al commesso se (a noi) .... porta quelle scarpe?

c Preferisco questa maglietta rosa, il nero non (a me) .... piace.

d I miei genitori non mettono mai i jeans. (a loro) .... piace essere eleganti.

e Oggi è il compleanno di Lucas. (a lui) .... ho comprato un cappello.

f Filippo, (a te) .... piace questa giacca?

2 Read these people's wishes and then encourage them or discourage them by using the imperative form and pronouns when needed.

Example: Vorrei comprare dei pantaloni rosa! *Comprali!*

a Vorrei mettere una gonna corta.

b Non vorrei indossare pantaloni di pelle.

c Vorrei dirti qualcosa.

d Vorrei comprare due borsette rosa.

e Non vorrei spendere molto.

f Vorrei cambiare questo completo di lana.

3 Complete the table with the correct articles and the endings of bello and quello.

Articolo		Quello	Bello
il	completo	Que .... completo è elegante.	È un be .... completo.
	giacca	Que .... giacca è alla moda.	È una be .... giacca.
	stivali	Que .... stivali sono di pelle	Sono dei be .... stivali.
	gonne	Que .... gonne sono lunghe	Sono delle be .... gonne.

La misteriosa donna in soffitta *The mysterious woman in the attic*

Let's have some fun with colors. What happens when you blend red and white together? The name of this new color will provide you with an additional letter to include in the name of our enigmatic woman featured in Annalisa and Cristian's attic.

Remember to use **My review** and **My takeaway** to assess your progress and reflect on your learning experience.

9

In this unit you will learn how to:

- Describe a house or an apartment.
- Recount situations and habits in the past using the **imperfetto**.
- Talk about school and education.
- Say what you are or were doing using the present progressive.
- Locate objects in space using **ci**.

Casa dolce casa

My study plan

I plan to work with Unit 9

- ○ Every day
- ○ Twice a week
- ○ Other ___________

I plan to study for

- ○ 5–15 minutes
- ○ 15–30 minutes
- ○ 30–45+ minutes

My progress tracker

Day / Date	Listening	Speaking	Reading	Writing	Conversation
	○	○	○	○	○
	○	○	○	○	○
	○	○	○	○	○
	○	○	○	○	○
	○	○	○	○	○
	○	○	○	○	○
	○	○	○	○	○

My goals

What do you want to be able to do or say in Italian when you complete this unit?

		Done
1	....	○
2	....	○
3	....	○

My review

SELF CHECK	
	I can ...
●	... describe a house or an apartment.
●	... talk about past experiences or situations in my life and the lives of others.
●	... say what is happening now.
●	... talk about school and subjects people learn in school.
●	... locate objects in space using ci.

CULTURE POINT 1

A casa mia *At my place*

According to a national survey in 2021, three quarters of the Italian population own their casa. Casa means both *home* and *house*, so when people say a casa mia, they indicate the place where they live, whether this is an appartamento, un palazzo (*a multi-story building*), una casa singola (*a detached house*), or una casa a schiera (*a terraced house*). Or even a villa or an attico (*penthouse*)! The typical Italian casa usually features a well-lit cucina (*kitchen*)—one of the most important rooms for Italians—one or more bagni (*bathrooms*) with either vasca (*tub*) or doccia (*shower*) and a bidet. In advertisements, bagni are often called servizi.

A very desirable feature of a house is un balcone (*balcony*) or una terrazza (*terrace*), or, even better, un giardino (*a garden*) where people can eat outside when il tempo è bello.

Answer the questions about your home.

a Quale tipo di casa hai?

b Quanti bagni ci sono?

c La cucina è grande o piccola?

d La casa è tua o in affitto (*rented*)?

VOCABULARY BUILDER 1

09.01

Look at the words and phrases and complete the missing English words and expressions. Then listen and try to imitate the pronunciation of the speakers.

TIPI DI CASA	*TYPES OF HOME*
il palazzo	....
la villa	*villa/mansion*
la casa singola/indipendente	....
la casa a schiera	....
l'attico	*penthouse*
il monolocale	*studio*

LE STANZE DELLA CASA	*TYPES OF ROOM*
l'ingresso	*entrance*
la cucina	*kitchen*
il soggiorno/il salotto/la sala da pranzo	*living/dining room*
la camera da letto (singola o matrimoniale)	.... *(single or double)*
il bagno	....
il giardino	....
il balcone	....
il garage	*garage*
la cantina	*cellar*

Vocabulary practice 1

Name the room in which people do the following actions.

Example: la stanza dove mettiamo l'auto *il garage*

a la stanza dove prepariamo il cibo
b la stanza dove dormiamo
c la stanza dove entriamo
d la stanza dove facciamo la doccia
e la stanza dove guardiamo la TV
f la stanza dove pranziamo o ceniamo.

CONVERSATION 1

Quando ero bambina *When I was a child*

09.02

1 Here are a few words and expressions to help you understand the following conversation. Note their meanings.

Ma dai!	*No way!*	cucinare	*to cook/prepare food*
dividere	*to share*		

09.03

2 Listen to the conversation without looking at the text. Then listen again and read the text. Pay attention to how Annalisa recounts what she used to do and where she used to live.

Annalisa is in Napoli, visiting her family. While there, she takes the opportunity to reconnect with her old friends from school. Now she is out having a drink with Eleonora, a volleyball friend who now plays for the national volleyball team! They are in Posillipo, a residential quartiere (***neighborhood***) in Napoli known for its cocktail bars by the sea and also where Annalisa's family used to live when she was a child (da bambina).

Annalisa Da bambina abitavo lì. Venti anni fa i miei genitori avevano un appartamento nel palazzo di *Un Posto al Sole*! Poi hanno comprato una casa indipendente e siamo andati al Vomero.

Eleonora Ma dai! E com'era?

Annalisa Non era grande, ma aveva un soggiorno con vista sul mare. Di solito guardavo il mare e immaginavo di andare lontano!

Eleonora Avevi una camera da letto per te?

Annalisa No, io e mio fratello dividevamo una camera da letto. La mia stanza preferita era la cucina: spesso stavo lì per ore e guardavo mio padre cucinare. Mi piaceva molto.

Eleonora Ma adesso non ti piace cucinare.

Annalisa (*laughs*) No, ora preferisco mangiare.

> Vomero is a neighborhood in Napoli. Posillipo is a neighborhood made famous by the show *Un Posto al Sole*.

3 Are the following statements vero (*true*) or falso (*false*), based on the conversation.

a	La famiglia di Annalisa ora abita a Posillipo.	vero	falso
b	La famiglia di Annalisa ora vive in un appartamento.	vero	falso
c	Da bambina Annalisa non aveva una casa grande.	vero	falso
d	Annalisa dormiva in una camera con suo fratello.	vero	falso
e	Il padre di Annalisa cucinava spesso.	vero	falso
f	Annalisa non ama cucinare.	vero	falso

LANGUAGE BUILDER 1

Language discovery 1

Read Annalisa's childhood memories below. Identify the subject of the verb from the given options. In the right column, complete with the infinitive of the verb.

a	Da bambina abitavo lì.	io/lui	....
b	I miei genitori avevano un appartamento.	noi/loro	....
c	Non era grande.	tu/lui	....
d	Avevi una camera da letto?	tu/io	....
e	Io e mio fratello dividevamo una camera.	io/noi	....

Imperfetto (part 1: forms)

Unit 7 looked at the passato prossimo. There is another past tense, called imperfetto, which is used to recount memories and past habits. This tense is very regular. To form it, remove -re from the infinitive and add the personal endings -vo, -vi, -va, -vamo, -vate, -vano. Notice that verbs keep the defining vowel if the infinitive is a, e, i.

	parlare	avere	dormire		parlare	avere	dormire
io	parlavo	avevo	dormivo	noi	parlavamo	avevamo	dormivamo
tu	parlavi	avevi	dormivi	voi	parlavate	avevate	dormivate
lui/lei/Lei	parlava	aveva	dormiva	loro	parlavano	avevano	dormivano

There are only very few irregular verbs: essere, fare, dire, and bere. Essere is quite irregular, but the other three verbs only have irregular stems (face-, dice-, and beve-) while the personal endings are the same as for all verbs.

essere				fare	dire	bere
io	ero	noi	eravamo	face-	dice-	beve-
tu	eri	voi	eravate			
lui/lei/Lei	era	loro	erano			

Non era grande, ma aveva un soggiorno con vista sul mare. — *It wasn't large, but it had a living room with a view of the sea.*

Example: Come dicevano i nonni: Chi dorme non piglia pesci.
Like our grandparents used to say: the early bird catches the worm (lit. *whoever sleeps late, catches no fish*).

Language practice 1

Eleonora and Annalisa continue reminiscing about their past. Complete their conversation with the verbs in the imperfetto.

Eleonora E cosa ti **a** .... (piacere) fare da bambina?

Annalisa **b** .... (amare) molto giocare con i Lego. **c** .... (costruire) piccoli oggetti, case, strade.

Eleonora [tu] **d** .... (essere) già una piccola ingegnera!

Annalisa Sì. Mio fratello invece **e** .... (avere) una passione per i libri: **f** .... (leggere) sempre! E per la musica: a 6 anni **g** .... (suonare) il piano abbastanza bene. E tu?

Eleonora Niente musica o Lego per me: da bambine io e mia sorella **h** .... (essere) appassionate di cucina e di sport. Noi **i** .... (giocare) a pallavolo tutti i giorni e io **j** .... (sognare – *to dream*) di giocare nella squadra nazionale.

Annalisa È vero! Beh, io ora faccio l'ingegnera, e tu sei una campionessa. Viva i sogni e le passioni!

LANGUAGE BUILDER 2

Language discovery 2

09.04

Listen to the conversation again and repeat each line in the pauses provided. Then look at these phrases in which the imperfetto is combined with an expression of time (underlined). Do these phrases indicate an event that happened once or an ongoing situation/a habit?

<u>Da bambina</u> abitavo lì.

<u>20 anni fa</u> i miei genitori avevano un appartamento

<u>Di solito</u> guardavo il mare

<u>Spesso</u> stavo in cucina per ore.

A tense for memory and habits: imperfetto (part 2: usage)

The imperfetto is used when talking about the past, but in particular to describe a situation or an action that constituted a habit in the past:

Quando ero bambina...	*When I was a child ...*
Da bambina giocavo con i Lego.	*As a child, I used to play with Legos.*

The imperfetto cannot be used to refer to an individual event or one that occurred once, but rather to an ongoing action or condition in the past:

Il tempo era bello.	*The weather was nice.* (describes a condition)
Spesso andavo in vacanza al mare.	*I often used to go on holiday to the seaside.* (describes a habit)

The imperfetto is often used with:

- expressions of time such as:

Di solito,	Usually	Da bambino/a	As a child
A (*number of years*) anni	At (years) old	Da giovane	When I was young

- adverbs of frequency: sempre, spesso, qualche volta, non...mai

With the expression (*number of years*) + fa (... years ago), the imperfetto describes a situation that was ongoing at that point in time.

Dieci anni fa abitavo a New York.	*Ten years ago I was living in New York.*

If, on the other hand, the reference is to an individual event which took place at that point in time, then the passato prossimo is used.

Dieci anni fa ho visto il musical Evita a New York.	*Ten years ago I saw the musical Evita in New York.* (Presumably, you only saw the show once.)

While there is no equivalent of the imperfetto in English, it is safe to assume that every sentence with *used to* corresponds to the imperfetto in Italian. Likewise, if you think of a point in the past and you want to say that at that point *you were doing something* or *were something/somewhere*, use the imperfetto in Italian. Nel 2010 lavoravo come segretario in un ufficio. *In 2010 I was working as a secretary in an office.* Nel 2010 ero in Giappone. *In 2010 I was in Japan.*

Language practice 2

1 Complete the sentences by either choosing one of the phrases in the list below or using the given verb in the imperfetto. Note: one of the phrases corresponds to a passato prossimo!

di solito	da giovane	a 25 anni	spesso	una volta	non... mai

a .... la nonna abitava vicino a Milano.

b Quando ero piccolo, non mi .... (piacere) andare a scuola.

c Quando era studente, Cristian .... (andare) spesso in biblioteca.

d Quando lavoravo in ufficio, io .... facevo .... sport.

e Quando abitavi in Cina, ... cosa mangiavi per colazione?

f ...., mio padre lavorava già (already) in un negozio di scarpe.

g Quando abitavamo a Napoli, noi cenavamo .... in pizzeria.

h Quando ero a Napoli, ... ho visto Sophia Loren.

CULTURE POINT 2

Scuola e istruzione *School and education*

L'istruzione (***education***) in Italy is broadly similar to that in other European countries. Children first attend l'asilo (***kindergarden***), then at six they begin la scuola elementare primaria (***primary school***). At 11 they start attending la scuola secondaria di primo grado (***lower secondary school***) until they are 14. Until then, all alunni (***students***) attend the same school. To progress, students need to attend two more years of compulsory education at the scuola secondaria di secondo grado (***high school***). Some continue until 19 when they must pass a state exam called la maturità (literally: ***maturity***, as at this point people are mature enough to vote). Unlike in other countries, there are many kinds of high school that students can choose according to their talents: liceo scientifico or classico, or linguistico (grammar schools with a focus on materie (***subjects***) like science, humanities, or modern languages), or a great variety of scuole professionali which prepare students for specific careers. If they wish, after la maturità they can progress to university and eventually get a laurea triennale (BA), a Master's, and a dottorato (Ph.D.).

Explore the website of the MIUR (Ministero dell'Istruzione e del Merito—*Ministry of Education, and merit.*).

a Is the Italian system similar to the one in your countr(ies)?

b A quanti anni (*at which age*) do people finish their compulsory education? And in your countr(ies)?

c Quali materie amavi quando andavi a scuola?

VOCABULARY BUILDER 2

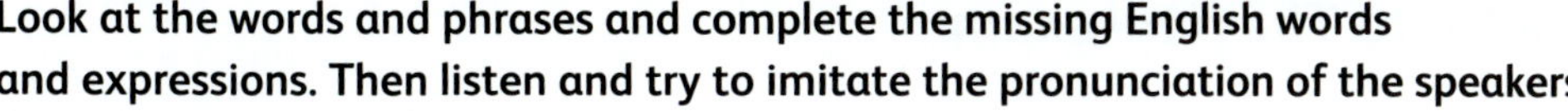

Look at the words and phrases and complete the missing English words and expressions. Then listen and try to imitate the pronunciation of the speakers.

L'ISTRUZIONE	*EDUCATION*
l'asilo	....
la scuola primaria e secondaria	*primary and secondary school*
il liceo	*high school*
la scuola professionale	*high school (for professional careers)*
il professore /la professoressa	*teacher/professor*
l'insegnante	*teacher*
il maestro/la maestra	*primary school teacher*
lo scolaro/la scolara	....
l'esame di maturità	*high school diploma*

LE MATERIE	*SUBJECTS*
la matematica	....
la storia	*history*
la letteratura	....
le lingue straniere	*foreign languages*
le scienze	....
la storia dell'arte	*history of art*
l'educazione fisica	*physical education (P.E.)*

VERBI ED ESPRESSIONI UTILI	*VERBS AND USEFUL PHRASES*
frequentare	*to attend*
imparare	*to learn*
insegnare	....
interessarsi a	*to be interested in*
andare bene/male a scuola	*to do well/poorly in school*
essere bravo in	*to be good at*

Vocabulary practice 2

Quale materia? **Indicate the subject that the below phrases refer to.**

- **a** La materia dei numeri e delle equazioni. ....
- **b** La materia dove impariamo a scrivere un testo e interpretare un libro. ....
- **c** Una parola generale per fisica, biologia, chimica e astronomia. ....
- **d** In questa materia gli italiani imparano l'inglese. ....
- **e** In questa materia gli alunni fanno sport. ....

CONVERSATION 2

La maturità *The final exam*

09.06

1 Here are a few words and expressions to help you understand the conversation. Note their meanings.

Cosa sta succedendo nel mondo?	*What's happening in the world?*
Il resto è storia	*The rest is history*
volentieri	*gladly*
Non ci credo!	*I don't believe it!*

09.07

2 Listen to the conversation without looking at the text. Then listen again and read the text.

Every year la maturità attracts national interest. I temi (*topics*) for the prova scritta (*essay exam*) are published in the newspapers and they usually generate a lively discussion: are they current, do they resonate with today's issues? This morning Annalisa is reading the news of la maturità on her laptop and sipping coffee, while Cristian is preparing his breakfast.

Cristian Cosa sta succedendo nel mondo?

Annalisa Sto leggendo le materie e i temi della maturità di quest'anno. Per il liceo scientifico una delle materie è fisica. Era la mia materia preferita quando andavo al liceo.

Cristian Io non ero bravo in fisica. Andavo male a scuola e non ci andavo volentieri.

Annalisa Tu??? Non ci credo!

Cristian Sí. Ma avevo un insegnante di storia dell'arte bravissimo. Io mi interessavo molto alle sue lezioni, come a una serie TV. Il resto è storia...

Annalisa Stai ancora pensando al lavoro a New York?

Cristian Certo. Ci penso tutti i giorni!

3 Decide whether the sentences below could be said by Annalisa (A) or Cristian (C).

a	Andavo benissimo a scuola.	A	C
b	Non mi piaceva andare a scuola.	A	C
c	Mi piacevano specialmente le materie scientifiche.	A	C
d	Gli insegnanti bravi fanno la differenza.	A	C
e	Mi interesso alle materie dell'esame di maturità.	A	C

LANGUAGE BUILDER 3

Language discovery 3

Look at the conversation again and find the sentences that match the following English expressions. What are the verbs used? What is the difference between the verbs in the last two examples?

English	Phrase in conversation	Verbs
a I'm reading ...		
b What is happening?		
c Are you still thinking?		
d I think about it every day.		

What's happening? The present progressive

To describe an action that is ongoing (such as *I am reading*), use the verb stare in the present tense plus the main verb in the gerund form. To form the gerund, for verbs ending in -are, replace -are with -ando. For verbs ending in -ere and -ire, use -endo. Note that, as with passato prossimo, only the helping verb, in this case stare, changes to indicate the subject.

	-are	-ere	-ire
io	sto studiando	sto leggendo	sto dormendo
tu	stai studiando	stai leggendo	stai dormendo
lui/lei/Lei	sta studiando	sta leggendo	sta dormendo
noi	stiamo studiando	stiamo leggendo	stiamo dormendo
voi	stiamo studiando	stiamo leggendo	stiamo dormendo
loro	stiamo studiando	stiamo leggendo	stiamo dormendo

Io sto studiando. *I am studying.* Lui sta leggendo. *He is reading.*

Il bambino sta dormendo. *The baby is sleeping.*

There are very few irregular verbs, and they are the same ones which are irregular in the imperfetto:

fare = facendo bere = bevendo dire = dicendo

Essere is regular and becomes essendo.

How do you translate *I was reading?* Simple: use the verb stare but in the imperfetto: Io stavo leggendo.

Language practice 3

Complete the sentences with the present progressive form of the verb.

a Anna .... (guardare) la TV.
b Cristian .... (leggere).
c Mark e Giorgio .... (andare) al supermercato.
d Noi .... (frequentare) un corso di italiano.
e Voi .... (fare) i compiti.
f Cosa (tu) .... (studiare)?

LANGUAGE BUILDER 4

Language discovery 4

Listen to the conversation again and repeat each line in the pauses provided. Then look at these sentences. What do you think ci stands for? Do you see a common element in the phrases in the right column? Match ci with what it stands for in the right column.

1 Andavo male a scuola e non <u>ci</u> andavo volentieri.
2 Non <u>ci</u> credo!
3 <u>Ci</u> penso tutti i giorni.

a al lavoro a New York.
b a scuola.
c all'idea che Cristian non andava bene a scuola.

The pronoun ci

You know that pronouns replace a word so that it does not have to be repeated twice in a short space of time. The pronoun ci is used in the expression c'è/ci sono (*there is/there are*). In fact, ci means *there*. Ci is used to indicate a place.

Vai all'università? – No, non ci vado. — *Do you go to university? – No, I don't go (there).*

Studi in biblioteca? – Sì, ci studio sempre. — *Do you study in the library? – Yes, I always study there.*

Ci replaces an element in the sentence preceded by a or in. It can be a physical place or a concept one thinks about—pensare a qualcosa (*to think about something*)—or one believes in—credere in/a qualcosa (*to believe in something*). The important thing is that ci replaces something preceded by a or in, whether it is real or imaginary:

Pensi al futuro? – Sì ci penso. — *Do you think about the future? – Yes, I do think about it.*

Like all object pronouns, ci goes before the verb.

Pensi alla tua famiglia? – Sì ci penso. — *Do you think about your family? – Yes, I think about them.*

Language practice 4

1 Combine the following sentences using the pronoun ci.

Example: Elisa va al supermercato. *Elisa va al supermercato.*
Elisa va al supermercato in bus e *ci va in bus.*

a Cristian pensa alla sua carriera. Lui pensa alla sua carriera tutti i giorni.
b Annalisa va al lavoro. Lei non va al lavoro volentieri.
c Aicha lavora a casa. Lei lavora spesso a casa.
d Matteo lavora in un'officina. Lui lavora in un'officina da lunedì a venerdì.
e I bambini vanno alla scuola primaria. Vanno alla scuola primaria per 5 anni.
f Cristian andava all'università. Lui andava all'università in treno.

09.09

2 Listen to the audio and respond to the questions using the pronoun ci.

a Da bambin* andavi volentieri a scuola?
b Da bambin* andavi spesso al mare?
c Pensi spesso alla carriera?
d Come vai al lavoro? (in macchina, in bus, in metro, in treno...)

SKILL BUILDER

1 Read the ads for rental homes. Which of the ads (1–4) would be suitable for each person (a–d)?

1 Villa in campagna a 8 km dalla città Giardino grande, 5 camere da letto, 3 bagni, cucina spaziosa, cantina, soffitta e garage. Possibilità di costruire la piscina.	**2** Monolocale in centro. Bagno con doccia. Vicino a supermercato, autobus, e a 500 metri dalla piazza centrale.
3 Appartamento completamente rinnovato in un palazzo antico a Bolzano. Una camera da letto, un bagno, cucina e salotto. Balcone con vista sulle montagne.	**4** Casa a schiera in zona residenziale. Piccolo giardino e garage. Tre camere da letto, doppi servizi. Lontano da mezzi pubblici. Supermercato a 2 km.

a Marco e Erich sono una coppia che ama la natura ma preferisce vivere in città.
b Paola è una pendolare (*commuter*) che lavora a Milano, non ha l'auto, e ha bisogno di una casa vicina al suo ufficio.
c Anna ha una famiglia molto grande e vuole una casa molto spaziosa.
d La famiglia di Amir vuole una casa con giardino. Loro hanno due macchine.

2 Answer these questions using ci and an expression of frequency: sempre, spesso, qualche volta, non ... mai, raramente (*rarely*).

a Vai a teatro?
b Vai in montagna?
c Lavori a casa?
d Vai in discoteca?
e Mangi al ristorante?

3 **Write an ad for your home. Say what type of house it is. List how many bedrooms, bathrooms there are and what other rooms it has. Say if it is close or far from the train station, the city center, the bus, the supermarket, etc.**

4 **Answer the questions using the imperfetto.**

a Di solito dove andavi in vacanza da bambin*?

b Dove sei andat* l'anno scorso?

c Cosa ti piaceva fare da bambin*?

d Dove abitavi 10 anni fa?

TEST YOURSELF

1 **Cristian describes his family home in Bolzano. Complete the text with the missing verbs in the imperfetto.**

Da bambino io **a** .... in un appartamento a Bolzano. L'appartamento non **b** .... grande, ma c'erano due camere da letto, una per me e una per mia sorella, e un soggiorno molto confortevole. Noi **c** .... lì perché i miei genitori **d** .... in città ma noi **e** .... spesso in montagna. Le Dolomiti sono molto vicine a Bolzano. Da bambino mi **f** .... fare lunghe escursioni nella natura.

2 **Turn the verbs in the sentences into present progressive.**

Example: Annalisa gioca a tennis. *Annalisa sta giocando a tennis.*

a Cristian legge un libro.

b Zhuang telefona a Lisa.

c Voi scrivete un'email.

d Io cucino il pranzo.

e Tu lavori in ospedale.

f Sandra e Pablo escono.

La misteriosa donna in soffitta *The mysterious woman in the attic*

In Conversation 2 you read that Annalisa was looking at the news on her laptop. What is the Italian word for news? The initial of this word will give us the next letter of the mysterious lady's name!

Remember to use **My review** and **My takeaway** to assess your progress and reflect on your learning experience.

10

In this unit you will learn how to:

- » Identify animals.
- » Locate and narrate events in the past using both **imperfetto** and **passato prossimo**.
- » describe actions using adverbs in **-mente**.
- » use direct object pronouns with the **passato prossimo**.
- » Describe a variety of Italian landscapes.

Che strano!

My study plan

I plan to work with Unit 10

- ○ Every day
- ○ Twice a week
- ○ Other ____________

I plan to study for

- ○ 5–15 minutes
- ○ 15–30 minutes
- ○ 30–45+ minutes

My progress tracker

Day / Date	Listening	Speaking	Reading	Writing	Conversation
	○	○	○	○	○
	○	○	○	○	○
	○	○	○	○	○
	○	○	○	○	○
	○	○	○	○	○
	○	○	○	○	○
	○	○	○	○	○

My goals

What do you want to be able to do or say in Italian when you complete this unit?

		Done
1	....	○
2	....	○
3	....	○

My review

SELF CHECK

	I can ...
●	... list many animals and briefly describe where they live.
●	... talk about past events switching from passato prossimo to imperfetto when needed.
●	... describe the variety of Italian landscape.
●	... use passato prossimo in combination with direct pronouns.
●	... explain how an action took place using adverbs in -mente.

CULTURE POINT 1

I parchi nazionali *National parks*

Italy's charm isn't limited to its cities; beyond the urban hubs lies a treasure trove of breathtaking destinations. Stretching from the Mediterranean's remote corners to the French border, Italy boasts remarkable parchi nazionali (*national parks*) teeming with indigenous wildlife and stunning vistas. These parks are a biodiversity haven, sheltering diverse flora and fauna. They unveil intricate ecosystems that epitomize the nation's natural legacy. For instance, il Parco Nazionale del Gran Paradiso showcases majestic stambecchi (*ibexes*) scaling alpine cliffs, while the thriving lupo (*wolf*) population in the Parchi Nazionali di Abruzzo, Lazio e Molise symbolizes conservation success. In the marine parks, like the Arcipelago Toscano (*Tuscan Archipelago*) and the Arcipelago de La Maddalena (*La Maddalena Archipelago*) in Sardinia, encountering rare marine species such as delfini (*dolphins*) and foche monache (*monk seals*) is possible. These sanctuaries not only safeguard Italy's biological richness but also invite explorers to embrace unspoiled landscapes and marvel at the wildlife's extraordinary diversity.

Il Parco Nazionale del Gran Paradiso

Il Parco Nazionale del Gran Paradiso is the oldest national park in Italy, covering the regions of Piemonte and Valle d'Aosta. Take a look at the park's informative and detailed website. If you head to the section fauna you will be able to see how many species today populate the park.

a How many can also be found in your own country?

b Which ones have you visited already?

VOCABULARY BUILDER 1

10.01

Look at the words and phrases and complete the missing English words and expressions. Then listen and try to imitate the pronunciation of the speakers.

a proposito	*by the way*
a un certo punto	*at a certain point*
cominciare	....
chissà	*who knows*
dentro/fuori/intorno	*inside/outside/around*
incredibile	....
DESCRIVERE UN ANIMALE	***DESCRIBE AN ANIMAL***
affamato/a	*hungry*
aggressivo/a	....
enorme	....
fedele	*loyal*
terrorizzato/a	*terrified*
ANIMALI DOMESTICI E AFFINI	***DOMESTIC ANIMALS AND SIMILAR***
il cane/il cavallo	...................../*horse*
il coniglio/il criceto	*rabbit/hamster*
il gatto/il pesce rosso	...................../*goldfish*
il piccione	*pigeon*
la specie	....
la tartaruga	*turtle/tortoise*
l'uccello	*bird*
VERBI	***VERBS***
ridere	*to laugh*
rubare	*to steal*
sembrare	*to seem*
succedere	*to happen*
volare	*to fly*

Vocabulary practice 1

Match animals with their description.

a ....: una specie che può volare.
b ....: è molto indipendente.
c ....: è grande e corre veloce.
d ....: è un uccello e abita in molte piazze italiane.
e ....: è considerato l'animale più fedele.

CONVERSATION 1

Un insolito ladro *An uncommon thief*

1 Here are a few words and expressions to help you understand the following conversation. Note their meanings.

Ridi pure!	*Laugh it up!*
Chissà che faccia avevi!	*Who knows what you looked like!*
Oddio!	*Oh my God!*

2 Listen to the conversation without looking at the text. Then listen again and read the text. Notice the tenses Annalisa uses while telling her story.

Annalisa has joined her friends at Matteo's place to celebrate his birthday. Upon spotting Matteo's dog, Kubo, memories of a recent disavventura (*misadventure*) with a pigeon come rushing back to her, and she's excited to recount this incident to the others.

Annalisa Che bello questo cane!

Matteo Grazie, si chiama Kubo, e abbiamo anche due criceti!

Annalisa Veramente? Ah, a proposito di animali! Sapete cosa mi è successo oggi?

Aicha No, racconta!

Annalisa Allora, ero in pausa pranzo su una panchina davanti all'ufficio, perché era davvero una bella giornata. Mentre mangiavo, è arrivato un piccione: era enorme e sembrava aggressivo. Probabilmente era affamato.

Aicha Poverino!

Annalisa Ha cominciato a volarmi intorno, così per paura mi sono alzata e... a un certo punto, mentre correvo dentro, mi ha rubato il panino! Incredibile!

Filippo (*laughs*) Oddio, chissà che faccia avevi!

Annalisa Ridi pure, ma io ero terrorizzata!

3 Answer the following questions in Italian.

- **a** Come si chiama il cane di Matteo?
- **b** Quanti animali ha Matteo?
- **c** In quale momento della giornata succede l'episodio di Annalisa?
- **d** Cosa stava mangiando Annalisa?
- **e** Cosa ha fatto il piccione?

LANGUAGE BUILDER 1

Language discovery 1

Can you spot the two sentences where Annalisa uses both imperfetto and passato prossimo? Which word introduce these sentences?

a .... un piccione.

b .... il panino!

Use of imperfetto and passato prossimo combined

Just as the name suggests, the action depicted by the imperfetto is inherently "imperfect," i.e., not finished. Consequently, a general tip for its usage is applying it when a specific time reference cannot be attributed. Imagine the imperfect tense as the frame surrounding a picture or the backdrop to the primary event. The frame (imperfetto) symbolizes the context (descriptions, feelings, emotions, ongoing actions), while the picture (passato prossimo) portrays a distinct event.

Mentre mangiavo (*background*),
è arrivato un piccione (*event*).
While I was eating,
a pigeon arrived.

Mentre correvo dentro (*background*),
mi ha rubato il panino (*event*).
While I was running inside,
he stole my sandwich.

The word mentre, when followed by a past tense, is exclusively paired with the imperfect tense.

This can happen with other words, like quando (*when*), siccome (*since*) or così (*so*).

Stavo tornando a casa, quando
ho visto Silvia.
I was going back home,
when I saw Silvia.

Siccome era una bella giornata,
ho portato il cane al parco.
Since it was a lovely day,
I took the dog to the park.

Il mio gatto non stava bene
e così l'ho portato dal veterinario.
My cat wasn't well,
so I took him to the vet.

Language practice 1

Choose the correct past forms to complete the sentences.

a Ieri sera la pizzeria è stata / era chiusa e così siamo rimasti / rimanevamo a casa.

b Mentre sono tornata / tornavo a casa, ho trovato / trovavo un gatto abbandonato.

c Siccome il frigorifero è stato / era vuoto, siamo andate / andavamo a fare la spesa.

d Due giorni fa ho visto / vedevo il tuo compagno mentre ho aspettato / aspettavo l'autobus.

LANGUAGE BUILDER 2

Language discovery 2

10.04

Listen to the conversation again and repeat each line in the pauses provided. Try to imitate the phrasing and intonation you hear.

Which two words from the conversation mean *truly* and *probably*? Can you tell which adjectives they originally came from?

veramente   allora   incredibile   probabilmente

Adverbs ending in -mente

Adverbs describe or clarify the way an action is performed, or they provide additional details about a verb, adjective, or another adverb. They are commonly used in response to the question come? (*how?*). They do not change for number or gender.

In English, many adverbs end in -ly (e.g., ***quickly***, ***naturally***, ***eventually***). The Italian adverb ending is -mente, which is added to the feminine singular form of an adjective.

vero (m) > vera (f) > veramente   true > truly

lento (m) > lenta (f) > lentamente   slow > slowly

grande (m/f) > grandemente   great > greatly

If the adjective ends in -ile or -ale, drop the final -e before adding -mente.

probabile > probabilmente   *probable > probably*

gentile > gentilmente   *kind > kindly*

Language practice 2

1 Form the correct adverb from the given adjectives.

a aggressivo > ....

b enorme > ....

c incredibile > ....

d allegro > ....

e freddo > ....

f felice > ....

g sportivo > ....

h formale > ....

i informale > ....

j corretto > ....

10.05

2 Now play Conversation 1 again, but this time you will play Annalisa's role. Speak in the pauses provided. Try to make up a fun story that happened to you involving an animal.

CULTURE POINT 2

Meraviglie d'Italia *Marvels of Italy*

Forty percent of Italy's landscape is made up of majestic montagne, a haven for both winter skiers and summer hikers. This wonderland reveals two mountain ranges: le Alpi (*the Alps*), crowning Italy, and gli Appennini (*the Apennines*), forming its backbone. Gracing the Alps on the French border, Monte Bianco (*Mont Blanc*) soars at 4807 meters. Down south, near Naples, Mount Vesuvius stands as Europe's lone active mainland vulcano (*volcano*), its fiery history woven with Pompeii, a history lover's gem. Sicily's heart beats with vibrant Mount Etna. Italy's mosaic extends beyond its peaks, revealing 1500 laghi (*lakes*) adorning the north. Italy's allure wanders to la costa (*the coast*), where wild, forest-fringed spiagge (*beaches*) entwine with turquoise shores. Amidst Sardinia's crystal waters lies a paradise rivalling the Maldives. Italy caters to every taste, weaving a rich symphony of paesaggi (*landscapes*) and experiences to savor.

Mount Etna

Take a glance at the ranking of the ten most breath taking natural wonders of Italy, as compiled by *Arché Travel* magazine:

a Have you visited any of these?

b Which ones would you like to see and why?

VOCABULARY BUILDER 2

10.06

Look at the words and phrases and complete the missing English words and expressions. Then listen and try to imitate the pronunciation of the speakers.

ELEMENTI DI GEOGRAFIA	*ELEMENTS OF GEOGRAPHY*
la collina	*hill*
la costa	....
il fiume	*river*
la foresta	....
il lago	....
il paesaggio	*landscape*
il territorio	....
il vulcano	....

ANIMALI SELVAGGI	*WILD ANIMALS*
l'aquila	*eagle*
il cervo	*deer*
il cucciolo	*pup, cub*
la volpe	*fox*
il lupo	*wolf*
l'orso	*bear*

VERBI E PAROLE UTILI	*USERFUL VERBS AND WORDS*
aspettare	*to wait*
circa	*around*
fermarsi	*to stop*
improvvisamente	*suddenly*
per terra	*on the ground*
scomparire	*disappear*
scoprire	*discover*
seguire	*to follow*
il sogno	*dream*
verso	*toward*

Vocabulary practice 2

Complete the crossword with some of the words from the table.

Orizzontali

1 Il Vesuvio è un...

4 Il Rio delle Amazzoni è un...

5 In Italia è famoso quello di Como

7 Quella italiana è lunga circa 8300km

8 Un posto dove ci sono molti alberi

Verticali

2 Un predatore che vola nel cielo

3 Una montagna piccola piccola

6 La specie di Winnie the Pooh

CONVERSATION 2

Che sogno! *What a dream!*

10.07

1 Here are a few words and expressions to help you understand the following conversation. Note their meanings.

il sogno	*dream*	preciso	*precise*
verso	*towards*	assurdo	*absurd*

10.08

2 Listen to the conversation without looking at the text. Then listen again and read the text. Listen for how the passato prossimo and imperfetto are combined when narrating events.

It's Monday morning and Annalisa is getting ready for an early morning run. As she prepares breakfast, she notices that Cristian ha una faccia– he's looking quite awful. Evidently, he had an unusual dream that disrupted his sleep. The enigmatic lady from the painting appeared to be a part of it, and he's struggling to decipher the dream's significance.

Annalisa Che succede? Hai una faccia!

Cristian Ho dormito male, perché ho fatto un sogno assurdo! Ero in una foresta enorme. A un certo punto, è arrivata una volpe. Si è fermata, mi ha guardato per circa due minuti, poi ha cominciato a correre verso un lago. Io l'ho seguita, ma dopo qualche minuto è scomparsa. Guardavo, guardavo... niente. Improvvisamente, dagli alberi, è uscita la signora del quadro. Camminava lentamente e aveva due cuccioli di lupo in mano.

Annalisa La signora del quadro in soffitta?

Cristian Sì, lei! Ha guardato i lupi, e li ha messi per terra. Poi ha detto: "Ti aspetto dal 1678. Andiamo?"

Annalisa Dal 1678? Così preciso, che strano!

Cristian Vero? Chissà cosa significa!

3 Displayed below are four images representing Cristian's story. Put them in the correct order to reconstruct the dream he recounted to Annalisa.

a

b

c

d

LANGUAGE BUILDER 3

Language discovery 3

Read the conversation and then look at the two phrases. Why is the imperfetto used in one and the passato prossimo in the other?

Mi ha guardato per circa due minuti | Guardavo, guardavo ...

Use of imperfetto and passato prossimo: duration of the action

When deciding which past tense to use, it's important to consider the duration of past actions. The imperfetto is used when referring to past actions or events with indistinct start and end points. In contrast, the passato prossimo is used for past events that occurred and concluded at specific moments in time.

Mi ha guardato per circa due minuti.	*She looked at me for about two minutes.*
Guardavo, guardavo...	*I was looking around ...*

In the first example, the duration of the action is precisely known: two minutes. In the second example, the duration is uncertain, leading to the use of the imperfetto. This principle is applicable to various scenarios where the beginning and end are known or unknown.

Ho camminato nel parco dalle 6 alle 8.	*I walked in the park from 6 to 8.*
Camminava lentamente.	*She was walking slowly.*

Remember that the passato prossimo is also used when an action is sudden, completed, and occurs only once, whereas the imperfetto is for past actions that were ongoing.

Improvvisamente è uscita la signora del quadro.	*Suddenly, the woman in the painting came out.*
Clara usciva con gli amici tutte le sere.	*Clara was going out with friends every night.*

Language practice 3

Complete the sentences with the correct past tense: passato prossimo or imperfetto?

a (noi – studiare) .... a Roma dal 2007 al 2010.
b Ieri sera Carlo (andare) .... a una festa. (essere) .... molto elegante: (indossare) .... una giacca di lana blu.
c Da bambine, Eva e Marina (giocare) .... a tennis tutte le settimane.
d Mentre (noi – passeggiare) .... in collina, (cominciare) .... a piovere.
e (tu – abitare) .... in Thailandia per sedici anni?
f L'anno scorso il 15 dicembre Lia e Luca (finire) .... l'università.
g Quando (voi – entrare) .... nella stanza, Polina (parlare) .... con un'amica.

LANGUAGE BUILDER 4

Language discovery 4

Listen to the conversation again and repeat each line in the pauses provided. Try to imitate the phrasing and intonation you hear. Then look at the conversation and focus on how the passato prossimo was used. What are the endings used for the following sentences? Can you spot the shared element between these sentences?

a L'ho seguit..... **b** Li ha mess..... per terra.

Using direct object pronouns with the passato prossimo

When using direct object pronouns in compound tenses like the passato prossimo (or any tense with a past participle), the past participle functions as an adjective and needs to match the gender and number of the object. This of course involves selecting the appropriate pronoun based on the object's gender and number in the first place. Afterward, adjust the past participle to agree accordingly, treating it as if it were an adjective.

Hai visitato il Parco Nazionale del Pollino? – Sì, l'ho visitato.	*Have you visited the Pollino National Park?—Yes, I visited it.*
Hai visitato la Sicilia? – No, non l'ho visitata.	*Have you visited Sicily? —No, I haven't visited it.*
Hai visitato le isole Eolie? – Sì, le ho visitate.	*Have you visited the Eolie islands? —Yes I visited them.*
Hai visitato i laghi italiani? – No, non li ho visitati.	*Have you visited the Italian lakes? —No, I haven't visited them.*

Both in writing and in speaking, the third person singular pronouns la and lo can be contracted if followed by a vowel or the letter h: l'ho seguita (= la ho seguita); l'abbiamo visto (= lo abbiamo visto). However, do not contract the plural pronouns: le ho seguite, li abbiamo visti.

It's important to remember that this applies only to direct objects and not indirect objects:

Hai scritto a Aicha? – Sí, le ho scritto. *Did you write to Aicha? – Yes, I wrote to her.*

Language practice 4

10.10

1 **Listen to the questions in the audio and answer by using a pronoun and the passato prossimo. Respond in the affirmative.**

a Sì, ...

b Sì, ...

c Sì, ...

d Sì, ...

e Sì, ...

f Sì, ...

g Sì, ...

h Sì, ...

i Sì, ...

j Sì, ...

10.11

2 **Now play Conversation 2 again, but this time play Cristian's role. Speak in the pauses provided and unleash your imagination: it's time to describe your own weird dream!**

SKILL BUILDER

1 **Search online and listen to the song "Gli animali" by Italian songwriter Mannarino. How many animals can you hear? List them, then check the lyrics to find any that you may have missed. Feel free to use a dictionary to identify new species!**

2 **Read the opening of the story. You might not recognize some words but try to grasp the main idea and determine whether the statements are true or false.**

In una foresta grande e misteriosa, da molti anni abitava un branco di lupi. Ogni giorno, la sera, i lupi si riunivano per cercare cibo e proteggersi dai pericoli. La luna era alta nel cielo mentre raccontavano storie di antichi tempi. Un giorno, un giovane lupo ha visto una creatura misteriosa al margine del bosco e ha immediatamente allertato gli altri lupi. Preoccupati, i lupi sono andati cautamente, e hanno scoperto che era un cucciolo di orso smarrito...

a I lupi abitavano nella foresta da qualche mese. vero falso

b I lupi si riunivano nel pomeriggio. vero falso

c La sera, i lupi raccontavano storie del passato. vero falso

d Un vecchio lupo ha trovato una creatura. vero falso

e La creatura era un piccolo orso. vero falso

3 **Now it's your turn: use your imagination and continue the story using the passato prossimo and imperfetto.**

10.12

4 **Do you want to know more about Cristian? Listen to Petra's description and complete the text with the words you hear.**

Mio fratello Cristian è un ragazzo speciale: è molto timido, ma ha grandi passioni. La natura, per esempio: le sue Dolomiti, e **a** .... in generale. E poi, **b** ...., l'arte: **c** .... da bambino e non **d** .... Quando era piccolo **e** .... disegnare e creare sculture con la terra del giardino. A quindici anni, **f** .... i giochi di ruolo: D&D e World of Warcraft: e altri con nomi strani. **g** .... subito e ogni settimana **h** .... tutta la notte con i suoi amici. Quando **i** .... a Venezia **j** .... molto triste, ma capisco che così può seguire i suoi sogni. **k** .... non è troppo lontano da Bolzano!

TEST YOURSELF

1 Read the conversation between Cristian and Matteo: Cristian is late for his party and he's making up excuses. Complete the conversation with the imperfetto or passato prossimo.

●●●○○ 100%

M Cristian dove sei? **a** .... (arrivare) tutti.

C Scusami, sto arrivando.

M Come "sto arrivando"? La festa **b** .... (cominciare) un'ora fa!

C Ehm, hai ragione: mentre **c** .... (farsi la doccia), **d** .... (sentire) un rumore.

M Un rumore?!

C Eh, la doccia **e** .... (rompersi), mentre **f** .... (io-lavarsi)

M Veramente?

C Sì, così **g** .... (chiamare) il tecnico immediatamente. Mentre **h** .... (aspettare) il tecnico, mia sorella mi **i** .... (telefonare).

M Ah. E poi?

C Quando **j** .... (finire) di parlare con lei **k** .... (uscire), ma **l** .... (dimenticare) il regalo e...!

M Cristian! È tardi, non perdere tempo!!

C Hai ragione, arrivo!

2 Match the questions with the answers.

1 Dove hai comprato quella camicia?
2 Abbiamo il mascarpone per il tiramisù?
3 Hai preso le chiavi?
4 Dov'è la tua macchina?
5 Da quanto tempo non senti Ugo e Jan?
6 Come hai imparato tre lingue?
7 Com'è l'ultimo film di Nolan?

a Sì, l'ha comprato Paolo ieri.
b Li ho chiamati due giorni fa!
c Le ho studiate a scuola.
d Bella, vero? L'ho presa in un negozio del centro.
e Mi dispiace, non l'ho visto.
f No, le ho dimenticate in macchina!
g L'ho portata dal meccanico.

3 Look at the sentences and decide whether the adverb ending in -mente is correct or not. Then correct the incorrect forms.

a Questo paesaggio è incredibilmente bello. (incredibile)
b Il lupo osserva aggressivomente l'altro lupo. (aggressivo)
c Abbiamo felicamente adottato un gatto! (felice)
d Il fiume scorre lentamente. (lento)
e Non siamo ancora arrivati al lago?! Io ho seguito le indicazioni correttemente! (corretto)
f La mamma orsa guarda i suoi cuccioli dolcemente. (dolce)

La misteriosa donna in soffitta *The mysterious woman in the attic*

Solve the riddle. The first letter of this new animal will add up to the name of Cristian's dream lady!

Sono molto grande e tutto il giorno cammino nella jungla o nelle foreste.

Ho una buona memoria e il mio colore è il grigio. Chi sono?

Remember to use **My review** and **My takeaway** to assess your progress and reflect on your learning experience.

In this unit you will learn how to:

» Talk about TV shows and the press.

» Express desires, suggestions, and making polite requests using the **conditional**.

» Use numbers from 100 onward.

11

Con un biglietto della lotteria

My study plan

I plan to work with Unit 11

○ Every day

○ Twice a week

○ Other ___________

I plan to study for

○ 5–15 minutes

○ 15–30 minutes

○ 30–45+ minutes

My progress tracker

Day / Date					
	○	○	○	○	○
	○	○	○	○	○
	○	○	○	○	○
	○	○	○	○	○
	○	○	○	○	○
	○	○	○	○	○
	○	○	○	○	○

My goals

What do you want to be able to do or say in Italian when you complete this unit?

		Done
1	....	○
2	....	○
3	....	○

My review

SELF CHECK

	I can ...
●	... talk about wishes and desires.
●	... talk about TV shows and the press.
●	... give suggestions.
●	... make polite requests.
●	... use irregular plural nouns.

CULTURE POINT 1

TV e intrattenimento in Italia *TV and entertainment in Italy*

Italian canali (*TV channels*) can be divided into three groups: first, la televisione statale (*state-run TV*), also known as RAI (Radiotelevisione Italiana), for which people must buy a canone (*licence*). RAI has several canali, offering a variety of programmi (*programs*), spanning from classic films to documentari (*documentaries*), telegiornali (*newscasts*), dibattiti politici (*political debates*) and programmi dedicated to sports. The second group consists of private TV channels owned by the Fininvest Group. Private TV contains more pubblicità (*commercials*) and is more geared toward intrattenimento (*entertainment*), for instance giochi a premi (*game shows*), reality shows, and films of various generi (*genres*): commedie romantiche (*rom coms*), dell'orrore (*horror*), polizieschi (*crime dramas*), and gialli (*thrillers*). The third group is represented by TV on demand, where people can pay and download content.

You can watch most RAI programs on the Rai Italia website called **RAIplay**. Most content is also available outside of Italy, depending on the region or country. Explore

the **RAIplay** website. Can you identify the genere and types of some of the programmi there?

Did you know? Thriller movies are called gialli because the first books of this genre were usually published with a yellow cover, so the name stuck!

VOCABULARY BUILDER 1

Look at the words and phrases and complete the missing English words and expressions. Then listen and try to imitate the pronunciation of the speakers.

LA TELEVISIONE E LA RADIO	*TV AND RADIO*
il programma	....
il telegiornale	....
il dibattito (politico)	*(political) debate*
il documentario	....
la serie TV	*TV series*
il giallo	....
la commedia (romantica)	*(romantic) comedy*
il film drammatico/il dramma	*drama*
il film storico	*period movie*
il film poliziesco	*detective film*
il film dell'orrore	*horror movie*
il canale	*channel*
il canone TV	....
il gioco a premi	*game show*
l'episodio/la puntata	....
i cartoni animati	*cartoons/animated films*

Note that all the nouns ending in -ramma are masculine even though they end in -a: diagramma, dramma. Some nouns end in -o but are feminine: la radio, la foto.

ESPRESSIONI UTILI	*USEFUL PHRASES*
seguire	*to follow*
raccontare/narrare	*to tell/to narrate*
scaricare	*to download*
fare l'abbonamento a	*to buy a subscription to*
smettere	*to quit/to stop (doing something)*
Fare una maratona di serie TV	*to binge-watch a TV series*
discutere	*to discuss*

Vocabulary practice 1

Read the descriptions and decide which genre they belong to.

a "Mare Fuori" racconta la storia, in dieci puntate, di dieci criminali in una prigione vicino al mare.

b In "Affari Tuoi" i partecipanti devono risolvere un enigma e ricevono molti soldi.

c "Montalbano" narra la storia di un detective in Sicilia.

d "Paradiso da salvare" parla del cambiamento del clima e il suo impatto sull'Italia.

e In "Agorà" gli ospiti discutono l'economia e le riforme fiscali.

f "Topo Gigio" è la storia di un topo gentile e romantico che adora il formaggio Emmenthal.

g "Io e Lei" è la storia dell'amore difficile tra Marina e Francesca.

CONVERSATION 1

Una maratona di TV! *Binge-watching TV!*

11.02

1 Here are a few words and expressions to help you understand the following conversation. Note their meanings.

crea dipendenza	*it's addictive*	cupo	*dark/gloomy*
al posto tuo	*if I were you*	io mi annoierei	*I would get bored*
su canale 5	*on channel 5*		

11.03

2 Listen to the conversation without looking at the text. Then listen to the conversation again and read the text.

Annalisa returns home from a late night out and finds Cristian glued to the TV. Fa una maratona della serie TV "The Michelangelo Code." That's how he deals with the nerve-racking stress of waiting for the outcome of his interview for the job in the U.S. Annalisa finds it very odd that he relaxes by watching serie TV e film storici that contain crimini (*crimes*) and vecchi relitti (*old relics*) but de gustibus non est disputandum ... which is Latin (but used in Italian as well) for: ***there is no arguing about tastes!***

Annalisa Cristian, sono le tre!

Cristian Lo so ma questa serie TV crea dipendenza. Non smetterei mai.

Annalisa Io al posto tuo andrei a letto... E poi... non guarderei questa serie così cupa, mamma mia, solo dramma, misteri e vecchi relitti! Non potrei dormire dopo! Al posto tuo seguirei le Olimpiadi su RAIplay, o un bel documentario sugli animali!

Cristian Atleti e animali marini... sarebbe perfetta per addormentarsi sul divano!

Annalisa De gustibus.... Senti... vorresti fare l'abbonamento a SkyTV? C'è una serie che vorrei guardare...

3 Decide if the following TV series or films are something that Annalisa (A) or Cristian (C) guarderebbe (*would watch*).

a La vita segreta dei delfini. A C

b Il nome della rosa. A C

c Il trono di spade (*Game of Thrones*). A C

d Ragazze vincenti (*A League of their Own*). A C

e L'esorcista. A C

4 C'è una serie TV che ti crea dipendenza? Cosa guarderesti tutta la notte?

Io guarderei...

LANGUAGE BUILDER 1

Language discovery 1

In the phrases below, Annalisa and Cristian are saying what they would do. Match the verbs with their infinitives. Can you see a pattern for the -are, -ere, or -ire verbs?

1	Non smetterei mai.	**a** seguire
2	Io non guarderei questa serie così cupa.	**b** smettere
3	Io seguirei le Olimpiadi.	**c** guardare

Condizionale

The conditional is often used to talk about a hypothetical situation or to express something we wish we could do but that we can't do. It can also be used to give a suggestion to someone else (*If I were you, I would ...*). To form the condizionale in Italian, remove -are, -ere, and -ire from the infinitive and replace them with the following endings:

Verbs ending in -are and -ere:	erei, eresti, erebbe, eremmo, ereste, erebbero
Verbs ending in -ire:	irei, iresti, irebbe, iremmo, ireste, irebbero

	guardare	**smettere**	**dormire**
io	guarder**ei**	smetter**ei**	dormir**ei**
tu	guarder**esti**	smetter**esti**	dormir**esti**
lui/lei	guarder**ebbe**	smetter**ebbe**	dormir**ebbe**
noi	guarder**emmo**	smetter**emmo**	dormir**emmo**
voi	guarder**este**	smetter**este**	dormir**emmo**
loro	guarder**ebbero**	smetter**ebbero**	dormir**ebbero**

Al posto tuo seguirei le Olimpiadi. *If I were you, I'd watch the Olympics.*

Notice that the same endings are added for all three groups to the infinitive. And note that for -are verbs -a changes to -e.

Language practice 1

Add the correct verb endings to form complete sentences.

a Annalisa guarder .... le Olimpiadi ma non ha tempo.
b Io smett .... di bere caffé, ma è molto difficile.
c Questa sera noi manger .... volentieri una pizza.
d Con i documentari sugli animali Cristian si annoiere ....
e Shuangyu e Hongfen uscir[illegible] .... stasera ma hanno molto lavoro.

LANGUAGE BUILDER 2

Language discovery 2

Listen to the conversation again and repeat each line in the pauses provided. Then find the phrases corresponding to the English sentences in the left column and add the infinitive. What do you notice about the verbs in the conditional? How are they built?

English	Italian	Infinitive
Would you want/like to subscribe to SkyTV?	Vorresti fare l'abbonamento a SkyTV?	volere
I would not be able to sleep.		
I would go to bed.		
It would be perfect to fall asleep on the couch.		

Irregular verbs in the conditional

By now you know that Italian is full of irregular verbs! And there is one irregular conditional you know already, vorrei (*I'd like*), which you used in Unit 3 to ask for things in a polite manner. Verbs that are irregular in the conditional have an irregular stem, but they all take the same endings: -ei, -esti, -ebbe, -emmo, -este, -ebbero. The stem for volere is vorr-: vorrei, vorresti, vorrebbe, vorremmo, vorreste, vorrebbero.

Vorremmo un caffè, per piacere. *We'd like a coffee, please.*

Let's group the most common ones to make them easy to remember.

ESSERE = sar- AVERE = avr-

POTERE = potr- VOLERE = vorr- DOVERE = dovr-

ANDARE = andr- VENIRE = verr-

FARE = far- DARE = dar- STARE = star-

Sarebbe perfetta per addormentarsi sul divano! *It would be perfect for falling asleep on the couch!*

Mi potresti aiutare? *Could you help me?*

Cosa farebbero al posto tuo? – Ci andrebbero. *What would they do in your place? —They would go there.*

There is a full list of irregular verbs in the Grammar summary.

Language practice 2

1 Change the underlined verbs in the present tense to the conditional.

- **a** Posso aprire la finestra? Fa molto caldo.
- **b** Al posto tuo, io vado dal dottore.
- **c** Annalisa vuole fare l'abbonamento a SkyTV ma costa molto.
- **d** Cristian deve andare a letto ma non è stanco.
- **e** Il gatto sta sul letto ma non è permesso.

2 Listen to the speaker asking you questions. Answer them with full sentences using the verb in the conditional.

Example: Dove andresti in vacanza? *Andrei in Cile.*

- **a** Cosa mangeresti volentieri per cena?
- **b** Ti piacerebbe una vacanza in Italia?
- **c** Vorresti salire sull'Everest?
- **d** Quale film guarderesti 100 volte?
- **e** Faresti l'abbonamento a SkyTV?
- **f** Al posto di Cristian, andresti a letto o finiresti la maratona di serie TV?

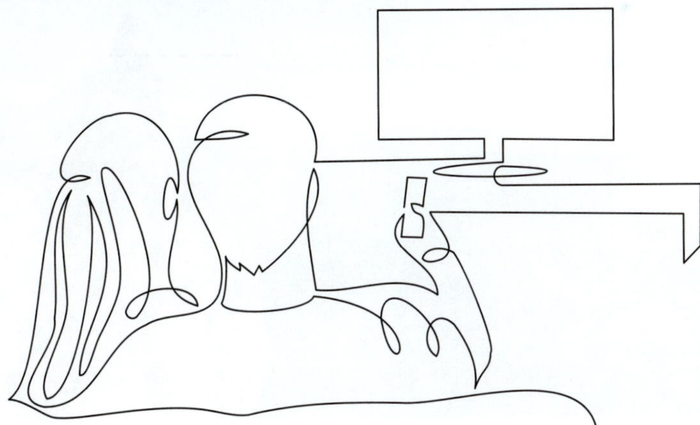

CULTURE POINT 2

Cosa sognano gli italiani? *What do Italians dream of?*

According to a sondaggio (*survey*) published in il giornale (*newspaper*) Corriere della Sera in 2023, Italians' dreams and goals changed after the Covid-19 pandemic. According to il giornalista (*the journalist*), a large percentage of people would like to have more time for personal development: physical and mental wellbeing and education figure prominently as life goals. Molti sognano (*many dream*) of owning a house, especially millennials. Some would prefer to live close to nature while others dream of living abroad. Many people giocano alla lotteria (*play the lottery*) in the hopes of achieving these goals. These sondaggi appear quite often in the national stampa (*press*) and give an idea of the new trends in Italian società (*society*).

Imagine you are taking part in a survey. Answer these questions in Italian, using the prompts given.

a Quali sono i tuoi obiettivi personali? Io vorrei...

b Dove ti piacerebbe vivere? Mi piacerebbe...

c Cosa sogni? Io sogno di + *infinitive*

VOCABULARY BUILDER 2

11.06

Look at the words and phrases and complete the missing English words and expressions. Then listen and try to imitate the pronunciation of the speakers.

LA STAMPA	*THE PRESS*
il giornale	....
la rivista	*magazine*
il/a giornalista	*journalist*
il/a giornalaio/a	*newsagent*
in edicola	*at the newsstand*
l'articolo	....
il titolo	*title*
la società	....
sul giornale	*in the newspaper*

VERBI UTILI	*USEFUL VERBS*
giocare alla lotteria	....
vendere	*to sell*
pubblicare	*to publish*
sognare	....
vincere	*to win*
dare in beneficenza	*to give to charity*

NUMERI DA 100	*NUMBERS FROM 100 ONWARDS*
cento	*a hundred*
duecento (trecento...)	....
mille	*a thousand*
duemila (tremila, quattromila...)	*two (three, four ...) thousand*
un milione, due milioni	....................., ...
un miliardo due miliardi	*a billion, two billion*

A hundred is cento. Numbers above 100 are very similar to English, but in Italian the number is written as one word: duecentocinquantacinque = 255. With mille, you can do the same, but mille becomes -mila in the plural: duemilacinquecentocinquantacinque = 2555. When dealing with milioni e miliardi, the subsequent digits are separated by e: un milione e cinquecentomila = 1,500,000.

Vocabulary practice 2

1 Write the following numbers in Italian.

a 2.000.000
b 8790
c 6923
d 348
e 4.000.000.000
f 7.560.000

2 Answer the questions based on the vocabulary.

a Chi scrive gli articoli sul giornale?
b Chi vende i giornali e le riviste?
c Dove possiamo comprare i giornali e le riviste?
d Quale parte dell'articolo dice il tema dell'articolo?

CONVERSATION 2

Il numero fortunato *The lucky number*

11.07

1 Listen to the conversation without looking at the text. Then listen to the conversation again and follow along in the text. Pay attention to the sentences using the condizionale.

Aicha and Annalisa are walking downtown, and Aicha is glued to her phone, as she is reading i titoli in the giornali online. Annalisa is a bit irritated as Aicha keeps bumping into people while her eyes are glued to the screen. They pass by an edicola. In Italy, edicole sell giornali and riviste but also biglietti della lotteria. One of the most popular lotterie is the Gratta e Vinci (*Scratch and Win*), a ticket that you scratch with a coin to reveal the numero fortunato.

Annalisa Potresti smettere di guardare il telefono?

Aicha Guarda questo articolo: studente vince 500.000 euro alla lotteria e dà tutto in beneficenza!

Annalisa I giornalisti pubblicano sempre titoli sensazionali!

Aicha Tu cosa faresti con quei soldi?

Annalisa Comprerei una casa al mare e vorrei lavorare meno e avere più tempo per me.

Aicha Io invece aprirei uno studio di fotografia a Berlino: una delle città più cool del mondo!

Annalisa Allora dovresti giocare alla lotteria! Ecco un'edicola!

Aicha (*al giornalaio*) Scusi, mi potrebbe dare un Gratta e Vinci?

2 Correct the mistakes in the sentences below based on the conversation.

- **a** Uno studente vince 500.000 euro e compra una casa al mare.
- **b** I giornalisti scrivono articoli noiosi.
- **c** Annalisa vorrebbe lavorare di più.
- **d** Aicha aprirebbe un negozio a Berlino.
- **e** In edicola Aicha e Annalisa comprano una rivista.

LANGUAGE BUILDER 3

Language discovery 3

Look at the sentences taken from the conversation. Which sentences express: a polite request (P), a suggestion (S), or a wish (W)? Which modal verbs are used to introduce these functions?

a Potresti smettere di guardare il telefono?

b Vorrei lavorare di meno.

c Dovresti giocare alla lotteria.

d Scusi, mi potrebbe dare un Gratta e Vinci?

Vorrei, potrei, dovrei: using the condizionale

As you have seen, the condizionale is used to express a hypothetical, unrealistic situation:

Io comprerei questa casa ma costa molto. — *I would buy this house, but it is too expensive.*

It can also be used to express a desire with volere in the conditional:

Annalisa vorrebbe lavorare meno. — *Annalisa would like to work less.*

The conditional is also used to give suggestions:

Al posto tuo, io giocherei alla lotteria. — *If I were you, I would play the lottery.*

In addition, suggestions can be made with the conditional of dovere, which is like *should* in English:

Dovresti giocare alla lotteria. — *You should play the lottery.*

Finally, the conditional is used to make polite requests. In this case, the verb potere is often used, like *could* in English:

Potresti smettere di guardare il telefono? — *Could you stop looking at your phone?*

The conditional of potere in polite requests is often associated with the polite form Lei:

Scusi, Lei mi potrebbe dire che ore sono? — *Excuse me, could you tell me what time it is?*

Language practice 3

1 Make a wish (W), a suggestion (S), or a polite request (P) using the conditional of volere (W), dovere (S), or potere (P).

Example: Annalisa è stanca. (fare una pausa S) — *Annalisa dovrebbe fare una pausa.*

a Chiudere la porta (P) — Tu... ....

b Dire dove è l'autobus (P) — Scusi, Lei... ....

c Aicha ama Berlino. (visitare la città S) — Aicha... ....

d Ordinare un caffè (W) — Io... ....

e Fare una maratona di una serie TV (W) Cristian... ....

f Vivere in campagna (W) Noi... ....

g Non telefonare in treno (P) Tu... ....

2 **A friend of yours is planning on visiting Italy. Based on what you know about the country, write a few suggestions about what they should see and do. If you were them (al posto tuo io...), what would you eat and drink?**

LANGUAGE BUILDER 4

Language discovery 4

11.08

Listen to the conversation again and repeat each line in the pauses provided. Try to imitate the phrasing and intonation you hear. Then look at these nouns. How are they pluralized in the conversation?

il giornalista	i giornalisti
la giornalista	le giornaliste
la città	le città
il dramma	i drammi

Plural form of irregular nouns

In the previous units, you have learned that most nouns end in -o or -e for masculine and -a or -e for feminine. The plural for nouns ending in -o and -e is always -i, whereas for nouns ending in -a the plural is -e. However, there are some nouns that do not fall into this pattern. Let's look at the most common groups.

1 Nouns ending in -ista and -eta/-auta. They mostly indicate professions, sports, or affiliations: dentista; atleta. These nouns have one form in the singular for masculine and feminine but two in the plural, ending in -i and -e.

Singular	Plural
il/la giornalista	i giornalisti, le giornaliste
l'atleta	gli atleti, le atlete

2 Nouns that end with an accented vowel: -à: città; -è: tè, caffè; -ò: comò (*commode*); -ù: gioventù (*youth*). They stay the same in the plural. Singular nouns ending in -i also stay the same in the plural: analisi, crisi.

Singular	Plural
la città	le città
il caffè	i caffè
la crisi	le crisi

3 Masculine nouns ending in -ema and -ramma form the plural by replacing the final -a with -i.

Singular	Plural
il problema	i problemi
il programma	i programmi

Language practice 4

1 Complete the following sentences with the correct word from the list and pluralize it, if needed.

dramma	giornalista	problema	pianista
atleta	caffè	città	maratoneta

a Vittorio Feltri è un .... famoso. Lui scrive sul giornale "Libero."

b Quanti .... bevi al giorno? Di solito ne bevo tre.

c L'articolo discute i .... della politica italiana.

d Le .... italiane sono di solito molto antiche.

e Ludovico Einaudi è un .... italiano.

f Federica Pellegrini e Vanessa Ferrari sono due .... italiane olimpioniche.

g Non mi piacciono i ....; preferisco le commedie.

h .... corrono 14 km.

11.09

2 Now play Conversation 2 again and play Aicha's role. At the end of the conversation, say what you would do if you win the lottery.

SKILL BUILDER

1 You are browsing a streaming video service in Italy. Look at some titles and plot summaries of various programmi and shows. What is their genere? Match the titles to the genres in the table.

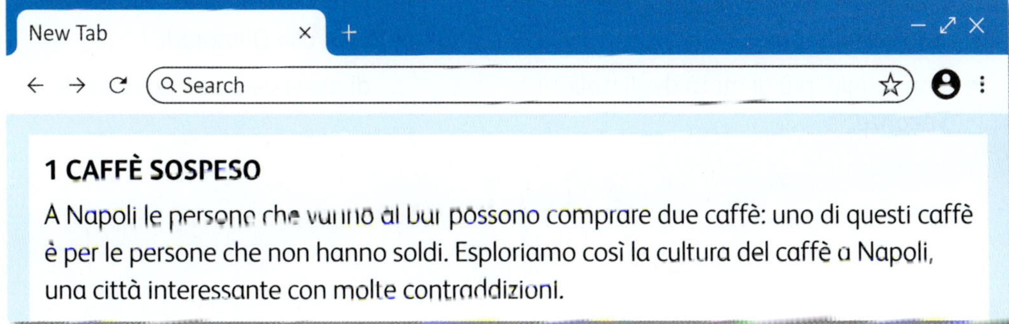

1 CAFFÈ SOSPESO

A Napoli le persone che vanno al bar possono comprare due caffè: uno di questi caffè è per le persone che non hanno soldi. Esploriamo così la cultura del caffè a Napoli, una città interessante con molte contraddizioni.

2 SOTTO IL SOLE DI RICCIONE

È la storia di un gruppo di teenagers in vacanza al mare nella città di Riccione. Drammi, amore, amicizia tra giovani con l'ossessione dei social media.

3 LA LEGGE DI LIDIA POET

Questa serie TV racconta la vita di Lidia Poet, la prima (first) avvocata (lawyer) in Italia. Un po' avvocata, un po' detective, Lidia deve risolvere molti casi difficili nella Torino del 1800.

4 CURON

Siamo vicino a Bolzano, in un piccolo villaggio sulle Alpi che si chiama Curon. A Curon c'è una cattedrale dentro un lago e il lago nasconde (hides) un mistero terribile.

Orrore/Thriller	Documentario	Giallo/Poliziesco	Commedia romantica

2 Correct the mistakes in the following sentences.

a Jannick Sinner è un tennisto italiano.
b Milano è una delle citte più interessanti in Italia.
c I programma della RAI sono anche su RAIplay.
d Cristian e Matteo prendono due caffí.

11.10

3 Il telegiornale. Listen to the news headlines and complete with the missing words.

a .... : un'estate con 40 gradi a Roma.
b Numero fortunato: signora di 90 anni vince .... euro e li spende per un viaggio intorno al mondo.
c Riforma fiscale: .... tra il governo e l'opposizione.
d Bravissimi! .... italiani vincono una medaglia alle Olimpiadi.
e Sondaggio: più di metà degli italiani .... di possedere una casa per le vacanze.

TEST YOURSELF

1 Complete the sentences with the conditional of the verbs.

a E tu, cosa .... (comprare) per il regalo di compleanno di Silva?
b Al posto tuo, io .... (decidere) di andare in vacanza in settembre.
c Mi .... (piacere) visitare questa città ma è molto lontana.
d Voi .... (studiare) spagnolo ma siete molto impegnati.
e Noi .... (avere) voglia di una vacanza ma non abbiamo tempo.
f .... (essere) una bella idea ma molto difficile da realizzare.
g I genitori di Annalisa .... (venire) spesso a Venezia ma il viaggio è lungo.
h E tu cosa .... (fare) al posto mio?

2 Pluralize the following sentences. Pay attention to irregular nouns, and add the appropriate articles. Modify the verbs, too.

a La città italiana è bella.
b Il giornalista è giapponese.
c Mi piace il programma.
d Il teorema è difficile.

3 Transform the underlined verb in the conditional to make polite requests and suggestions.

a <u>Puoi</u> parlare più lentamente?
b <u>Devi</u> contattare il dottore.
c <u>Vuoi</u> un caffè?
d <u>Posso</u> usare il tuo telefono?
e <u>Volete</u> un bicchiere d'acqua?

La misteriosa donna in soffitta *The mysterious woman in the attic*

Let's help Cristian with his quest. This time we need the first letter of the name of the movie director who made *La vita è bella*.

Remember to use **My review** and **My takeaway** to assess your progress and reflect on your learning experience.

12

In this unit you will learn how to:

- Talk about objects of everyday life.
- Explain the function of objects.
- Compare items.
- Use the pronoun **ne** with verbs in **passato prossimo**.

Made in Italy

My study plan

I plan to work with Unit 12

- ○ Every day
- ○ Twice a week
- ○ Other ____________

I plan to study for

- ○ 5–15 minutes
- ○ 15–30 minutes
- ○ 30–45+ minutes

My progress tracker

Day / Date	Listening	Speaking	Reading	Writing	Conversation
	○	○	○	○	○
	○	○	○	○	○
	○	○	○	○	○
	○	○	○	○	○
	○	○	○	○	○
	○	○	○	○	○
	○	○	○	○	○

My goals

What do you want to be able to do or say in Italian when you complete this unit?

		Done
1	....	○
2	....	○
3	....	○

My review

SELF CHECK

	I can ...
●	... talk about objects of everyday life.
●	... explain the function of objects.
●	... make comparisons between items and activities.
●	... connect sentences using relative pronouns.
●	... talk about quantity in the past using ne.

CULTURE POINT 1

Il Salone Internazionale del Mobile *Milan Furniture Fair*

Made in Italy—is there a better label across moda (*fashion*), cibo e bevande (*food and beverages*), automobili (*cars*), e arredamento di design (*interior design*)? More than a simple tag, it's the talented embrace of Italy's artigianato (*craftsmanship*) and innovazione (*innovation*). An influential hotspot for innovazione e design is the Salone Internazionale del Mobile (*Milan Furniture Fair*), initiated in 1961 in Milan. A key global hub for interior design and the world's largest event of its kind, today the fair encompasses 150,000 m^2 of exhibition space. With 1000 Italian and over 300 international exhibitors, il Salone annually draws nearly 300,000 specialized attendees, half of whom come from abroad. Beyond this, Milan's yearly array of complementary events has supported the fair's tradition and triumph, including university gatherings, Design Districts, and the renowned Fuorisalone (*Outside the fair*). This includes an extensive range of mostre (*exhibitions*), incontri (*gatherings*), and presentazioni (*presentations*) across Milan's cultural, artistic, and design spaces.

Explore the official website of the Salone Internazionale del Mobile, particularly the prodotti (*products*) section. Is there a design piece you'd love to have in your home?

VOCABULARY BUILDER 1

12.01

Look at the words and phrases and complete the missing English words and expressions. Then listen and try to imitate the pronunciation of the speakers.

OGGETTI D'ARREDAMENTO	*FURNITURE*
la caffettiera	*coffee machine*
la cosa / il coso	*thing*
la lampada	....
la libreria	*bookshelf*
il manico	*handle*
il mobile	*furniture*
la moka	*moka pot*
l'oggetto	*item*
la poltrona	*armchair*
la possibilità	....
la sedia	*chair*
il vaso	....
MATERIALI	***MATERIALS***
la gomma	*rubber*
il metallo	....
la plastica	....
COM'E?	***HOW IS IT?***
colorato/a	....
comodo/a	*comfortable*
di design	....
funzionale	....
moderno/a	....
VERBI UTILI	***USEFUL VERBS***
A cosa serve/servono?	*What is the use?*
serve/servono a	*to serve a purpose*
bruciarsi	*to get burned*

Vocabulary practice 1

Unscramble the letters to reveal the different furniture items.

a adlamap
b lonpatro
c desia
d rielabir
e rcfieatfeaa
f oavs

CONVERSATION 1

Un oggetto di design *A design item*

12.02

1 Listen to the conversation without looking at the text. Then listen again and read the text.

While making breakfast, Cristian's eyes fall upon an unfamiliar, shiny oggetto. Unsure about its purpose, he is standing there contemplating it when Annalisa enters la cucina. With a patient smile, she proceeds to unveil the object's function and its operation, surprised by Cristian's evident lack of affinity for contemporary aesthetics. As their conversation flows, it becomes apparent that they hold contrasting views about modern design. Listen to how they compare objects and activities.

Cristian Che cos'è questo?

Annalisa Come, che cos'è?! È la nuova caffettiera di Alessi che ho comprato ieri. È perfetta per la nostra cucina: moderna e di design. Non ti piace?

Cristian È sicuramente più moderna della mia vecchia moka, ma non capisco. A cosa serve questo... questo coso lungo e colorato?

Annalisa Cristian, è il manico! Vedi: è di gomma, serve a tenere la caffettiera e a non bruciarsi.

Cristian Non so, mi sembra meno funzionale di quella che abbiamo. E poi lo sai: preferisco gli oggetti vintage, che hanno una storia!

Annalisa Dalle una possibilità: forse scopri che fare il caffè con questa è più facile che prepararlo con la tua moka del paleolitico.

Cristian Ehi, non parlare male della mia Moka!

The expression servire a expresses the idea of "to be used for" or "to be needed for." It indicates the purpose or function of an object, action, or situation in relation to a specific context. It's often used in the third person singular or plural, depending on the subject: il coltello serve a tagliare il pane / i coltelli servono a tagliare il pane (*the knife is used for cutting the bread / the knives are used for cutting the bread*).

2 Answer the questions in Italian.

a What is the item, which Annalisa and Cristian are discussing, used for?
b Which two names are used for the item?
c Why does Annalisa think the new coffee maker is perfect for their kitchen?

LANGUAGE BUILDER 1

Language discovery 1

1 Look at the following sentences from the dialogue and choose the appropriate word.

a Mi sembra più / meno funzionale di / che quella che abbiamo.

b Forse scopri che fare il caffè con questa è più / meno facile di / che prepararlo con la tua moka

2 In the conversation, Cristian compares the new coffee machine and the old one. Which key words does he use? How is the item of comparison introduced?

Making comparisons

In Italian, to compare two items or qualities use più (*more*) or meno (less) followed by the adjective.

Questa caffettiera è più moderna di quella.	*This coffee machine is more modern than that one.*
Torino è meno turistica di Firenze.	*Turin is less touristy than Florence.*

When introducing the second element of comparison, there are two choices: di or che. Use di when contrasting nouns or pronouns, and che when comparing two actions (verbs) or qualities (adverbs or adjectives).

Carlos è più giovane di Clara.	*Carlos is younger than Clara.*
Giocare a pallavolo è più divertente che pulire la casa.	*Playing volleyball is more fun than cleaning the house.*
Andare a lavoro in bicicletta è meno veloce che in macchina.	*Going to work by bike is slower than by car.*
Questa moka è più bella che utile.	*This moka pot is more beautiful than it is useful.*

Remember that di combines with a definite article to form one word (del, dei, della, delle...):

È più moderna della mia vecchia moka.	*It's more modern than my old moka pot.*

To express that two things are the same, use the word quanto.

Lucas è alto quanto Delia.	*Lucas is as tall as Delia.*

Language practice 1

Write full sentences using the comparative più (+) or meno (-).

a Londra / grande / Roma (+) ....

b Cucinare le lasagne / veloce / cucinare la pasta (-) ....

c Le poltrone / comode / le sedie (+) ....

d La tua lampada / moderna / la mia (-) ....

LANGUAGE BUILDER 2

Language discovery 2

12.03

Listen to the conversation again and repeat each line in the pauses provided. Try to imitate the phrasing and intonation you hear. Then look at these sentences from the conversation. What does che mean in each one?

a Che cos'è?
b La caffettiera che ho comprato ieri.
c Forse scopri che fare il caffè è più facile.

The many functions of che

The word che has several meanings in Italian, based on the context. When initiating a question, it signifies *what* or *which*.

Che cos'è?	*What is it?*

If it comes after a verb, it serves as a link between two sentences, meaning "*that*":

Dico che non capisci niente di design!	*I say that you don't have a clue about design.*
So che le lampade di Alessi sono molto costose.	*I know that Alessi lamps are very expensive.*

Che can also act as a relative pronoun, meaning *who* or *what/which*, when combining two sentences.

L'architetto che ha progettato l'oggetto è italiano.	*The architect who designed the item is Italian.*
La ragazza che parla si chiama Luna.	*The girl who is speaking is called Luna.*
Mi piacciono gli oggetti vintage, che hanno una storia.	*I like retro items, which have a history.*
La sedia che hai comprato è di plastica.	*The chair that you bought is made of plastic.*

And as you just learned, when comparing actions or qualities, che also takes on the meaning of "than."

Fare il caffè è più facile che prepararlo con la tua moka.	*To make coffee it's easier than to prepare it with your moka pot.*

Lastly, positioned just before an adjective in an exclamation, che signifies "how."

Che bello!	*How nice!*

Language practice 2

12.04

1 **Listen to the sentences and choose the correct translation of che.**

	What?/ Which?	That (link)	That/ Which (relative)	Who	Than	How
a						
b						
c						
d						
e						
f						
g						
h						
i						
j						

2 **Match 1–6 with a–f to form sentences.**

1 Viaggiare in treno è più rilassante
2 Sonia mi ha detto
3 È nuova questa borsa?
4 Andiamo al mare domani?
5 L'architetto
6 Vorrei usare la moka

a che è in ritardo.
b che ha progettato questo edificio è Renzo Piano.
c che ti ho prestato ieri.
d Sì, ma dipende. Che tempo fa?
e che viaggiare in aereo
f Che bella, mi piace molto!

12.05

3 **Now play Conversation 1 again, but this time you will play Annalisa's role. Think of a peculiar object and describe it to Cristian, including what its purpose is.**

CULTURE POINT 2

Vespa: una corsa italiana verso la rinascita *Vespa: Italy's ride to rebirth*

After World War II, in 1945, a sense of speranza (*hope*) for a better future emerged, marked by joyful celebrations and the rise of rock and roll music. People's desire for libertà (*freedom)* and divertimento (*leisure*), constrained during the war, began to flourish. However, public services remained limited, presenting a challenge. Enrico Piaggio teamed up with engineer Corradino d'Ascanio to create an affordable, compact, and durable transportation solution. A year later, the Vespa was born, named for its resemblance to a vespa (*wasp*) and its sleek design. The Vespa quickly gained global fame, produced in 13 countries, and distributed across 114. With over 19 million units produced, its success symbolized rebellion and the era's spirit of youthful liberation. Italy's motor industry also thrived, epitomized by the Motor Valley Development in Emilia Romagna, home to major automobili (*car*) and moto (*motorcycle*) designers like Ferrari, Maserati, Lamborghini, and Ducati.

Explore the Motor Valley website. Can you locate the Italian city where the following brands have their headquarters?

a Ferrari **b** Lamborghini **c** Maserati
d Ducati **e** Dallara

VOCABULARY BUILDER 2

12.06

Look at the words and phrases and complete the missing English words and expressions. Then listen and try to imitate the pronunciation of the speakers.

di seconda mano	....
la marca	*brand*
il motorino	*moped*
TECNOLOGIA	***TECH***
l'applicazione/app	....
gli auricolari	*earphones*
la cassa bluetooth	*bluetooth speaker*
il cavo	*cable*
il cellulare/telefonino	....
il computer	....
il contapassi	*step counter*
il dispositivo	*the device*
la notifica	....
l'orologio digitale	....
il portatile	*laptop*
il selfie	....
i social media	....
la stampante	*printer*
il tablet	....
il televisore/la TV	....
VERBI UTILI	***USEFUL VERBS***
caricare	*to upload*
cliccare	....
googlare	....
navigare	*to browse*
perdere	*to lose/to miss*
ricevere	*to receive*
zoomare	....

With the advancement of technology and the influx of new foreign vocabulary, Italian has both incorporated and modified numerous foreign words. This is evident in terms like computer, tablet, selfie, and social media. However, in the realm of verbs, a distinct pattern emerges. There's either an Italian counterpart (e.g., scaricare—*to download*) or the English verb is Italianized, usually adopting the -are group ending. Examples include cliccare (*to click*), zoommare (*to zoom in/out*), googlare (*to google something*), spoilerare (*to spoil the ending of a book/film*), and many others.

Vocabulary practice 2

Identify the object that matches the description given.

a Serve a vedere quanti passi fai ogni giorno: ....
b Serve a viaggiare in modo leggero e veloce: ....
c Serve a navigare su internet, ma anche a scrivere documenti: ....
d Servono ad ascoltare la musica in autobus: ....
e Serve a chiamare gli amici e la famiglia: ....

CONVERSATION 2

Qualcosa di nuovo *Something new*

12.07

1 Here are a few words and expressions to help you understand the following conversation. Note their meanings.

fuori città	*out of town*	magari	*perhaps*
è vietato	*it's forbidden*	circolare	*to circulate*

12.08

2 Listen to the conversation without looking at the text. Then listen again and read the text.

Cristian has just received his tredicesima (*thirteenth*—a year-end bonus equivalent to one month's salary) and is pondering how to spend the money. He would like to purchase some new prodotti tecnologici (*tech products*), but Matteo has a better idea. Listen to the features of some products and how they are introduced.

Cristian Forse potrei comprare un televisore nuovo?
Matteo Non guardi mai la TV.
Cristian Auricolari wireless?
Matteo In sei mesi, ne hai già persi quattro, direi di no.
Cristian Un orologio digitale?
Matteo Quello con cui puoi contare i passi?
Cristian Sì, su cui scarichi anche le applicazioni del cellulare e ricevi tutte le notifiche.
Matteo Non so. Ma perché non compri un motorino invece?
Cristian Un motorino a Venezia? È vietato circolare in centro.
Matteo Lo so, ma lo potresti usare per andare ai cosplay, che sono sempre fuori città. Magari una Vespa! Ne ho vista una di seconda mano nel negozio accanto a cui lavoro. Andiamo?

3 Decide if the following statements are vero (*true*) or falso (*false*), based on the conversation.

a	Cristian guarda spesso la televisione.	vero	falso
b	Secondo Matteo un orologio digitale non è una buona idea.	vero	falso
c	Con un motorino Cristian potrebbe andare a lavoro in centro.	vero	falso
d	Con un motorino Cristian potrebbe andare ai cosplay che sono fuori città.	vero	falso
e	La Vespa di cui parla Matteo è nuova.	vero	falso

LANGUAGE BUILDER 3

Language discovery 3

Read the conversation again. Then look at the following sentences that form the conversation. What is the meaning of the underlined expressions? How is the word cui different from che?

a Quello <u>con cui</u> puoi contare i passi?

b Nel negozio accanto <u>a cui</u> lavoro.

c <u>Su cui</u> scarichi le applicazioni

d I cosplay, <u>che</u> sono sempre fuori città.

The relative pronoun cui

The Italian pronouns che and cui are frequently interchanged in English translations, yet they have distinct uses and meanings. Similar to che, cui translates to *which* or *whom* but it is always preceded by a preposition. The preposition changes based on the verb in the relative clause.

Quello con cui puoi contare i passi? (= Puoi contare i passi con un orologio digitale.)	*The one you can count your steps <u>with</u>? > You can count the steps with a smart watch.*
Su cui scarichi le applicazioni. (= Scarichi le applicazioni su un dispositivo.)	*<u>On which</u> you download the apps. > You download the apps <u>on</u> a device.*

Note that at times, the relative pronoun is omitted in English; however, it is always necessary in Italian.

Paolo è l'amico di cui ti parlo sempre.	*Paolo is the friend I am always talking about.*

Language practice 3

1 Decide which relative construction with cui is more appropriate in the following sentences.

- **a** Siete arrivati nel momento **in cui/a cui** di solito preparo la cena.
- **b** Questa è la marca della cassa bluetooth **per cui/di cui** ti ho parlato ieri.
- **c** L'appartamento **su cui/in cui** vivono Serena e Ahmed è in centro.
- **d** La ragazza **a cui/in cui** abbiamo regalato il contapassi si chiama Hongfen.
- **e** Non posso dire il motivo **di cui/per cui** Claire non viene alla festa.

2 Now decide whether che or cui is needed.

- **a** Ho comprato dei nuovi auricolari **di cui/che** sono wireless.
- **b** Il negozio di tecnologia **in cui/che** ho comprato questo televisore è chiuso.
- **c** La stampante **su cui/che** hai visto non è molto moderna.
- **d** Filippo è la persona **con cui/che** faccio sempre shopping.
- **e** Il tiramisú è il dolce **per cui/che** preferisco.

LANGUAGE BUILDER 4

Language discovery 4

12.09

Listen to the conversation again and repeat each line in the pauses provided. Then read the conversation and find the past tenses preceded by ne.

a ....

b ....

What do they have in common? Can you see a pattern?

Using the passato prossimo with ne

Remember that the pronoun ne is used in association with a quantity, meaning "of it" or "of them." When ne is used with the passato prossimo, the past participle agrees in gender and number with the noun replaced by ne when this noun is a direct object.

Gli auricolari > ne hai già persi quattro.	*The earphones* (masc. pl.) > *you have already lost four of them.*
La Vespa > ne ho vista una.	*The Vespa* (fem. sing.) > *I have seen one of it.*

Remember: the past participle does not agree with the noun ne stands for when it isn't a direct object.

Avete parlato delle vacanze? – No, non ne abbiamo parlato.	*Have you talked about holidays? —No, we haven't talked about it.*

Language practice 4

1 Find the mistakes in the sentences and correct them. Not all sentences have mistakes.

- **a** Quanti auricolari hai perso? – Questo mese ne ho perso già sei.
- **b** Quante stampanti avete messo in ufficio? – Ne abbiamo messe due.
- **c** I tuoi zii hanno comprato una nuova lampada per il soggiorno? – Sì, ne hanno comprate una molto moderna.
- **d** Quanti computer dell'ufficio hanno riparato i tecnici? Sono molto lenti. – Oggi ne hanno riparato solo cinque.
- **e** Hai comprato un nuovo televisore? – Sì, ne ho comprati uno di seconda mano.
- **f** Cosa è successo al tuo motorino nuovo? – È dal meccanico. Ne ho ricevuto uno in sostituzione.
- **g** Quanta gente hai visto al Salone del Mobile ? – Ne ho vista molta.

12.10

2 Now play Conversation 2 again, but this time you will play Cristian's role. Speak in the pauses provided and try to come up with some new items. Also, how would you react to Matteo's idea? Try to formulate an answer!

SKILL BUILDER

1 Combine the sentence pairs with a relative pronoun (either che or cui + appropriate preposition). The first one is done for you as an example.

- **a** Il cellulare consuma molta batteria. – Ho comprato il cellulare un mese fa.
  Il cellulare che ho comprato un mese fa consuma molta batteria.
- **b** Il mio amico abita in Colombia. – Ho fatto una videochiamata con il mio amico.
- **c** La poltrona è di design. – Mio nonno si siede sempre sulla poltrona.
- **d** Sei andato all'evento del Salone del Mobile? – L'evento era alle 5pm.
- **e** In città circolo solo con la Vespa. – Ho comprato la Vespa di seconda mano.
- **f** Gli amici sono i miei compagni di cosplay. – Tu mi hai visto con gli amici.
- **g** L'ufficio è in centro. – Felipe e Tatiana lavorano nell'ufficio.

12.11

2 Listen to the following questions and answer using ne with the correct agreement of the past participle.

- **a** Sì, ... due per mia sorella.
- **b** Sì, ... quattro.
- **c** .... almeno venti.
- **d** Sì, ... una molto moderna.
- **e** .... molta.
- **f** Sì, ... una di seconda mano.

3 **Compare the items. Make sentences with the given adjective and the comparativo di maggioranza (+) o minoranza (–).**

a Questa lampada / antico / quella lampada / -
b Questi auricolari / moderno / quegli auricolari / +
c Lamborghini / veloce / Fiat 500 / +

TEST YOURSELF

Match to form sentences.

1 Viaggiare in treno è più rilassante
2 Sonia mi ha detto
3 L'app che ho scaricato
4 È nuova questa borsa?
5 Cuanti libri hai letto questa settimana?
6 Andiamo al mare domani?
7 Dov'è l'ufficio
8 L'architetto
9 Come si chiama
10 Vorrei usare la moka

a che è in ritardo.
b che ha progettato questo edificio è Renzo Piano.
c Ne ho letti due.
d che ti ho prestato ieri.
e non funziona.
f Sì, ma dipende. Che tempo fa?
g la donna con cui stavi parlando?
h che viaggiare in aereo
i in cui lavora Annalisa?
j Che bella, mi piace molto!

La misteriosa donna in soffitta *The mysterious woman in the attic*

Read the message Cristian has just sent to Annalisa, informing her about a recent purchase. Feel free to look up any unfamiliar words in a dictionary. The initial letter of the item described will contribute to forming the name of the enigmatic woman in the attic.

Annalisa, l'ho comprato! È un modello moderno, ma ha anche un tocco vintage, perché il cinturino è di pelle. È fantastico perché può fare molte cose: serve a controllare le notifiche del cellulare in diretta, ma serve anche a contare i passi e, ovviamente, a telefonare.

Remember to use **My review** and **My takeaway** to assess your progress and reflect on your learning experience.

In this unit you will learn how to:

» Answer a phone/video call.
» Write a formal email.
» Use courtesy formulas.
» Say that you are about to do something.

Pronto?

My study plan

I plan to work with Unit 13

○ Every day
○ Twice a week
○ Other ________

I plan to study for

○ 5–15 minutes
○ 15–30 minutes
○ 30–45+ minutes

My progress tracker

Day / Date	Listening	Speaking	Reading	Writing	Conversation
	○	○	○	○	○
	○	○	○	○	○
	○	○	○	○	○
	○	○	○	○	○
	○	○	○	○	○
	○	○	○	○	○
	○	○	○	○	○

My goals

What do you want to be able to do or say in Italian when you complete this unit?

		Done
1	....	○
2	....	○
3	....	○

My review

SELF CHECK

	I can ...
●	... make a phone or video call.
●	... write a formal or informal email.
●	... use courtesy formulas.
●	... say that I am about to do something.

CULTURE POINT 1

Smart working in Italia *Working from home in Italy*

The practice of smart working (***remote work***) in Italy, which peaked during the Covid 19 pandemic and remains popular in many places, quickly reversed in Italy. A lucky minority remains eligible for this modalità (*arrangement*), with a mere 14.9 percent of Italian dipendenti (*employees*) enjoying partial work-from-home setups. Certain positions are inherently unsuited for smart working, contributing to this proportion. Although Italians believe smart working allows for more flessibilità (*flexibility*), there seems to be a degree of resistance to embracing novel work models from the datori di lavoro (*employers*). Nevertheless, in an era where attention to benessere (*wellbeing*) is paramount, it's encouraging to observe that a growing number of compagnie (*companies*) are incorporating at least one day per week of smart working. This gradual shift suggests a developing acceptance of modalità di lavoro flessibile (*flexible working practices*) within the country's panorama lavorativo (*employment landscape*).

Answer the questions in Italian.

a How about you? Can you work from home in your profession?

b What are the advantages? What are the disadvantages?

c Do you think there should be a dress code for remote working video calls?

VOCABULARY BUILDER 1

13.01

Look at the words and phrases and complete the missing English words and expressions. Then listen and try to imitate the pronunciation of the speakers.

PRONTO?	*HELLO?*
la chiamata	*call*
la connessione	....
connesso/a	....
il documento	*file*
il microfono	....
il nome utente	*username*
la riunione	*meeting*
lo schermo	*screen*
la telecamera	....
la videochiamata	....
VERBI UTILI	***USEFUL VERBS***
attaccare	*to hang up*
attivare/disattivare il microfono	*to unmute/to mute oneself*
condividere	*to share*
connettersi	....
disconnettersi	....
lavoro da casa/lo smart working	....
riuscire	*to manage*
vedersi	*to see each other/to meet*
FRASI UTILI	***USEFUL EXPRESSIONS***
Mi vedi?/Mi senti?	*Can you see me?/Can you hear me?*
Non ti vedo!/Non ti sento!	....
Ti vedo bene!/Ti sento bene!	....

Vocabulary practice 1

Annalisa has just joined a work video call and her colleague Daniele has some issues and asks her in a chat to help him. Complete the dialogue with the correct words.

Daniele Non riesco a **a** connettermi / condividere, ho problemi di **b** connessione / nome utente e la **c** telecamera / videochiamata comincia tra poco.

Annalisa Oh no, come ti posso aiutare?

Daniele Guarda, adesso sono **d** connesso / schermo. Mi senti?

Annalisa No, **e** mi vedi / ti vedo, però non **f** ti sento / mi senti?

Daniele Che strano, non capisco. Sembra tutto regolare.

Annalisa Daniele devi **g** condividere / attivare il microfono!

Daniele Oddio, hai ragione! ☺☺☺

CONVERSATION 1

Una videochiamata da incubo *A nightmarish video call*

13.02

1 Here are a few words and expressions to help you understand the conversation.

Lasciamo perdere.	*Let's forget it.*	Imbarazzante!	*Embarrassing!*
Possiamo dire addio.	*We can say goodbye.*	incubo	*nightmare*
comportarsi	*to behave*	lamentarsi	*to complain*
impazzire	*to get crazy*		

13.03

2 Listen to the conversation without looking at the text. Then listen again and read the text.

Today, Annalisa is working from home. After enduring a nightmarish video call with her boss, she decides to give Aicha a call to unwind and share what happened. Listen to the dialogue and pay attention to how they use the past tense in contrast to what is about to occur.

Aicha Pronto? Annalisa? Non sei in ufficio?

Annalisa No, oggi lavoro da casa e sto per impazzire. Ho appena finito una riunione in videochiamata con la mia capa. Un incubo.

Aicha Perché? Come si è comportata?

Annalisa Lasciamo perdere. Era una riunione importante e la sua connessione era terribile. Poi, non riusciva a condividere lo schermo con i documenti del progetto.

Aicha Oh no!

Annalisa Ha ricevuto una telefonata e si è dimenticata di disattivare il microfono: imbarazzante! Secondo me, gli investitori stavano per attaccare, possiamo dire addio al progetto.

Aicha E tu non ti sei lamentata?

Annalisa Con lei? Sei matta! Senti, sto per cominciare un'altra videochiamata, a dopo!

3 Answer the questions in Italian.

a Where is Annalisa?
b What are the three issues Annalisa's boss is facing?
c Did Annalisa complain to her boss?

LANGUAGE BUILDER 1

Language discovery 1

Look at the conversation and find the sentences with the past tense of the verbs comportarsi, dimenticarsi, and lamentarsi. What do they have in common?

Passato prossimo of reflexive verbs

To form the passato prossimo of reflexive verbs, start with the reflexive pronouns (mi, ti, si, ci, vi, si) followed by essere and the past participle, which can be regular (ending in -ato, -uto or -ito) or irregular.

Come si è comportata?	*How did she behave?*
Si è dimenticata di disattivare il microfono.	*She forgot to unmute herself.*
Per la festa mi sono messo una giacca rosa.	*For the party I wore a pink jacket.*

The past participle must agree with the subject.

Ci siamo dimenticati i biglietti!	*We forgot the tickets!*
Fatma e Alexa si sono alzate alle sei.	*Fatma and Alexa got up at 6 a.m.*

alzarsi (*to get up*)

io	mi sono alzato/a	noi	ci siamo alzati/e
tu	ti sei alzato/a	voi	vi siete alzati/e
lui/lei/Lei	si è alzato/a	loro	si sono alzati/e

Language practice 1

Complete the sentences with the correct past tense form of the verb.

a A che ora (alzarsi – tu) .... questa mattina?

b Ieri sera alla festa (divertirsi – noi) ....

c Oh no, (dimenticarsi – io) .... le chiavi di casa!

d Anya (arrabbiarsi) .... perché il computer non funzionava.

e Durante la vacanza, i miei genitori (lamentarsi) .... molto per il caldo.

f Scusate, (lavarsi – voi) .... le mani prima di venire a tavola?

LANGUAGE BUILDER 2

Language discovery 2

13.04

Listen to the conversation again and repeat each line in the pauses provided. Note three expressions that indicate that something is about to happen. Put the words below in order to rebuild these expressions. Do you notice a pattern?

impazzire stavano sto (x2) attaccare cominciare per (x3)

a .... **b** ....

c ....

Imminent future: stare per + infinitive

To express that something is about to happen, use the verb stare followed by the preposition per and then the infinitive of the action.

Sto per impazzire.	*I am about to go crazy.*
Sto per cominciare un'altra video chiamata.	*I am about to start another video call.*
Stiamo per uscire.	*We are about to go out.*

To say that something ***was about to happen***, use the imperfetto of stare.

Stavano per attaccare.	*They were about to hang up.*
Stavi per dire qualcosa?	*Were you about to say something?*

Language practice 2

1 Match the sentence halves.

1 Devo connettermi perché...
2 Quando ieri ho visto Tom e Louis, loro...
3 Prendi l'ombrello, perché...
4 No, non ti possiamo aiutare, perché
5 Se vuoi parlare con Lea, chiamala, perché...
6 Ieri in stazione abbiamo corso, perché...

a ...il treno stava per partire.
b ...sta per prendere l'aereo.
c ...stavano per entrare in un negozio.
d ...sta per piovere.
e ...la videochiamata sta per iniziare.
f ...stiamo per uscire.

13.05

2 Now play Conversation 1 again, but this time play Annalisa's role. Speak in the pauses provided and try to describe a nightmarish video call of your own.

CULTURE POINT 2

Una questione di titoli *A matter of titles*

Italian has a clear distinction between formal spoken and written language. Writing formal letters or emails is not unlike doing it in English, with more options for i saluti (*greetings*) and addresses and a wide range of formulas. Notably, using titoli (*titles*) is quite significant: in Italy, titles are numerous and varied. Graduates of professional schools are addressed by their occupation, i.e., Avvocato/Avvocata (*contracted* Avv.) or Ingegnere/Ingegnera (*contracted* Ing.). Post-elementary school teachers are called Professore (*contracted* Prof.) or Professoressa (*contracted* Prof.ssa) and even some secondary schools grant titles, like Ragioniere/Ragioniera (*accountant*) for individuals with a diploma in accounting. Any degree holders, from bachelor to doctorate, are titled Dottore (*contracted* Dott.) or Dottoressa (*contracted* Dott.ssa) and so are doctors, of course! For those without degrees, Signore (*contracted* Sig.) or Signora (*contracted* Sig.a) are suitable. Unlike in English, nobody would ever start a formal email with Caro/a (*dear*) followed by the first name, as this is reserved for friends and family.

Have a look at the most famous Italian encyclopaedia: *La Treccani*. Here you can find a list of all the titles you can use in Italy.

- Do you have equivalents in your own language?
- How many would you use in your correspondence today?

VOCABULARY BUILDER 2

13.06

Look at the words and phrases and complete the missing English words and expressions. Then listen and try to imitate the pronunciation of the speakers.

UNA LETTERA FORMALE	*A FORMAL LETTER*
distinti/cordiali saluti	*best/kind regards*
egregio/a	*dear*
gentile	*dear*
in attesa di una sua risposta	*waiting for your answer*
la ringrazio	*Thank you*
le scrivo	*I am writing to you*

per la sua disponibilità	*for your kindness*
vorrei chiederle	*I would like to ask you*
UNA LETTERA INFORMALE	***AN INFORMAL LETTER***
caro/a	*dear*
ciao/a presto	....
fammi sapere	*let me know*
per la tua disponibilità	....
ti ringrazio	....
ti scrivo	....
vorrei chiederti	....
UNA LETTERA/EMAIL	***A LETTER/EMAIL***
l'allegato	*attachment*
destinatario/a	*recipient*
fare domanda	*to apply*
la firma	*signature*
in anticipo	*in advance*
la lettera di referenza	....
mandare	*to send*
il mittente	*sender*
l'oggetto	*letter/email subject*
per qualsiasi domanda	*if you have any questions*
presso	*by*
via	....

Vocabulary practice 2

Complete the table using expressions from the vocabulary builder.

	Informal	Formal
How to address the recipient		
How to introduce the reason for contact		Le scrivo per
How to start a question		
How to say you are waiting for an answer	Fammi sapere!	
How to thank the recipient		
Final greetings		

CONVERSATION 2

Una richiesta *A request*

While Cristian thoroughly enjoys teaching, he is actively seeking a new opportunity where he can fully express his passion for art. During his web search, he stumbled upon an intriguing position as a consulente (*consultant*) at a renowned art gallery. Now he only needs a letter of recommendation from the headmaster at the school where he currently teaches. Read the email below. Notice the expressions he uses and take note of pronoun placement and the accompanying verbs.

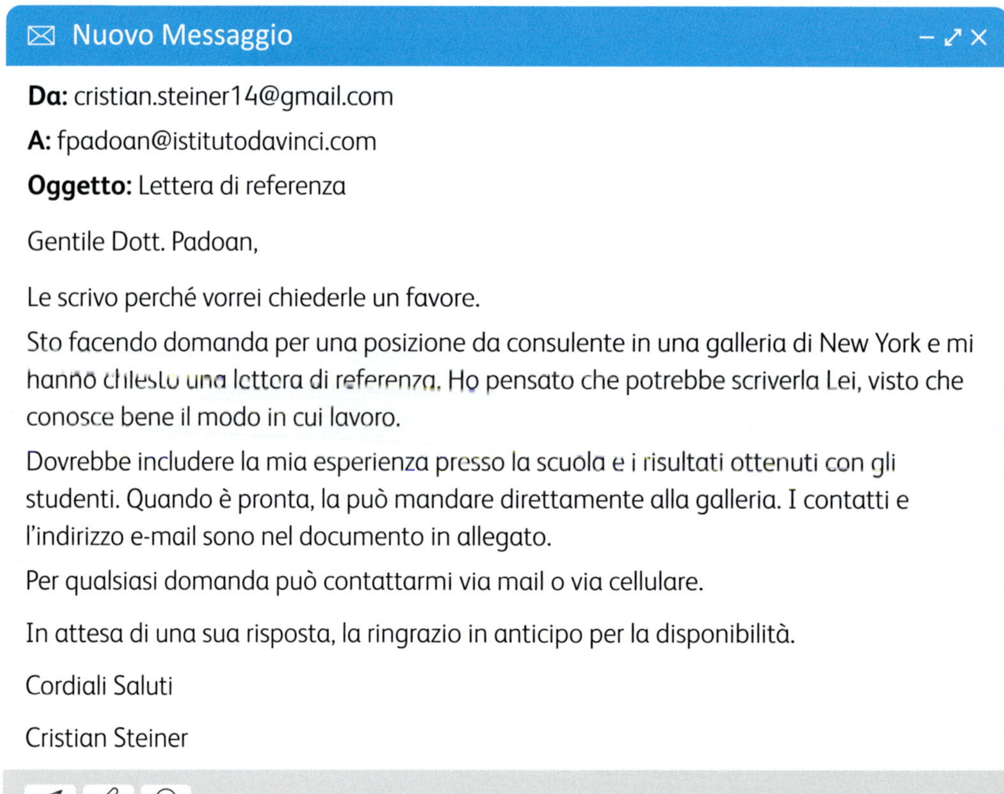

Nuovo Messaggio

Da: cristian.steiner14@gmail.com

A: fpadoan@istitutodavinci.com

Oggetto: Lettera di referenza

Gentile Dott. Padoan,

Le scrivo perché vorrei chiederle un favore.

Sto facendo domanda per una posizione da consulente in una galleria di New York e mi hanno chiesto una lettera di referenza. Ho pensato che potrebbe scriverla Lei, visto che conosce bene il modo in cui lavoro.

Dovrebbe includere la mia esperienza presso la scuola e i risultati ottenuti con gli studenti. Quando è pronta, la può mandare direttamente alla galleria. I contatti e l'indirizzo e-mail sono nel documento in allegato.

Per qualsiasi domanda può contattarmi via mail o via cellulare.

In attesa di una sua risposta, la ringrazio in anticipo per la disponibilità.

Cordiali Saluti

Cristian Steiner

Which of the statements accurately reflect the contents of the email?

a Cristian scrive al Dott. Padoan una mail formale.
b La galleria dove Cristian vorrebbe lavorare è in Inghilterra.
c Cristian scrive al Dott. Padoan perché sono molto amici.
d Cristian chiede al Dott. Padoan di scrivere una referenza per lui.
e Il Dott. Padoan deve mandare la lettera a Cristian.

LANGUAGE BUILDER 3

Language discovery 3

Look at the phrases below and choose the correct form without looking at the email.

a Vorrei le chiedere / Vorrei chiederle un favore.
b Mi hanno chiesto / Hanno chiestomi una lettera.
c Potrebbe la scrivere / Potrebbe scriverla.
d La può mandare / Può la mandare.

What do you notice about the position of the pronouns? Is there any connection with the verb?

Position of pronouns with modal verbs

Pronouns are typically positioned before the verb. Nonetheless, when dealing with modal verbs (dovere, potere, volere), pronouns can either go before the modal verb or be attached to the end of the infinitive (after removing the final -e).

La può mandare. = Può mandarla. *You can send it.*

Mi può contattare. = Può contattarmi. *You can contact me.*

This rule applies to modal verbs across all moods and tenses.

La potrebbe scrivere? = Potrebbe scriverla? *Could you write it?*

When an infinitive appears without a modal verb, pronouns are always attached to the end of the infinitive (after removing the final -e).

Scrivo per chiederle un favore. *I am writing to ask you for a favor.*

Language practice 3

13.07 **Dott. Padoan calls Cristian to make sure he understood what he needs to do. Rewrite some sentences of the conversation by moving the pronoun before or after the verb, like in the example in the first sentence. Then listen to the conversation and check your answers.**

Dott. Padoan Salve dott. Steiner Vorrei farle una domanda. > Le vorrei fare una domanda.

Cristian Certo. Mi può dare un secondo (**a** ....)? Sto uscendo di casa adesso.

Dott. Padoan Naturalmente, ma non voglio rubarle (**b** ....) tempo, vorrei solo delle informazioni. La lettera di presentazione che mi ha chiesto, la devo scrivere (**c** ....) su carta o in formato elettronico?

Cristian	Può scriverla (**d** ....) in formato elettronico e poi può mandarla (**e** ....) via mail.
Dott. Padoan	Benissimo. Il suo tutor diretto è la Dottoressa Manzoni, le posso chiedere (**f** ....) un commento da inserire nella lettera?
Cristian	Naturalmente.

LANGUAGE BUILDER 4

Language discovery 4

Based on what you saw in the email, insert the correct pronouns in the gaps. All the pronouns refer to Dott. Padoan in formal address. Why is an indirect object pronoun used in some instances while a direct object pronoun is used in others?

a .... **scrivo** **b** Vorrei .... chieder

c .... **ringrazio**

Verbs with direct and indirect object pronouns

As you know, Italian uses both direct object pronouns and indirect object pronouns to refer back to an object. Direct object pronouns are used with verbs that answer the question cosa? (*what?*) or chi? (*who?*), while indirect object pronouns are used with verbs that answer a chi? (*to whom?*) or per chi? (*for whom?*), and typically replace people.

Le scrivo. (a chi? > Al Dott. Padoan) — *I am writing to you. (formal)*

Potrebbe scriverla. (cosa? > la lettera) — *You could write it.*

Some verbs in Italian may take indirect objects even if they take direct objects in English, and vice versa. For instance, the Italian verb chiedere takes an indirect object (chiedere a qualcuno) whereas the English equivalent takes a direct object (*to ask someone*). To determine which pronoun to use, consult a dictionary for the specific verb.

Language practice 4

1 Answer the following questions by using a direct or indirect object pronoun.

a	A che ora prendi il treno?	.... prendo alle 7:25.
b	Conosci quelle ragazze?	No, ... non conosco.
c	Hai scritto al professore?	Sì, ... ho scritto ieri.
d	Prepari tu il risotto?	Sì, ... preparo adesso!
e	Guardate la TV tutte le sere?	No, ... guardiamo solo il venerdì.
f	Cosa hai regalato ai tuoi genitori?	.... ho regalato un libro.
g	Compri i broccoli, quando vai al supermercato?	Sì, ... compro stasera.

13.07

2 Now listen to the questions and answer freely using the correct pronoun.

a ....

b ....

c ....

d ....

e ....

f ....

g ....

SKILL BUILDER

13.09

1 Listen to Annalisa recounting her day and note what she did using the correct form of the past tense.

a ....

b ....

c ....

d ....

e ....

f ....

2 Now transform the sentences from 1 to the first person plural (noi). Use both the masculine and the feminine.

a ....

b ....

c ....

d ....

e ....

f ....

3 You are Dott. Padoan and you want to inform Cristian you have sent the reference letter he asked for. Write an email using the correct formulas and style.

✉ Nuovo Messaggio

Da: fpadoan@istitutodavinci.com

A: cristian.steiner14@gmail.com

Oggetto: Lettera di referenza

....

....

....

....

....

4 Read this paragraph about the rules for a perfect formal written communication and check (✓) the information you can infer from the text.

Nella comunicazione formale è importante seguire alcune regole. Per cominciare, dobbiamo usare il titolo corretto per la persona a cui stiamo scrivendo. Se la persona è laureata, usiamo 'Dottore' o 'Dottoressa', altrimenti 'gentile' è sufficiente. Se scriviamo a una compagnia, dobbiamo usare la forma plurale, 'voi' e il titolo 'Spettabile'. Se scriviamo a un individuo, possiamo usare il 'Lei'. È importante ricordare che tutti i pronomi e i verbi devono essere nella stessa forma (lei o voi), così come i possessivi (suo, vostro).

Se abbiamo una richiesta, meglio usare il modo condizionale e non l'imperativo. Infine, è importante ricordarsi di ringraziare il nostro destinatario per la sua disponibilità e il suo tempo.

a Scrivere la data in lettere e non in numeri. ☐
b Usare il titolo appropriato per il destinatario. ☐
c Chiedere se il destinatario sta bene. ☐
d Chiedere se è possibile usare la forma "tu". ☐
e Usare la forma "voi" per le compagnie. ☐
f Usare sempre la forma appropriata, con pronomi, possessivi e verbi. ☐
g Usare il modo condizionale per le richieste. ☐
h Non scrivere una lettera lunga. ☐
i Ringraziare per la disponibilità e il tempo del destinario. ☐
j Usare solo il cognome nella firma. ☐

TEST YOURSELF

1 Unscramble the sentences.

a anticipo La cominciata in è riunione
b chiederle Le perché scrivo un vorrei favore
c disattivare il microfono Puoi
d fare perché videochiamata casa da Preferisco una lavoro
e La per la anticipo in ringrazio anticipo

2 Change the sentences from the present to the past.

a Eva si sveglia.
b Paolo e Mariam si connettono.
c Io mi comporto.
d Noi ci facciamo la doccia.
e Jonas si veste.
f Voi vi lamentate.

3 Look at the activities in parentheses. Create questions about doing them using the verb potere, like in the example.

Example: (mangiare la pasta – io) *Posso mangiarla? / La posso mangiare?*

a (provare le scarpe – lei)
b (parlare al direttore – noi)
c (pagare il conto – tu)
d (chiamare Valentina – voi)
e (scrivere a Vikram – lui)
f (usare il coltello – tu)

La misteriosa donna in soffitta *The mysterious woman in the attic*

Do you remember how to say "mail" in Italian? If not, consult a dictionary. The first letter of this word will continue to form the name of the woman depicted in Cristian and Annalisa's painting.

Remember to use **My review** and **My takeaway** to assess your progress and reflect on your learning experience.

14

In this unit you will learn how to:

- Identify body parts.
- Identify symptoms and discuss physical and mental health.
- Give suggestions and commands using the formal imperative.

Mens sana in corpore sano

My study plan

I plan to work with Unit 14

- ○ Every day
- ○ Twice a week
- ○ Other ________

I plan to study for

- ○ 5–15 minutes
- ○ 15–30 minutes
- ○ 30–45+ minutes

My progress tracker

Day / Date	Listening	Speaking	Reading	Writing	Conversation
	○	○	○	○	○
	○	○	○	○	○
	○	○	○	○	○
	○	○	○	○	○
	○	○	○	○	○
	○	○	○	○	○
	○	○	○	○	○

My goals

What do you want to be able to do or say in Italian when you complete this unit?

		Done
1	....	○
2	....	○
3	....	○

My review

SELF CHECK

	I can ...
●	... talk about illnesses and health issues.
●	... recognize body parts in Italian.
●	... give orders, suggestions, and instructions while addressing people formally and informally.
●	... discuss what is good or bad for me.

CULTURE POINT 1

La salute è importante *Health is important*

Italy can boast a very comprehensive and generous sistema sanitario nazionale (*national healthcare system*). Il medico di base (*general practitioner*), l'ospedale (*hospital*) e il Pronto Soccorso (*Emergency Room*) are gratis (*free*) for all. For medicine (*medicines*), visite specialistiche (*consultations with a specialist*), or esami (*tests*), people above a certain income must pay a contribution. In general, Italians are very health conscious and well informed about la salute mentale e fisica (*mental and physical health*) and benessere (*wellbeing*). One of the aspects of la vita sana (*a healthy life*) is adherence to la dieta mediterranea (*the Mediterranean diet*), a way of eating focusing on plants, fish, and healthy fats, which has been part of UNESCO's Intangible Heritage since 2013.

The Mediterranean diet

Take a look at the UNESCO description of the Mediterranean diet.

a Look at the pictures in the link. Can you identify some of the food items in Italian?

b What represents la vita sana for you? Think of a few elements that constitute la salute fisica e mentale.

VOCABULARY BUILDER 1

14.01

Look at the words and phrases and complete the missing English words and expressions. Then listen and try to imitate the pronunciation of the speakers.

LE PARTI DEL CORPO	*BODY PARTS*
la testa	*head*
il braccio (plurale: le braccia)	*arm*
la mano	*hand*
il torso	....
la gamba	*leg*
il ginocchio (plurale: le ginocchia)	*knee*
la pancia	*belly*
il piede	*foot*
lo stomaco	*stomach*
il collo	*neck*
le orecchie	*ears*
il naso	*nose*
le dita	*fingers and toes*
le spalle	*shoulders*
la bocca	*mouth*
i denti	*teeth*
gli occhi	*eyes*

Some words indicating body parts have an irregular plural: il braccio, le braccia. The gender changes into feminine in the plural, and the word ends in -a. These are words that retain the Latin neuter plural in -a. Another example: l'osso, le ossa (*bone*). Le orecchie is plural feminine but the singular is masculine: l'orecchio.

LA SALUTE E LA MALATTIA	*HEALTH AND ILLNESS*
dal dottore	*at the* ....
all'ospedale/al Pronto Soccorso	*at the* .... / ....
ho male a/ho mal di....	*I feel pain in ....*
essere stanco/a	*to be tired*
sotto stress	*under stress*
avere il raffreddore	*to have a cold*
avere l'influenza	*to have the flu*
avere la tosse	*to have a cough*
avere la febbre	*to have a fever*
soffrire di	*to suffer from*
l'allergia	....
essere allergico a	*to be allergic to*
prescrivere	*to prescribe*
una ricetta	*a prescription*
la medicina	....
in farmacia	*at the* ....

Vocabulary practice 1

Complete the sentences.

a Quando mangio troppo io ....

b Quando cammino molto io ....

c Quando ho l'influenza io ....

d ....: 38 Celsius!

e In primavera io ....

f Non vado al cinema perché io ....

CONVERSATION 1

Dal dottore *At the doctor's*

14.02

1 Listen to the conversation without looking at the text. Then listen again and read the text. Pay attention to the suggestions the doctor gives Annalisa. What is good and what is bad for her? Are they addressing each other formally or informally?

Annalisa is not feeling well. She's working hard on the MOSE project, eating and sleeping little e soffre di mal di testa. Dovrebbe andare dal dottore! As she is usually healthy, she has only met her medico di base (*GP*), but he reassures her that all she needs is una vacanza, il sonno regolare (*regular sleep*) and cibo nutriente.

Dottore Dorme bene?

Annalisa No, dormo tre-quattro ore per notte. Sono sempre stanca.

Dottore Mmmm, dorma almeno otto ore per notte. E non guardi la televisione o il computer prima di dormire, le fa male.

Annalisa Ma mi rilassa...

Dottore Faccia una passeggiata. Un po' di attività fisica le fa bene. Mangi una cena leggera ma nutriente e beva poco caffè durante il giorno. Il caffè e le bevande con caffeina fanno male quando uno è sotto stress.

Annalisa E il mal di testa?

Dottore Le prescrivo questa medicina. La prenda una volta al giorno. E vada un po' in vacanza... troppo lavoro non fa bene alla Sua salute.

2 Based on the conversation, which things are bene and which are male for la salute?

BENE: ....

MALE: ....

LANGUAGE BUILDER 1

Language discovery 1

Look at the sentences from the conversation. What do fa bene and fa male agree with?

Guardare la televisione prima di dormire fa male.

Il caffè e le bevande con caffeina fanno male.

Troppo lavoro non fa bene alla salute.

Ti fa bene *(it's good for you)*

To talk about things that are beneficial or detrimental, the verb fare is used, paired with bene or male. Fare agrees with the thing that is good or bad, and the person affected is usually expressed with an indirect object pronoun. This is similar to piace/piacciono and ci vuole/vogliono, which appeared in Unit 3.

Il caffé ti fa male.	*Coffee is bad for you.*
Dormire le fa bene.	*Sleep is good for her.*

The person or element affected can also be introduced by the preposition a:

Dormire fa bene a Annalisa.	*Sleep is good for Annalisa.*
Il fumo e l'alcool fanno male alla salute.	*Smoke and alcohol are bad for your health.*

To keep the preposition to emphasize the person use a special form of the indirect object pronouns used when they follow a preposition: a me, a te, a lui/lei/Lei, a noi, a voi, a loro. Note that, except for me and te, they are the same as the subject pronouns.

Dormire fa bene a Annalisa.	= Dormire le fa bene.	= Dormire fa bene a lei.
Fare sport fa bene a Matteo.	= Fare sport gli fa bene.	= Fare sport fa bene a lui.

Language practice 1

Complete the following sentences with either fa or fanno.

Example: Fumare fa/fanno male alla salute. *Fumare fa male alla salute.*

a Bere molta acqua fa/fanno bene alla salute.
b Troppo caffè fa/fanno male alla salute.
c Il pesce fa/fanno male alla salute.
d Le bevande alcooliche fa/fanno male alla salute.

LANGUAGE BUILDER 2

Language discovery 2

14.03

Listen to the conversation again and repeat each line in the pauses provided. Try to imitate the phrasing and intonation you hear. Annalisa and the doctor address each other formally. Look at these phrases, spoken by the doctor. Is he stating a fact or commanding/suggesting something? What tense have you learned before that is used to command/prescribe/firmly suggest?

(Lei) dorma almeno otto ore per notte

(Lei) non guardi la televisione prima di dormire

(Lei) la prenda una volta al giorno

(Lei) faccia una passeggiata

(Lei) vada un po' in vacanza.

The formal imperative

Unit 8 looked at the informal imperative. To prescribe/command/suggest something in a formal manner, use the formal imperative. Let's see how it's formed: take the io form of the verb in the present tense, remove -o, and replace it with -i for -are verbs, and -a for -ere and -ire verbs.

	Presente (io)	Imperativo formale (lei)
guardare	guardo	guardi!
prendere	prendo	prenda!
dormire	dormo	dorma!

Notice that the same form is used in the affirmative and negative:

Mangi una cena leggera! *Eat a light dinner!*

Non guardi la television prima di dormiré! *Don't watch television before sleep!*

Verbs that are irregular in the present tense always replace -o with -a.

faccio = faccia! vado= vada! vengo = venga! bevo = beva! esco = esca!

Faccia una passeggiata! Vada in vacanza!

There are some verbs that are super irregular, and they all end in -ia.

sono = sia! ho = abbia! sto = stia! do = dia!

Abbia pazienza! *Be patient!*

See the Grammar Summary for a full list of irregular verbs: the ones that are irregular in the present are also irregular in the formal imperative.

Language practice 2

1 You have been giving advice to your friends and family but now you need to advise people you don't know very well. Transform the sentences from the informal imperative to the formal imperative.

Example: Parla lentamente! *Parli lentamente!*

a Bevi un litro d'acqua al giorno!
b Non guardare quella serie TV!
c Fa' una colazione nutriente!
d Va' dal dottore!
e Prendi l'autobus!
f Telefona al Pronto Soccorso!
g Sta' a casa!
h Non fumare!
i Scrivi questo numero!
j Non comprare la cioccolata!

14.04

2 Now play Conversation 1 again, but this time you will play the doctor's role. Speak in the pauses provided. Suggest a few things Annalisa should do to feel better. Try not to refer to the text.

CULTURE POINT 2

Vacanze benessere *Wellbeing vacations*

Modern life can be very stressante (*stressful*) so sometimes what you need is a vacanza entirely dedicated to your benessere. Italy offers several different possibilities. You can opt to stay in un convento (*convent*). The region of Umbria is famous for i conventi that offer hospitality nestled among the charming hills. The rules are no phones, no alcohol or smoking, and there is usually a curfew. But you can enjoy la tranquillità nella natura (*tranquillity in nature*) and accommodation in medieval buildings, as well as take corsi di meditazione o di yoga (*meditation or yoga classes*). Or you can go to the Dolomites, which are majestic mountains towering over green valli (*valleys*). This area specializes in centri benessere: hotels and B&Bs that offer sauna, spa, and special treatments with alpine herbs. And, of course, fare una passeggiata in this amazing landscape, breathing the clean air scented with the alpine flowers fa bene alla mente (*mind*) e al corpo!

Ti piacerebbe una vacanza in un convento? Immagina la routine di un turista in convento. A che ora si alza? A che ora si addormenta? Cosa fa durante il giorno?

VOCABULARY BUILDER 2

14.05

Look at the words and phrases and complete the missing English words and expressions. Then listen and try to imitate the pronunciation of the speakers.

IL BENESSERE	*WELLBEING*
lo stress	*stress*
stressante/stressato/a	.... /*stressed*
la calma	*calm* (n.)
calmo/a	*calm* (adj.)
riposarsi	*to rest*
rilassarsi	*to relax*
rilassante/rilassato/a	*relaxing/relaxed*
il relax	....
la mente	....
la salute mentale	....
sentirsi bene/male	*to feel well/unwell*
prendersi cura di	*to take care of*
guarire	*to heal*
andare dallo psicologo	....
essere in forma	*to be in good shape/fit/healthy*
tranquillo/a	*quiet*
camminare	*to walk*
meditare	....
fare yoga/ginnastica	*to do yoga/ fitness exercises*
in palestra	*at the gym*
respirare	*to breathe*

Vocabulary practice 2

Complete the following short text with words and phrases from this list.

yoga	calma	tranquillo	rilassarvi	camminare
si prendono cura	respirare	palestra	stress	

"La stella alpina": Relax e bellezza

Il B&B "La Stella Alpina" si trova nelle Dolomiti. Qui gli ospiti possono e trovare un'oasi di "**a** ...." lontana dallo "**b** ...." della vita moderna. Petra e Clara vi aspettano in un ambiente confortevole e "**c** ...." immerso nella meravigliosa natura alpina. Qui potete **d** .... nei boschi, "**e** ...." l'aria pura delle montagne e "**f** ...." nella spa del B&B, che include anche una moderna "**g** ...." e dà la possibilità di fare corsi di "**h** ....". Petra e Clara "**i** ...." della vostra salute fisica e mentale!

CONVERSATION 2

Un fine settimana in montagna *A weekend in the mountains*

14.06

1 Listen to the conversation a few times without looking at the text. Then listen to the conversation again and read the text. Pay attention to how Cristian rates the various options Annalisa and Aicha are considering.

After seeing the doctor, Annalisa has decided to take a break from work and go on a vacanza benessere. She and Aicha will go together, so they are browsing possible destinations on Annalisa's computer. Annalisa is interested in trying a convent in Umbria, but Aicha is adamant that she cannot survive a weekend without her phone... and there is no vacanza without foto da postare! So they compromise on a centro benessere in the Dolomiti. Cristian catches them as they are about to prenotare un fine settimana in montagna a Cortina d'Ampezzo, a very popular tourist destination, at the hotel Belvedere. He is from that area, so he can give good advice, and in fact, he has a better idea...

Cristian	Non andate all'hotel Belvedere! Costa un sacco ma la qualità è peggiore che in posti meno cari!
Annalisa	Ah! Hai un'idea migliore?
Cristian	Mia sorella minore e la sua compagna hanno aperto un B&B vicino a Dobbiaco. È in uno chalet di legno, ma ha una spa moderna e una palestra, con corsi di yoga, meditazione e ginnastica.
Aicha	Mi ispira!
Cristian	È in una valle tranquilla, dove potete camminare, respirare l'aria buona e riposarvi. Petra e Clara sono due guru del benessere!
Annalisa	Prenotiamolo!
Cristian	Telefonatele e ditele che siete mie amiche. Vi potrebbe offrire un prezzo inferiore...
Aicha	Costa molto?
Cristian	Costa meno del Belvedere e il servizio è decisamente superiore!

2 Which of these three summaries describes the gist of the conversation?

a Aicha and Annalisa vogliono andare in montagna ma Cristian dice che gli hotel sono troppo cari.

b Aicha ed Annalisa vogliono andare al B&B della sorella di Cristian, ma la qualità non è buona e il prezzo è alto.

c Aicha ed Annalisa vogliono andare all'hotel Belvedere ma Cristian dice che il B&B di sua sorella è un'opzione migliore.

LANGUAGE BUILDER 3

Language discovery 3

Look at the conversation and find the corresponding Italian phrases for these English phrases. What do you notice about the ending of the words corresponding to those underlined in English?

a The service is definitely superior.
b The quality is worse than in cheaper places.
c Do you have a better idea?
d She might offer you a lower price.
e My younger sister

Special comparatives

In English, we don't say *more good*: the correct form is *better.* We don't say *more bad* but *worse*. Likewise, in Italian certain adjectives: buono, cattivo/brutto, grande, piccolo, alto, and basso, when used with più have a second, alternative form ending in -iore/i.

buono/a	più buono/a = migliore	*better*
cattivo/a-brutto/a	più cattivo/a- brutto/a = peggiore	*worse*
grande	più grande = maggiore	*bigger/greater/older*
piccolo/a	più piccolo/a = minore	*smaller/younger*
alto	più alto/a = superiore	*higher/taller*
basso	più basso/a = inferiore	*lower*

The special forms tend to be used in reference to concepts or age, whereas the forms with più are more common with reference to physical descriptions.

Marta è mia sorella maggiore. — *Marta is my older sister.*

Questa baita è più grande di quella. — *This cabin is larger than that one.*

Bene and male also have irregular comparatives: meglio and peggio. In this case, più bene/male are not correct.

Annalisa vive meglio a Venezia Naples. — *Annalisa lives better in Venice than in che a Napoli.*

Language practice 3

Complete the sentences with the comparatives in the list.

inferiore	maggiore	superior	migliore	meglio	peggio	peggiore

a Cristian è il fratello "....................." di Petra.

b Dopo una vacanza in montagna, Annalisa si sente "....................." di prima.

c La qualità di un hotel a 5 stelle è "....................." di quella di un hotel a 3 stelle.

d Con i saldi posso comprare questo vestito ad un prezzo ".....................".

e Con lo stress la qualità della vita è ".....................".

f Il cibo è "....................." in questo ristorante che in quello.

g Dormo "....................." se guardo la TV prima di andare a letto.

LANGUAGE BUILDER 4

Language discovery 4

Listen to the conversation again and repeat each line in the pauses provided. Try to imitate the phrasing and intonation you hear. Then look at these sentences. Are the speakers stating facts or suggesting/encouraging? If there are pronouns, where are they placed?

Non andate all'hotel Belvedere!

Prenotiamolo!

Telefonatele...

Ditele che siete mie amiche

Let's do it! Imperative in the **noi** and **voi** forms

The imperative with tu and Lei is used to give someone a suggestion or instructions, informally or formally. But it can also be used to encourage ourselves to do something: *Let's go!* Andiamo! or tell a group of people what to do: Andate! *Go!* The forms of the imperative for noi and voi are the same as for the present tense. The only difference is that pronouns are attached to the end of the verb, just like in the imperative for tu. (Remember, however, that with the formal imperative, Lei, pronouns go before the verb.) Let's see how it works with prendere la medicina, rilassarsi, and non telefonare a lei.

Tu	Noi	Voi	Lei formale
Prendila!	Prendiamola!	Prendetela	La prenda!
Rilassati!	Rilassiamoci!	Rilassatevi!	Si rilassi!
Non telefonarle!	Non telefoniamole!	Non telefonatele!	No le telefoni!

Language practice 4

1 Complete the following sentences with the imperative of the given verb and a pronoun to replace the underlined item, when applicable.

Example: Ragazzi, questo hotel è bellissimo, (prenotate) = *Prenotatelo!*

a <u>L'aria</u> della montagna è pura, (noi – respirare) = ...

b <u>Voi</u> siete stanchi e stressati, (riposarsi) = ...

c <u>Lo yoga</u> fa bene alla salute, (noi – praticare) = ...

d Signora, Lei ha bisogno di <u>una pausa</u>, (fare) = ...

e Mi piace andare <u>in palestra</u>, (noi – andare) domani! = ...

f Bere <u>acqua</u> fa bene alla salute, (tu – bere)! = ...

g Guardare <u>il computer</u> prima di dormire non favorisce il sonno, (noi – non guardare)!= ....

h Se non hai ancora visto <u>quel film</u>, (tu – guardare) = ...

i Signor Steiner, se vuole parlare <u>al direttore</u>, (Lei – telefonare) = ...

14.08

2 Now play Conversation 2 again. You have learned about the B&B Cristian presents. Talk about it to a friend and give advice: "Call the number!" "Book a vacation!" "Relax!"

SKILL BUILDER

1 The following sentences containing the imperative are scrambled. The pronouns have also been separated from the verb. Put the words in the sentences in the correct order, reattaching the pronoun to the verb if necessary. The word that is capitalized is the first in the sentence. Punctuation is included.

a si – Signora, – molto – è- stressata,- rilassi.

b è – Il – yoga- facciamo – corso – lo – di – bellissimo,.

c economico, – hotel – L' – lo – prenotiamo – è

d Dottore, – devo – cosa – mi – fare – dica, - ?

e questa – Compri – medicina – tutti – giorni – la – i – prenda –e.

2 Read the text about Italians and their health and say whether the statements are vero or falso.

Gli italiani, in generale, conoscono molto bene l'anatomia del corpo umano e sono molto attenti alla salute. Per questo, soffrono di malattie che sono misteriose per gli inglesi o gli americani. Una di queste è "il colpo d'aria" (*being hit by the air*). Infatti quando fa freddo gli italiani si mettono vestiti pesanti e sciarpe sul collo perché hanno paura (*they fear*) dell'aria. L'aria causa problemi come "la cervicale": il misterioso male al collo, unicamente italiano! Ma anche il mal di pancia e il mal di stomaco. Pancia e stomaco sono due organi differenti per gli italiani, che sanno distinguere tra i due: in inglese esiste solo il *tummy ache!* I bambini italiani non possono nuotare dopo il pranzo o la cena: questa è una cosa molto pericolosa (*dangerous*) che fa molto male alla salute. Uscire con i capelli bagnati (*wet*) dopo la doccia è un rischio (*risk*) molto grande. Andare al ristorante e sedersi vicino alla porta in inverno è particolarmente rischioso: lo spiffero (*draft*) mentre le persone mangiano in una stanza calda è praticamente letale. Il giornalista conclude che essere un po' ignoranti dell'anatomia e delle malattie è meglio: essere italiani fa male alla salute!

a Gli italiani conoscono le parti del corpo meglio delle persone in altri paesi. vero falso
b Secondo gli italiani, l'aria è pericolosa per la salute. vero falso
c Per gli italiani è una buona idea nuotare dopo cena. vero falso
d Al ristorante gli italiani vogliono sedersi vicino alla porta. vero falso
e La cervicale è una malattia che esiste solo in Italia. vero falso

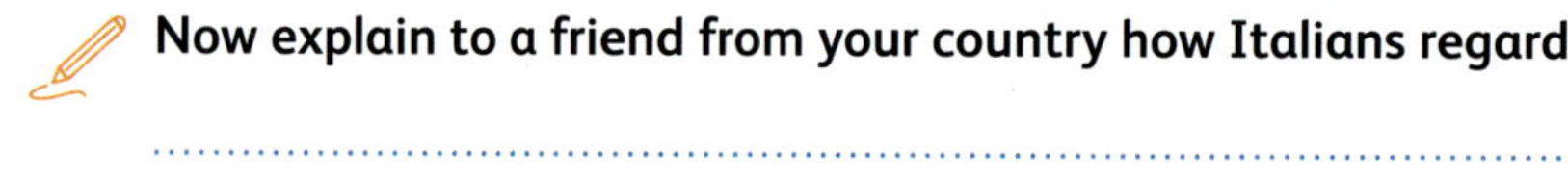

Now explain to a friend from your country how Italians regard health issues.

....

....

....

14.09

3 Listen to the following interaction dal dottore. List the complaints of the patient and the doctor's advice.

Il paziente ha ...	Il medico suggerisce ...

TEST YOURSELF

1 Turn the suggestions from formal to informal.

a Dormi almeno 8 ore per notte =

b Non guardare la televisione o il computer prima di dormire =

c Fa' sport =

d Mangia pesce fresco =

e Bevi poco caffé =

f Prendi questa medicina =

g Va' in palestra =

2 Complete the sentences with the appropriate body part or illness from the list.

i denti	la febbre	testa	la pancia	i piedi

a Quando cammino molto mi fanno male ....

b La mia temperatura è molto alta: ho ....

c Ho mangiato troppo e mi fa male ....

d Se ti fanno male .... va' dal dentista.

e Quando ho il raffreddore, ho spesso anche mal di ....

La misteriosa donna in soffitta *The mysterious woman in the attic*

Knowing the parts of the human body can help you figure out the name of the woman in the painting. This time, look for the central bone of your ginocchia.

The word is the same in Italian and English! The first letter will continue creating the name of the woman.

Remember to use **My review** and **My takeaway** to assess your progress and reflect on your learning experience.

In this unit you will learn how to:

- Talk about customs and habits using the **si impersonale**.
- Identify activities and items needed when traveling.
- Compare objects in a group using the superlative.
- Plan and discuss the outcome of a trip.
- Describe what should have, could have, or would have happened.

Turista o esploratore?

My study plan

I plan to work with Unit 15

- ○ Every day
- ○ Twice a week
- ○ Other ___________

I plan to study for

- ○ 5–15 minutes
- ○ 15–30 minutes
- ○ 30–45+ minutes

My progress tracker

Day / Date	Listening	Speaking	Reading	Writing	Conversation
	○	○	○	○	○
	○	○	○	○	○
	○	○	○	○	○
	○	○	○	○	○
	○	○	○	○	○
	○	○	○	○	○
	○	○	○	○	○

My goals

What do you want to be able to do or say in Italian when you complete this unit?

		Done
1	....	○
2	....	○
3	....	○

My review

SELF CHECK

	I can ...
●	... talk about customs and habits using the si impersonale.
●	... identify activities and items that are needed when traveling.
●	... compare objects in a group using the comparative superlative.
●	... plan and discuss the outcome of a trip.
●	... describe what should have, could have, or would have happened.

CULTURE POINT 1

L'italia a piedi *Italy on foot*

One of the best ways to discover the beauty of the Italian paesaggio and its numerous hidden gems is to viaggiare a piedi (*hike*) through Italy. Venezia, Roma, and Firenze may still be top destinazioni turistiche, but it would be a pity to miss out on the many things you can admire from one città to the next: rolling colline (*hills*), antiche chiese (*old churches*), and castelli (*castles*). From North to South, there are many sentieri (*paths*) which used to be pilgrim routes or old Roman or medieval roads. One of the most famous is the Via Francigena that goes from Canterbury, UK, to Rome, attraversando (*crossing*) Francia, Svizzera e quasi tutta l'Italia (*France, Switzerland, and almost all of Italy*). This type of tourism is becoming more and more popular in Italy, as it is slow and sostenibile (*sustainable*). Put on your scarponi (*boots*), prepare your zaino (*backpack*), and be ready for an adventure in the footsteps of the ancient pilgrims!

Via Francigena

Guarda la mappa della via Francigena.

a Quali regioni italiane attraversa?

b Quali sono le tappe (*stages*) più famose?

VOCABULARY BUILDER 1

Look at the words and phrases and complete the missing English words and expressions. Then listen and try to imitate the pronunciation of the speakers.

PREPARARSI PER UN VIAGGIO	*PREPARING FOR A TRIP*
la valigia	*suitcase*
lo spazzolino da denti	*toothbrush*
il dentifricio	*toothpaste*
il pigiama	....
gli occhiali da sole	....
gli scarponi	....
la biancheria	*underwear*
il sapone	*soap*
la giacca impermeabile	*raincoat/rain jacket*
i trucchi	*make-up*
il pettine	*comb*
il kit di pronto soccorso	*first-aid kit*
la schiuma da barba	*shaving foam*
lo sciampo	....
il caricatore del cellulare	*phone charger*
gli assorbenti/tampax	*sanitary pads/tampons*

VERBI ED ESPRESSIONI UTILI	*VERBS AND USEFUL PHRASES*
fare tappa	*to do a stop-over/do one stage of a journey*
fermarsi a	*to stop in/at*
fare la valigia/lo zaino	*to pack a suitcase/backpack*
portare	*to bring*
percorrere	*to cover (a distance)*
il sentiero	....
attraversare	*to cross*
attraverso	*across*
lungo	*along*
da... a...	*from ...* ....
a piedi	*on* ....
in barca/nave/treno/macchina/autobus	*by +boat/ship/train/car/bus*

With means of transportation, use the preposition in: viaggio in macchina; preferisco viaggiare in treno. Except one: your feet! When you walk, you say: vado a piedi.

Vocabulary practice 1

Find the odd one out.

a il pettine – lo sciampo – il caricatore – il sapone

b il pigiama – la giacca impermeabile – il pettine – la biancheria

c lo zaino – il dentifricio- lo spazzolino da denti – la schiuma da barba

d fermarsi – attraverso – percorrere- attraversare

CONVERSATION 1

Zaino in spalla e via! *Backpack is ready and go!*

15.02

1 Here are a few words and expressions to help you understand the following conversation. Note their meanings.

leggerissimo	*very light*	Beh	*Well, ...*
e basta!	*and that's it!*	aspettare	*to wait*

15.03

2 Listen to the conversation without looking at the text. Then listen again and read the text. Pay attention to how Matteo and Cristian talk about what one does/people do on this kind of vacation.

Annalisa, Aicha, e la loro amica Sandra sono al pub con Matteo e Cristian. Parlano delle loro prossime (*next*) vacanze. Che piani hanno? Matteo ha un'idea brillante: zaino in spalla e via: un viaggio a piedi lungo la Via degli Dei, un sentiero che va da Bologna a Firenze. Con grande entusiasmo, Matteo presenta i dettagli (*details*) del suo piano ai suoi amici, un po' scettici (*skeptical*)...

Matteo Di solito si parte la mattina presto, si percorrono circa 30 km al giorno...

Aicha 30 km? È moltissimo!

Matteo La Via degli Dei è il sentiero più corto del mio programma...

Aicha Sarebbe il viaggio a piedi più lungo della mia vita...

Matteo Si fa lo zaino leggerissimo: giacca impermeabile, biancheria, spazzolino da denti, dentifricio... e basta!

Annalisa Beh, certo non si portano i trucchi! Vero, Aicha?

Matteo Si attraversano gli Appennini e si arriva da Bologna a Firenze in quattro o cinque giorni.

Cristian E si vedono dei castelli bellissimi lungo il sentiero...

Aicha Io vado in treno e vi aspetto in un bel bar di Firenze!

3 Decide if the statements are vero or falso based on the conversation.

a	La Via degli Dei è lunga circa 30 km.	vero	falso
b	La Via degli Dei è il sentiero più lungo di tutti.	vero	falso
c	Nello zaino mettiamo solo oggetti essenziali.	vero	falso
d	La Via degli Dei è un sentiero in montagna.	vero	falso
e	Aicha è molto contenta di partecipare al viaggio a piedi.	vero	falso

LANGUAGE BUILDER 1

Language discovery 1

Find the phrases in the text that correspond to the following English sentences. What form is used in Italian to express a general habit or a custom, or something people do as a rule? Can you guess how it works?

a One usually leaves early in the morning.
b One does roughly 30 km a day.
c People pack a very light backpack.
d One certainly does not bring make-up.

Dos and don'ts: si impersonale

To say how something is generally done (e.g., to describe a tradition, a habit or a custom), the "impersonal si" is used:

In Italia non si beve il cappuccino dopo pranzo. — *In Italy people don't drink cappuccino after lunch.*

Impersonal si indicates that no particular subject is performing the action, rather it is a common practice. English typically uses the subject *people*, *you*, *one* or the passive voice (si parla italiano; *Italian is spoken*).

Si is followed by the lui/lei form of the verb if there is no direct object or if the direct object is singular:

Di solito si va a piedi. — *People usually go on foot.*

Si fa lo zaino leggerissimo. — *One packs a very light backpack.*

If there is a plural direct object, then the verb is in the plural loro form:

Si percorrono circa 30 km al giorno. — *You cover roughly 30 km a day.*

Verb alone	Verb + singular direct object	Verb + plural direct object
si va	si fa lo zaino leggerissimo	si percorrono circa 30 km

What if a reflexive verb in the impersonal form is required? The third person of reflexive verbs already contains si: Matteo si sveglia alle 7. (*Matteo wakes up at 7*.) To say that people usually wake up at 7, it would be si si sveglia. However, to avoid repeating si, turn the first si into ci: ci si ferma in un hotel. The verb is always in the third person singular (lui/lei) form.

Language practice 1

Is it just you or is it something people in your country do? Transform the sentences about a particular subject into a general statement about a cultural norm in Italy. Then try to guess if the new statement is vero or falso.

a	Annalisa fa sempre colazione al bar. In Italia...	vero	falso
b	Matteo mangia molta pasta. In Italia...	vero	falso
c	Cristian si veste elegante per andare al matrimonio. In Italia...	vero	falso
d	Sandra mangia antipasto, primo, secondo e dolce tutti i giorni. In Italia...	vero	falso
e	Aicha va in vacanza solo al mare. In Italia...	vero	falso
f	Eleonora si mette il costume per la festa di Carnevale. In Italia...	vero	falso

LANGUAGE BUILDER 2

Language discovery 2

15.04

Listen to the conversation again and repeat each line in the pauses provided. Then look at the text and find how Matteo says "the shortest path in my program?" How does Aicha say, "the longest journey of my life?"

The best of the group: the superlative

When comparing two objects or qualities, use the comparative (più or meno di/che). When comparing items in a group of three or more, use the superlative to indicate the highest or lowest degree of a quality. It is formed by using the definite article with più or meno di. The article agrees with the item being compared, but the item itself can be stated or omitted.

Il Kilimanjaro è la (montagna) più alta delle montagne in Africa.	*Kilimanjaro is the tallest (mountain) of all the mountains in Africa.*
La Via degli Dei è il (sentiero) più corto dei sentieri in Italia.	*La Via degli Dei is the shortest (path) of all walking paths in Italy.*

Più or meno goes before the quality you are discussing:

Aicha è la (persona) meno sportiva del gruppo.	*Aicha is the least athletic (person) in the group.*

The reference group is preceded by di. Remember that di combines with the definite article to form a single word: del, della, dell', dello, dei, degli, delle.

Venezia è la città più antica del Veneto.	*Venice is the oldest city in Veneto.*
Annalisa è la più giovane delle sue amiche.	*Annalisa is the youngest among her friends.*

The superlative cannot be used with adjectives ending in -issimo/a/i/e, as those express absolute qualities, without any comparison. Venezia è la città più bella del Veneto (*Venezia is the most beautiful relative to a specific group of cities in Veneto*); Venezia è bellissima (*Venezia is very beautiful in a general sense*).

Similarly, words like ottimo (*very good*), pessimo (*very bad*), massimo (*very high/big*), and minimo (*very low/small*) can't be used in the superlative, as they already express absolute qualities. Instead use il/la migliore; il/la peggiore, il/la maggiore; il/la minore: È il modo migliore di vedere Italia. (*It's the best way to see Italy.*)

Language practice 2

1 Complete the following text with the missing words expressing superlatives.

La Via Francigena è indubbiamente **a** .... sentiero più ricco di bellezza artistica e naturale **b** .... Italia. Questa strada, che collega Canterbury a Roma, è **c** .... più lunga di tutta l'Europa. Lungo la via si incontrano città medievali come Siena o Lucca, forse **d** .... città meno famosa **e** .... Toscana, ma comunque bellissima . Inoltre, la Via Francigena attraversa la regione dell'Umbria, famosa per la sua cucina e il suo vino, che è probabilmente **f** .... migliore **g** .... vini rossi dell'Italia centrale. La Via Francigena attraversa anche la valle del Gran San Bernardo, e qui si vede il Monte Bianco, che è **h** .... montagna **I** .... alta **j** .... Europa.

15.05

2 Now play Conversation 1 again, but this time you will play Aicha's role. Comment about Matteo's plan. Speak in the pauses provided. Try not to refer to the text.

CULTURE POINT 2

Ultraturismo o turismo slow *Overtourism or "slow" tourism*

The United Nations World Tourism Organization (UNWTO) defines ultraturismo as "the impact of tourism on a destination that excessively influences the quality of life of citizens and/or quality of visitor experiences in a negative way." In some parts of Italy ci sono troppi turisti, especially Venezia, Roma, and Le Cinque Terre in Liguria. Many locals don't live there anymore, as il costo della vita è troppo alto. Therefore, tourists do not get to experience la cultura italiana autentica. I turisti e i locali possono invece scoprire (*discover*) the many hidden gems of Italy by practicing il turismo slow in less crowded but equally beautiful destinations. For instance, instead of going to one of the major città, people could visit a borgo. Borghi are villages of medieval origin, usually su una collina o montagna. Most of them are very charming, featuring artigianato locale, castelli, and picturesque views. You can attend their local sagra (*fair*), degustare i prodotti tipici, and witness ancient rituals often from the Middle Ages. Tourists can often pernottare (*lodge*) in alberghi diffusi. The albergo diffuso is a form of hotel where guest rooms are spread out in various buildings within a small town or community, generally of historical significance. The concept was launched in Italy in the early 1980s as a means of reviving small, historic borghi off the beaten path.

Castelmezzano

1 Guarda il sito con la lista dei borghi più belli d'Italia. Scegli (*choose*) un borgo.

- **a** Dove si trova?
- **b** Cosa si fa in questo borgo?
- **c** Quali cibi tipici si mangiano?
- **d** Cosa si può comprare?

2 Guarda il sito degli alberghi diffusi.

Dove ti piacerebbe pernottare? Perché?

VOCABULARY BUILDER 2

Look at the words and phrases and complete the missing English words and expressions. Then listen and try to imitate the pronunciation of the speakers.

ATTIVITÀ DURANTE UN VIAGGIO	*ACTIVITIES DURING A TRIP*
fermarsi in/a	*to stop in/at*
pernottare	*to lodge/to spend the night*
esplorare	....
fare shopping/fare le spese	....
fare una deviazione	*to take a detour*
guidare	*to drive*
assaggiare/degustare	*to taste*
fare una passeggiata/camminare	....
scoprire	*to discover*
fare una visita guidata	*to do a guided tour/visit*
salire su	*to go up/climb*
scendere da	*to go down from*
dormire in tenda	.... *in a tent*
campeggiare	*to camp*
guardare le stelle	*to stargaze*
andare a funghi	*to go foraging for mushrooms*
pagare la tassa di soggiorno	*to pay the visitor's tax (in hotels)*

I LUOGHI	*PLACES*
il bosco	*wood*
il borgo	....
il castello	*castle*
la chiesa	*church*
il museo	....
la sagra	*country fair*

Vocabulary practice 2

Classify the activities according to the type of person who would like to do.

Ama la natura	Ama il cibo	Ama l'arte e la storia.

CONVERSATION 2

Mi è piaciuto! *I liked it!*

1 Here are a few words and expressions to help you understand the following conversation. Note their meanings.

non lo rifarei	*I would not do it again*
Lo spero!	*I hope so!*
la rievocazione storica	*historical reenactment*
per fortuna	*fortunately*
a tutti i costi	*at all costs*
peccato che	*pity that/too bad*

2 Listen to the conversation without looking at the text. Then listen again and read the text. Pay attention to how they say that they liked something, and what they could do, wanted to do, and had to do.

Annalisa, Aicha, Sandra, Cristian e Matteo sono tornati a casa dopo il viaggio a piedi sulla Via degli Dei. Loro parlano del viaggio: cosa è stato bello e cosa hanno fatto.

Matteo	Di' la verità, Aicha: questa esperienza ti è piaciuta!
Aicha	Sì, ma non la rifarei, eh! Abbiamo dovuto camminare un sacco!
Cristian	A me sono piaciuti i castelli, e la rievocazione storica che abbiamo potuto vedere!
Annalisa	Lo spero! Hai voluto a tutti i costi fare una deviazione di 5 km per andare alla sagra di quel borgo!
Matteo	A me è piaciuto dormire in tenda. Abbiamo potuto guardare le stelle che è difficile vedere in città.
Sandra	Peccato che non siamo potuti salire sulla montagna per vedere quel borgo pittoresco. Avrei voluto anche assaggiare i prodotti tipici...
Aicha	Per fortuna! Dopo il viaggio non ho potuto camminare per due giorni!

3 Answer the following questions based on the text.

a Qual è l'opinione di Aicha sul viaggio a piedi?
b Cosa è piaciuto a Matteo?
c Quale esperienza è piaciuta molto a Cristian?
d Chi ama le degustazioni?

LANGUAGE BUILDER 3

Language discovery 3

Look back to the conversation and find the sentences below. Complete the verbs with the missing endings.

a Dì la verità Aicha: questa esperienza ti è piaciut ....?

b A me sono piaciut ....? i castelli.

c A me è piaciut ....? dormire in tenda.

What pattern do you see in the endings? What verb is used here as the helping verb?

The passato prossimo of piacere

To say that you liked something, use piacere in the passato prossimo, which is formed with essere in the third-person singular or plural:

Ti è piaciuta la degustazione? *Did you like the tasting?*

Ti sono piaciuti i castelli? *Did you like the castles?*

Remember that the participle agrees with the thing that you liked. Literally, the thing that was pleasing:

La visita guidata mi è piaciuta. *I liked the guided tour.*

When referring to activities, i.e., verbs in the infinitive, they are considered masculine, singular:

Dormire in tenda mi è piaciuto. *I liked sleeping in a tent.*

	Masculine	Feminine
Singular	mi è piaciuto	mi è piaciuta
Plural	mi sono piaciuti	mi sono piaciute

The passato prossimo of piacere is used to evaluate a past experience from today's perspective. The imperfetto—mi piaceva/mi piacevano—means I used to like it, prompting the question: *and now?* E ora?

Language practice 3

1 Change these sentences into passato prossimo.

a A Annalisa piacciono i borghi.

b Mi piace pernottare nell'albergo diffuso.

c Ti piacciono le visite guidate?

d A Aicha non piace salire sulla montagna.

e Vi piacciono molto i prodotti tipici.

2 Pensa a una vacanza recente. Cosa ti è piaciuto? Cosa non ti è piaciuto?

LANGUAGE BUILDER 4

Language discovery 4

1 Listen to the conversation again and repeat each line in the pauses provided. Then choose the right option to complete the sentences from the conversation.

a Sì, ma non la rifarei, eh! Abbiamo / Siamo dovuto camminare un sacco!

b A me sono piaciuti i castelli, e la rievocazione storica che abbiamo / siamo potuto vedere!

c Abbiamo / Siamo potuto guardare le stelle che è difficile vedere in città.

d Peccato che non abbiamo / siamo potuti salire sulla montagna per vedere quel borgo pittoresco.

e Hai / Sei voluto a tutti i costi fare una deviazione di 5 km per andare alla sagra di quell borgo.

2 Voluto, potuto, dovuto are the past participles of the modal verbs volere, potere, dovere, which are in the passato prossimo. Can you see a pattern in the auxiliary? When do we use essere and when do we use avere?

The passato prossimo of modal verbs

Unit 7 covered the rule of the auxiliary for the passato prossimo. Verbs that indicate motion from point A to B (andare, venire, salire, scendere, entrare, uscire, partire, arrivare...), verbs that indicate a lack of motion (stare, restare, rimanere), and verbs that indicate physical or psychological change (diventare, nascere, morire...) all take essere as their auxiliary.

What about the modal verbs potere, volere, and dovere? These verbs are usually followed by the infinitive: Io voglio viaggiare. In the past tense, it is not the modal verb that determines the auxiliary but the infinitive that follows: io ho viaggiato → io ho voluto viaggiare. BUT io sono rimasto → io sono voluto rimanere. So, use the auxiliary you would need for the second verb. The participles of potere, volere, dovere are regular: potuto, voluto, dovuto.

Visitare. → Io ho potuto visitare il castello.	*I could have visited the castle.*
Andare. → Io sono dovuta partire alle 7.	*I had to leave at 7.*

Remember that, with essere, the participle works as an adjective, agreeing in gender and number with the logical subject of the sentence.

This rule works for all the tenses that have an auxiliary. Look at this sentence from the conversation: Avrei voluto assaggiare i prodotti tipici. *I would have wanted to taste the typical products.*

Language practice 4

1 Change the following text into the past. Make sure that the sentences with modal verbs are formed with the appropriate auxiliary.

Oggi Aicha vuole passare una giornata in totale relax. Prima però deve fare alcune cose in ufficio poi finalmente può uscire. Vuole andare al museo per vedere una mostra di fotografia e vuole anche fare un giro in centro per fare un po' di shopping prima di incontrare un'amica per un aperitivo. Purtroppo però la sua amica non può venire perché deve lavorare fino a tardi e così Aicha beve uno spritz da sola in piazza.

Ieri...

....

....

....

....

....

....

15.10

2 Now play Conversation 2 again. Imagine you have also participated in this journey. Say what you liked or disliked, and what was the best thing in the program.

SKILL BUILDER

1 Read the following reviews written by people who hiked along the various sentieri. Complete the texts with the missing auxiliaries and endings of the participles.

La Via Francigena in Lazio ...

Con mia moglie **a** .... **b** volut .... percorrere la parte della Via Francigena che attraversa il Lazio. È stata un'esperienza che ci **c** .... **d** piaciut .... moltissimo. Abbiamo sempre pernottato in piccoli alberghi o B&B lungo il cammino, dove **e** .... **f** potut .... dormire e fare colazione per prezzi onesti. La Via Francigena non è così organizzata come il Cammino di Santiago, quindi **g** .... **h** dovut .... comprare una guida e prenotare tutto in anticipo.

La Via Della Lana

L'anno scorso ho fatto la Via degli Dei e quest'anno **i** .... **j** volu .... andare a camminare sulla via della Lana. **k** .... **l** potut .... percorrere i 130 km della via in 6 giorni grazie ai suggerimenti della guida "La Via della Lana". Purtroppo **m** .... **n** dovut .... fare una deviazione perché una parte del sentiero era chiusa.

Il Cammino Celeste

Ciao a tutt*! Dopo due anni di lockdown finalmente io e i miei amici **o** .... **p** potut .... partire per il Cammino Celeste. Noi **q** .... **r** volut .... dividere il viaggio in 7 tappe invece che 10 perché abbiamo viaggiato a giugno e **s** .... **t** potut .... sfruttare (*take advantage of*) i giorni lunghi dell'estate. Questo cammino ci **u** .... **v** piaciut .... moltissimo e lo consigliamo a tutt*.

2 The following blog extract contains some rules on how to travel in Italy. They are expressed as le persone/i turisti. Turn the sentences into general statements with si.

Example: I viaggiatori portano vestiti per tutti i climi *Si portano vestiti per tutti i climi.*

- **a** I viaggiatori prenotano i musei nelle grandi città in anticipo (advance).
- **b** Nel Centro e Sud Italia, le persone non mangiano prima delle otto di sera.
- **c** Normalmente nei ristoranti e nei bar le persone non danno la mancia (tip).
- **d** In Italia le persone guidano a destra.
- **e** Negli alberghi i clienti pagano la tassa di soggiorno.
- **f** I viaggiatori pagano per guidare in autostrada.

3 Form sentences using the superlative and the elements given. Note that you have to modify the adjective as needed.

Example: lasagne – buono – menu *Le lasagne sono le più buone del menu.*

- **a** Il viaggio in Italia – bello – anno
- **b** La vacanza al mare – lungo – anno.
- **c** Lucy – alto – gruppo.
- **d** Pablo – giovane – classe.

4 An Italian friend of yours is traveling to your country. Write a list of dos and don'ts in your country with si.

TEST YOURSELF

1 **Look at the data below and for each group form a sentence using the superlative.**
Example: *Milano è la più popolosa delle città del Nord Italia.*

a Laghi della Lombardia		**b** Vulcani d'Italia		**c** Città dell'Umbria	
Lago di Como	145,9 km²	Etna	3329 m	Perugia	166 mila abitanti
Lago di Garda	370 km²	Stromboli	926 m	Terni	111 mila abitanti
Lago d'Iseo	65 km²	Vesuvio	1281 m		
Lago Maggiore	212 km²				
Lago di Varese	15 km²				

La misteriosa donna in soffitta

The mysterious woman in the attic

Guarda ancora il sito.

In quale regione si trova il borgo di Monterosso Almo, chiamato "il piccolo Eden di montagna"? La prima lettera del nome della regione è la lettera n. 15 del nome della donna nel quadro.

Remember to use **My review** and **My takeaway** to assess your progress and reflect on your learning experience.

16

In this unit you will learn how to:

- Talk about the environment and current challenges.
- Explain how to recycle in your city.
- Make predictions using the future.
- Talk about indefinite quantities or people with indefinite pronouns and adjectives.

Il pianeta verde

My study plan

I plan to work with Unit 16

- ○ Every day
- ○ Twice a week
- ○ Other ___________

I plan to study for

- ○ 5–15 minutes
- ○ 15–30 minutes
- ○ 30–45+ minutes

My progress tracker

Day / Date	Listening	Speaking	Reading	Writing	Conversation
	○	○	○	○	○
	○	○	○	○	○
	○	○	○	○	○
	○	○	○	○	○
	○	○	○	○	○
	○	○	○	○	○
	○	○	○	○	○

My goals

What do you want to be able to do or say in Italian when you complete this unit?

		Done
1	....	○
2	....	○
3	....	○

My review

SELF CHECK

	I can ...
●	... explain how recycling works in my city.
●	... talk about environmental issues.
●	... make predictions using future tense.
●	... use some common indefinite adjectives and pronouns.
●	... correctly use the pronoun ne.

CULTURE POINT 1

Riciclare in Italia *Recycling in Italy*

In Italia, la raccolta differenziata (*waste sorting*) dei rifiuti (*waste*) è molto comune, anche se le modalità possono variare da una regione all'altra. Le famiglie e le imprese devono separare i rifiuti in categorie specifiche come carta (*paper*), vetro (*glass*), plastica (*plastic*), organico (*organic waste*) e rifiuti indifferenziati (*undifferentiated waste*). I bidoni (*bins*) per la raccolta differenziata sono solitamente di colori differenti per indicare quale tipo di materiale deve andare al loro interno: ad esempio, il verde per il vetro, il giallo per la plastica, il blu per la carta, il marrone per l'organico e così via. Le città spesso seguono (*follow*) un calendario di raccolta (*collection schedule*) programmato, con giorni specifici della settimana in cui il servizio comunale (*municipal service*) raccoglie (*collects*) i diversi tipi di rifiuti. I cittadini devono quindi mettere i loro rifiuti fuori nei giorni prestabiliti (*established*).

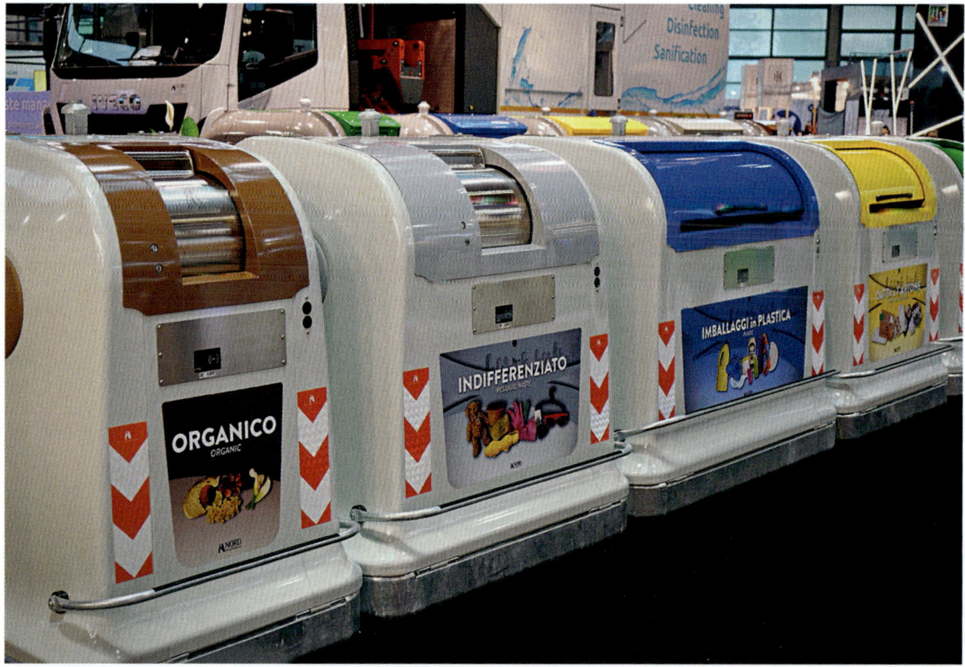

Osserva il sito web per la raccolta differenziata nella città di Trento, capoluogo della regione Trentino. In quali giorni il servizio comunale passa nelle vie del centro storico per raccogliere:

a La carta?
b I rifiuti organici?
c Il vetro?

VOCABULARY BUILDER 1

Look at the words and phrases and complete the missing English words and expressions. Then listen and try to imitate the pronunciation of the speakers.

LA RACCOLTA DIFFERENZIATA	*WASTE SORTING*
attento/a	*careful*
Il bidone	*bin*
la carta	*paper*
il cartone	*cardboard*
il metallo	....
la multa	*fine*
nessuno/a	*nobody*
niente	*nothing*
l'organico	*organic waste*
la plastica	....
qualcosa	....
qualcuno/a	*someone*
la raccolta porta a porta	*door-to-door collection*
i rifiuti	*waste*
i rifiuti indifferenziati	....
la spazzatura	*trash/garbage*
il vetro	*glass*

VERBI UTILI	*USEFUL VERBS*
conseguire	*to follow from an action*
buttare	*to throw*
raccogliere	....
riciclare	....
seguire	*to follow*

Vocabulary practice 1

Look at the pictures. Can you identify the correct bin for each of them?

raccolta vetro	raccolta carta e cartone	raccolta organico
raccolta indifferenziato	raccolta metalli	raccolta plastica

a .... **b** .... **c** .... **d** .... **e** .... **f** ....

CONVERSATION 1

L'importanza del riciclare *The importance of recycling*

16.02

1 Here are a few words and expressions to help you understand the following conversation. Note their meanings.

Ferma!	*Stop!*
sbagliare	*to make a mistake*

16.03

2 Listen to the conversation a few times without looking at the text. Then listen to the conversation again and read the text.

Una mattina, Cristian vede Annalisa che sta per buttare un oggetto nel bidone del riciclaggio sbagliato. Dalla sua reazione nasce una piccola conversazione sui diversi modi di fare raccolta differenziata nelle loro regioni di origine. Ascolta la conversazione e fai attenzione all'uso di alcuni pronomi, in particolare il pronome ne.

Cristian Annalisa, ferma! Stai mettendo la plastica nel bidone del vetro!

Annalisa Ah, grazie! Senza occhiali, non vedo niente.

Cristian La raccolta differenziata è qualcosa di molto importante: nella mia città, se sbagli, ricevi una multa. Ne consegue che siamo moooolto attenti. [ride]

Annalisa Nel mio quartiere a Napoli non abbiamo il bidone del vetro in casa. Ne abbiamo solo tre per la raccolta porta a porta: indifferenziato, organico e carta… gli altri in strada.

Cristian Nessuno vi fa la multa, se sbagliate?

Annalisa Non saprei, non ne ho sentito parlare. Forse non ho mai sbagliato prima! [ride]

3 Answer the questions in Italian.

a Che errore sta per fare Annalisa?

b Qual è la ragione di questo errore?

c Cosa succede nella città di Cristian se qualcuno sbaglia a fare la raccolta differenziata?

d Qual è la differenza nella raccolta differenziata a Napoli?

LANGUAGE BUILDER 1

Language discovery 1

In the conversation, you encountered again the pronoun ne. Find the relevant sentences and explain how ne was used. What is it referring to each time?

The pronoun ne: more usages

The pronoun ne is very versatile! It can substitute for a direct object when referring to a quantity:

Ne abbiamo solo tre. *We only have three of them.*

Ne prendo cinque. *I'll take five of them.*

Ne can stand in for a phrase or even an entire sentence introduced by the preposition di:

Non ne ho mai sentito parlare. = Non ho mai sentito parlare di questo. *I have never heard of that.*

Vorrei comprare una macchina nuova. Cosa ne pensi? = Cosa pensi di questa mia idea? *I would like to buy a new car. What do you think?*

Ne can also take the place of a noun or a sentence that was previously introduced by the preposition da:

Ne consegue che... *From this, it follows that ...*

È una situazione difficile. Non ne usciamo. *It's a difficult situation. We can't escape from it.*

Language practice 1

Rephrase these sentences using ne.

a Ho letto un articolo sulla raccolta differenziata e sono stato molto impressionato dall'articolo sulla raccolta differenziata

....

b Hanno cambiato il modo di fare la raccolta. Secondo me viene fuori un grande caos dal cambiamento del modo di fare la raccolta.

....

c Hai visto cosa ha fatto il primo ministro? Tutti parlano di quello che ha fatto il primo ministro.

....

d Abbiamo finito le carote. Compri un chilo di carote, per favore?

....

e Quel ristorante è molto rumoroso. Sono uscita da quel ristorante con il mal di testa!

....

LANGUAGE BUILDER 2

Language discovery 2

16.04

Listen to the conversation again and repeat each line in the pauses provided.

Senza occhiali, non vedo niente. È qualcosa di molto importante.

What do you think niente and qualcosa mean? How is their structure different from your language? What words do you think are extra?

Indefinite pronouns: qualcosa, qualcuno – niente, nessuno

Indefinite pronouns serve as useful tools for referring to unspecified things or persons. Qualcuno and qualcuna both mean *someone* and are used exclusively in their singular forms. Qualcosa means *something* and remains unchanged. When accompanied by an adjective, qualcosa is followed by the preposition di.

Qualcuno fa la raccolta differenziata. *Someone recycles.*

Ho molte amiche. Qualcuna è italiana. *I have many friends. Someone is Italian.*

È qualcosa di molto importante. *It's something very important.*

Vorrei qualcosa di dolce. *I would like something sweet.*

Nessuno and nessuna both mean *nobody*. Meanwhile, niente means *nothing* and, like qualcosa, it requires the preposition di when an adjective follows. As negatives, they pair with non when placed after the verb (but don't need non if they begin a sentence).

Non ho visto nessuno. *I have seen nobody.*

Nessuno vi fa la multa? *Nobody fines you?*

Senza occhiali non vedo niente. *Without glasses, I see nothing.*

Cosa ho fatto ieri? Niente di interessante. *What did I do yesterday? Nothing interesting.*

Language practice 2

1 Complete the sentences with the correct indefinite pronoun (qualcuno/a, qualcosa, nessuno/a, niente).

a .... ha dimenticato di mettere fuori il bidone della plastica.

b Vorrei comprare .... di elegante per la festa.

c Non ho trovato .... di interessante nel negozio.

d .... ha risposto alla mia domanda durante la lezione.

e .... ha suonato alla porta, ma non ho aperto perché non aspettavo ....

f Voglio cucinare .... di speciale per la cena stasera.

16.05

2 **Now play Conversation 1 again, but this time you will play Annalisa's role. Speak in the pauses provided and try to explain how recycling works in your city.**

CULTURE POINT 2

Sfide ambientali italiane *Italian environmental challenges*

Insieme alle sfide ambientali globali, da risolvere a livello internazionale, l'Italia deve anche affrontare (*face*) numerosi problemi interni, che richiedono attenzione e azioni immediate. Una delle principali preoccupazioni (*worries*) è l'instabilità sismica (*seismic instability*), per la presenza di vulcani attivi come l'Etna e il Vesuvio. L'erosione costiera (*coastal erosion*) è invece un problema critico delle coste e include anche la città di Venezia, con effetti negativi sull'habitat marino e sulle comunità costiere. Un'altra priorità sono le risorse idriche (*water resources*), soprattutto (*mostly*) nelle regioni del Sud che spesso hanno lunghi periodi di siccità (*drought*). La buona gestione (*management*) di queste risorse è fondamentale per l'agricoltura. Per affrontare queste sfide assistiamo a un impegno (*commitment*) continuo da parte del governo e delle comunità, che ha già portato alla creazione di strategie e grandi opere ingegneristiche (*engineering works*) come il MOSE di Venezia.

Vulcano Vesuvio

Osserva la pagina Wikipedia dedicate al MOSE di Venezia e prova a rispondere alle domande.

a Quando è cominciato il progetto?

b Perché il MOSE ha questo nome?

c Come si chiama la compagnia che lavora alla costruzione del MOSE?

VOCABULARY BUILDER 2

16.06

Look at the words and phrases and complete the missing English words and expressions. Then listen and try to imitate the pronunciation of the speakers.

SALVIAMO IL PIANETA!	*LET'S SAVE THE PLANET!*
l'ambiente	*environment*
il cambiamento climatico	....
la diga	*dam*
l'effetto serra	*greenhouse effect*
l'erosione	....
l'impegno	*commitment*
l'inondazione	*flood*
l'inquinamento	*pollution*
il livello	....
la marea	*tide*
la minaccia	*threat*
il mondo	*world*
preoccupato/a	*worried*
le previsioni	*forecast*
rinnovabile	....
le risorse	*resources*
la siccità	*drought*
il sistema	....
sostenibile	....

VERBI UTILI	*USEFUL VERBS*
abbassare	*to lower*
affrontare	*to face*
aumentare	*to increase*
conservare	*to save*
monitorare	....
proteggere	....

Vocabulary practice 2

Complete the text with the given words.

proteggere	ambiente (x2)	inquinamento	mondo
risorse	sostenibile	cambiamento	climatico

Nel **a** .... di oggi, l' **b** .... è al centro delle nostre preoccupazioni. Il **c** .... sta modificando le temperature, l'**d** .... è una minaccia per le nostre **e** .... naturali e la salute del pianeta. È essenziale adottare uno stile di vita **f** .... per **g** .... il nostro **h** .... e le **i** .... limitate che abbiamo.

CONVERSATION 2

La sfida dell'alta marea *The high tide's challenge*

1 Here are a few words to help you understand the following conversation. Note the meaning.

Stiamo facendo il possible.	*We are doing everything we can.*

2 Listen to the conversation a few times without looking at the text. Then listen to the conversation again and read the text.

Piove da diversi giorni. Cristian e Annalisa discutono del meteo e del MOSE, un sistema ingegneristico contro l'acqua alta a Venezia. Annalisa, che lavora sul progetto MOSE, racconta a Cristian come funziona il sistema. Ascolta attentamente la conversazione e osserva quali sono i verbi usati per parlare di azioni future.

Cristian Hai visto le previsioni? Pioverà tutta la settimana.

Annalisa Sì, e probabilmente il MOSE si alzerà. Dovrò monitorare i livelli dell'acqua.

Cristian Giusto, voi lavorate su questo progetto! Come funziona esattamente?

Annalisa Il MOSE è come una grande diga che si alza o si abbassa per proteggere la città dall'alta marea, quando piove troppo. Il sistema è automatico, e noi stiamo lavorando per migliorarne alcune funzioni.

Cristian C'è stato qualche problema?

Annalisa Sì, abbiamo avuto dei problemi in passato, ma speriamo che non ne avremo altri. Stiamo facendo il possibile per finire prima dell'inverno!

3 Match the sentence halves.

1 Cristian	**a** è un sistema per proteggere Venezia.
2 Annalisa	**b** dovrebbero finire.
3 Il MOSE	**c** si occupa del MOSE.
4 Le previsioni	**d** mettono pioggia per la settimana
5 I problemi	**e** vuole sapere come funziona il MOSE.

LANGUAGE BUILDER 3

Language discovery 3

Look at these sentences from the conversation. They contain a new tense.

Pioverà tutta la settimana.
Probabilmente il MOSE si alzerà.
Dovrò monitorare i livelli.
Speriamo che non ne avremo altri.

Where would you place these actions on a timeline? Do the verb forms remind you of another tense you have already studied?

The future tense

In Italian, you can use the present tense to talk about the future, provided that a time reference is included:

Il mese prossimo andiamo in Cambogia. — *Next month we are going to Cambodia.*

However, for plans that aren't definite, distant events in the future, or when making predictions, the future tense is used:

Dovrò monitorare i livelli. — *I will have to monitor the levels.*

Probabilmente il MOSE si alzerà. — *Probably the MOSE will rise.*

To form the **futuro** in Italian, remove the final -e from the infinitive and add the following endings: -ò, -ai, -à, -emo, -ete, -anno. Remember to change the a in the -are group to an e.

	conservare	proteggere	finire		conservare	proteggere	finire
io	conserv**erò**	protegg**erò**	fin**irò**	noi	conserv**eremo**	protegg**eremo**	fin**iremo**
tu	conserv**erai**	protegg**erai**	fin**irai**	voi	conserv**erete**	protegg**erete**	fin**irete**
lui/lei	conserv**erà**	protegg**erà**	fin**irà**	loro	conserv**eranno**	protegg**eranno**	fin**iranno**

The stem of the future tense is the same as in the present conditional, it just requires a new set of endings. This rule also applies to irregular verbs, such as sarò, dovrò, andrò, avrò, vorrò, and so on.

Language practice 3

Complete the sentences with the correct form of the future tense.

a Ho deciso che (cominciare) .... ad avere un nuovo stile di vita più sostenibile.

b Jasmin e Lucia (andare) .... al cinema la settimana prossima.

c (noi – scrivere) .... un articolo sul cambiamento climatico.

d Il governo (dovere) .... affrontare molte sfide connesse all'ambiente.

e A che ora (voi – finire) .... la riunione sulle energie rinnovabili? I miei colleghi (venire) .... alla conferenza più tardi.

f L'esame (essere) .... il 19 giugno.

g A causa della siccità, non (noi – potere) .... usare molta acqua questa estate.

h Claire è stanca, credo che (rimanere) .... a casa.

LANGUAGE BUILDER 4

Language discovery 4

16.09

Listen to the conversation again and repeat each line in the pauses provided. How would you translate the following expression?

dei problemi = ...

Can you find an equivalent in the conversation? There is also another way to express an indefinite quantity, referring to a different noun. What is it?

Indefinite adjectives: qualche, alcuni, di + article

Indefinite adjectives are used to express unspecified quantities or amounts, e.g., "some," "a few," or "any" in English. In Italian, this can be expressed with qualche, alcuni, or di + article.

Qualche is always followed by a singular noun and used in questions or positive statements:

C'è stato qualche problema?	*Was there any problem?*
Ho comprato qualche libro.	*I bought some books.*

Alcuni and alcune are always followed by plural nouns and used in positive statements:

Stiamo lavorando per migliorarne alcune funzioni.	We are working to improve some functions.
Ho alcune domande sul progetto.	I have some questions about the project.

Di + definite article can be used with singular nouns if the noun is uncountable (e.g., latte, pane, natura, etc.) or with plural nouns if they are countable. Di + article can be used in positive and negative statements, as well as in questions. Remember the combined forms of di + article.

Abbiamo avuto dei problemi.	*We had some problems.*
Non ho delle buone notizie.	*I don't have any good news.*
Puoi comprare del latte?	*Can you buy some milk?*

Language practice 4

1 Complete the sentence with the appropriate indefinite adjective (qualche, alcuni, alcune, di + article). Sometimes multiple options are possible.

a Vado a fare la spesa. Devo prendere .... pane?

b Ho cucinato .... ricette italiane deliziose per la cena.

c Mi piacerebbe leggere .... libro sul cambiamento climatico.

d Sono uscito con .... amico ieri sera.

e Abbiamo invitato .... parenti alla festa di compleanno di mia madre.

f .... previsioni sul futuro del nostro pianeta non sono molto positive.

g Dobbiamo cominciare a produrre energia con .... risorsa rinnovabile.

16.10

2 Now play Conversation 2 again, but this time you will play Annalisa's role. Speak in the pauses provided. Try to talk about a fictional project related to the environment you are supposedly working on.

SKILL BUILDER

1 Choose the correct indefinite pronoun/adjective.

a Per preparare una buona torta è spesso necessario usare del / qualche latte e del / qualche burro.

b Nella nostra area, recentemente, ci sono state alcune / qualche inondazioni.

c Nessuno / alcuni può dire che la sostenibilità non sarà essenziale per il futuro del nostro pianeta.

d Qualcosa / nessuno di positivo sta succedendo: sempre più persone stanno adottando uno stile di vita sostenibile.

e Qualche / alcuni governi stanno lavorando per fermare l'aumento dell'effetto serra.

f Dobbiamo fare qualcosa / qualcuno per proteggere le foreste, perché sono importanti per il clima.

g Abbiamo bisogno di fare qualcosa / niente: qualche / delle soluzioni ai problemi ambientali sono necessarie.

h Niente / del è più prezioso dell'acqua pulita, e dobbiamo proteggerla a tutti i costi.

i Qualcuno / qualche dovrebbe portare l'educazione ambientale nelle scuole, per le future generazioni.

j Sfortunatamente, non ho niente / qualcosa da dire su questo argomento.

2 Rewrite the paragraph, replacing the words in bold with the pronoun ne.

Il MOSE di Venezia è un sistema di dighe mobili che sono posizionate in diversi punti. Troviamo alcune **di queste dighe** all'ingresso delle bocche di mare principali che collegano la laguna di Venezia al Mar Adriatico. Le dighe si trovano sul fondo del mare ed escono **dal mare** solo quando è necessario evitare inondazioni. Perché questo sistema?

Perché Venezia ha molto bisogno **di questo sistema**. Quando le dighe sono alzate, creano una barriera contro l'acqua. La città ha avuto molte inondazioni nel passato, ma il MOSE è stato creato per proteggerla.

Il MOSE di Venezia...

....

....

....

....

....

....

TEST YOURSELF

16.11

1 Listen to the presentation by a climatologist and note the predictions you hear.

2 Do you agree with the climatologist's predictions? Why? Comment on the presentation and make your own predictions by using the future tense, the pronoun ne, and some indefinite pronouns/adjectives.

Example: *Non credo che useremo solo energie rinnovabili. Useremo anche l'energia nucleare.*

3 Change the sentences from the present tense to the future tense.

a La settimana prossima andiamo al mare.
b Carlos e Regina studiano geografia ambientale.
c Se abbiamo sete, beviamo l'acqua.
d Partite domani per il Sudafrica?
e Fa freddo in montagna?
f Lukas scrive un documento di lavoro.
g I ricercatori ricevono un premio per il loro studio sul cambiamento climatico.

La misteriosa donna in soffitta

The mysterious woman in the attic

The MOSE's dams are situated at four key points: the Barriera di Lido Nord, Barriera di Lido Sud, Barriera di Malamocco, and the Barriera di...? The initial letter of this fourth barrier's name will provide you with a clue to assemble the name of the lady depicted in the painting.

Remember to use **My review** and **My takeaway** to assess your progress and reflect on your learning experience.

17

In this unit you will learn how to:

» Talk about personality traits.
» Talk about feelings and emotions.
» Express personal opinions using the subjunctive.

Incontro online

My study plan

I plan to work with Unit 17

○ Every day
○ Twice a week
○ Other ________

I plan to study for

○ 5–15 minutes
○ 15–30 minutes
○ 30–45+ minutes

My progress tracker

Day / Date	Listening	Speaking	Reading	Writing	Conversation
	○	○	○	○	○
	○	○	○	○	○
	○	○	○	○	○
	○	○	○	○	○
	○	○	○	○	○
	○	○	○	○	○
	○	○	○	○	○

My goals

What do you want to be able to do or say in Italian when you complete this unit?

		Done
1	....	○
2	....	○
3	....	○

My review

SELF CHECK

	I can ...
●	... describe my personality and that of others.
●	... talk about relationships.
●	... talk about feelings and make subjective statements.
●	... answer direct questions using combined pronouns.

CULTURE POINT 1

Italiano lingua romantica: amore e musica

L'italiano ha una reputazione di lingua romantica, probabilmente anche a causa di un gioco di parole (*wordplay*) tra la parola romantico (*romantic*) e lingua romanza (*romance language*). L'italiano è infatti una lingua romanza perché, come il francese, lo spagnolo e il portoghese, viene dal latino, la lingua dell'impero di Roma. L'italiano però è forse considerato una lingua romantica perché ha un suono (*sound*) molto melodioso. Grazie alle molte vocali (*vowels*), l'italiano è perfetto per il canto (*singing*) e la musica. In Italia c'è una tradizione musicale molto importante. L'italiano è non solo la lingua dell'opera, ma gli italiani amano molto anche la canzone (*song*) melodica, un tipo di musica molto orecchiabile (*easy listening*) con un testo (*lyrics*) che normalmente parla d'amore e di sentimenti (*feelings*). Questa canzone si chiama anche romanza (da non confondere con la parola romanzo, che significa novel, e originariamente indicava una storia d'amore). Romantico, lingua romanza, romanza, romanzo, che confusione!

Si possono ascoltare molte canzoni melodiche al Festival di Sanremo, un festival e competizione di musica che si svolge ogni anno in febbraio. Lo sapevi? Il/la cantante (*singer*) e la canzone che vince il Festival di Sanremo rappresenta l'Italia all'Eurovision l'anno dopo.

Sanremo

Guarda lo slideshow della storia del Festival di Sanremo.

a In quale regione si trova la città di Sanremo?

b In quale anno c'è stato la prima edizione del Festival di Sanremo?

c Chi ha vinto la prima edizione del Festival e con quale canzone?

VOCABULARY BUILDER 1

17.01

Look at the words and phrases and complete the missing English words and expressions. Then listen and try to imitate the pronunciation of the speakers.

LA PERSONALITÀ	*PERSONALITY TRAITS*
allegro/a	*cheerful*
sensibile	*sensitive*
affascinante	*charming*
simpatico/a	*nice/likeable*
antipatico/a	....
impulsivo/a	....
riservato/a	....
timido/a	....
aperto/a	*open-minded*
permaloso/a	*touchy*

LE RELAZIONI	*RELATIONSHIPS*
l'amore	....
innamorarsi di	*to fall in love with*
uscire con qualcuno	*to go out with someone/to have a date*
avere un/a/*ragazzo/a/*	*to have a boyfriend/girlfriend/partner*
avere una relazione (aperta) con	*to have an (open) relationship with*
la storia d'amore	....
l'attrazione	....
convivere	*to live together*
fidanzarsi	*to get engaged*
fidanzato/a/*	*fiancé*
lasciarsi	*to break up*
divorziare	*to get divorced*
in una relazione complicata	*it's complicated*
essere single	....

In italiano non c'è una parola per *date*. La parola appuntamento significa, genericamente, appointment. Per dire che uno ha un date, si può usare l'espressione uscire con qualcuno: stasera esco con Paolo.
Attenzione al falso amico sensibile, che significa *sensitive* e non *sensible*. *Sensible* si traduce con sensato o ragionevole.

Vocabulary practice 1

Complete the sentences with the correct word or expression. Use correct verb forms.

a Paolo è una persona che si offende facilmente: è molto ....

b Da qualche mese Lara non è più single: lei ora .... con Elia.

c Clara e Petra hanno comprato una casa insieme in montagna e ora .... ,

d Cristian è una persona ....: non gli piace parlare della sua vita privata.

e Oh no! Ho sentito che Eleonora e Carlo ....: la loro storia d'amore è finita dopo un anno.

f La capa di Annalisa è sempre arrabbiata e risponde male: è davvero ....

CONVERSATION 1

La persona giusta! *The right one!*

17.02

1 Here are a few words and expressions to help you understand the conversation.

serata	*evening*	la data	*date* (indication of time)
la mostra	*exhibition*	mi informo	*I will get the information*

17.03

2 Listen to the conversation without looking at the text. Then listen again and read the text. Pay attention to how the speakers answer questions.

Aicha e Annalisa prendono un caffè insieme. Aicha cerca una relazione e usa un'app con un algoritmo per trovare persone compatibili. Ieri sera, infatti, ha incontrato una persona molto interessante e ne parla con Annalisa, che, invece, è sempre un po' scettica riguardo agli algoritmi dell'attrazione.

Aicha Ieri sera sono uscita con uno che ho incontrato grazie alla nuova app, quella che per ognuno trova dieci persone compatibili... e l'algoritmo ha funzionato: secondo me è la persona giusta!

Annalisa Ehm, me lo dici ogni volta...

Aicha Non essere antipatica! È sensibile, affascinante... e mi ha già mandato un messaggio... Se vuoi te lo leggo... se vuoi, eh!

Annalisa Permalosa! Sì, leggimelo.

Aicha Scrive: "Grazie per la bella serata. Sei molto simpatica."

Annalisa Simpatica??

Aicha Aspetta, poi continua: "Mi scrivi la data della mostra di cui abbiamo parlato?" E io: "Sì, mi informo e te la scrivo subito!"

Annalisa E quindi? Ti ha chiesto di andare alla mostra insieme?

Aicha No, non me lo ha chiesto. Non ancora... forse è timido.

Annalisa Forse. Perché non glielo chiedi tu?

3 Answer the questions in Italian.

a Perché Annalisa è un po' scettica dell'entusiasmo di Aicha?
b Perché "simpatico/a" non è la parola giusta?
c Cosa suggerisce Annalisa per continuare la relazione?

LANGUAGE BUILDER 1

Language discovery 1

Look at these sentences from the conversation. What do you think the underlined pronouns refer to? Match the sentences (1–4) with what they refer to (a–c).

1 Se vuoi te lo leggo.
2 Mi informo e te la scrivo subito.
3 No, non me lo ha chiesto.
4 Perché non glielo chiedi tu?

a Andare alla mostra
b La data della mostra
c Il messaggio

What do you notice about the pronouns that are used?

Combined pronouns

In previous units you learned that there are two sets of pronouns: direct object pronouns (lo, la, li, le...) and indirect object pronouns (mi, ti, gli, le, ci, vi...). Pronouns replace a word or phrase so that it does not have to be repeated: Mi compri il latte? Okay, te lo compro. Lo replaces the direct object il latte. However, in this sentence there is also the indirect pronoun te = a te. When two pronouns find themselves in the same sentence, the indirect object pronoun comes first, and mi, ti, ci, vi change the vowel into e:

	lo	la	li	le
mi	me lo	me la	me li	me le
ti	te lo	te la	te li	te le
ci	ce lo	ce la	ce li	ce le
vi	ve lo	ve la	ve li	ve le

The indirect object pronouns le and gli (singular and plural) combine into a single word with the direct object pronoun: glielo, gliela, glieli, gliele.

Note that lo can be used to replace an entire phrase or sentence: Gli hai detto che sei in ritardo? Sì, glielo ho detto.

Combined pronouns always go before the verb. Io glielo ho chiesto; Me lo hai già detto. However, with the informal (tu) imperative, the combined form is attached to the end of the verb: leggimelo!

Language practice 1

Answer the questions using a combined pronoun.

a Ti ho già detto che ti amo?
b Per favore, mi dai il tuo numero di telefono?
c Le scrivi che arriviamo alle 5?
d Mi mandi la lista della spesa?
e Gli hai detto che è stata una bella serata?
f Ci scrivi il tuo indirizzo?
g Vi mando i documenti per email?
h Perché non ti compri un telefono nuovo?
i Mamma, mi compri un gelato?
j E Aicha e Annalisa? Gli hai mandato l'invito?

LANGUAGE BUILDER 2

Language discovery 2

17.04

Listen to the conversation again and repeat each line in the pauses provided. Try to imitate the phrasing and intonation you hear. Match the English words/ expressions (1–3) with their Italian equivalents (a–c).

1 every time
2 everyone/everybody
3 one/someone

a Me lo dici ogni volta.
b Sono uscita con uno.
c L'app che per ognuno trova dieci persone compatibili.

What is the difference between ogni and ognuno?

Someone, everyone

In Italian there are several ways of saying *everyone/everybody*.

We can say tutti/e/*:

In estate tutt* vanno al mare.	*In the summer, everyone goes to the sea.*

To emphasize "each and every one," use ognuno/a/*. Unlike tutti/e/*, which is always plural, ognuno/a/* is always singular:

Ognuno ha il suo compito.	*Everyone has their task.*

Ognuno/a/* is a pronoun and can stand alone. If to keep the noun and say *every*, use the adjective ogni:

Ogni giorno mangio i cereali per colazione. *Every day I eat cereal for breakfast.*

Ogni is an adjective because it describes a noun, but it is special because it does not change to agree with the noun, and it is always singular.

In spoken Italian it is not possible to not specify gender when using words like ognuno/a or uno/a, which just means *one* or *someone*. So, to talk about "someone" without indicating their gender, use una persona. In written Italian, the last vowel can be replaced with *.

Language practice 2

1 Complete the sentences with either tutti/e/*, ogni, uno/a/*, or ognuno/a/*.

a Stasera .... escono e io resto a casa.
b Che gentile: hai portato un regalo per .... di noi.
c .... mattina mi alzo e non ho mai voglia di andare al lavoro.
d .... le mie amiche abitano a Napoli.
e Queste sono Carla e Anna: .... di loro ha una storia interessante da raccontare.
f Ieri sera ho conosciuto .... grazie alla nuova app.

17.05

2 Now play Conversation 1 again. Play Aicha's role and perhaps describe someone you've recently met instead.

CULTURE POINT 2

La fuga dei cervelli *Brain drain*

Da alcuni anni in Italia esiste il fenomeno della fuga dei cervelli. Molti italiani, spesso giovani e molto qualificati (*qualified*) vanno a lavorare all'estero (*abroad*), dove i salari sono più alti e ci sono migliori opportunità di carriera. Non solo persone nelle discipline umanistiche (*humanities*) ma anche medici, ingegneri e scienziati scelgono di lasciare l'Italia per vivere in altri paesi, soprattutto negli Stati Uniti, Regno Unito e Europa del Nord. Gli italiani all'estero sono una grande comunità: nel 2022 erano circa 5,8 milioni. Molti espatriati (*expats*) sentono nostalgia (*homesickness*) e gli mancano (*miss*) la famiglia e il contesto sociale di origine, ma molti sono perfettamente integrati nei loro nuovi paesi e sono entusiasti delle possibilità che questi paesi offrono.

Italian New Yorkers at the annual Italian Heritage Day Parade along Fifth Avenue in New York City

a Ti piacerebbe abitare e lavorare all'estero? Se sì, in quali paesi?

b Che cosa ti manca (*what do you miss*) quando viaggi all'estero?

VOCABULARY BUILDER 2

17.06

Look at the words and phrases and complete the missing English words and expressions. Then listen and try to imitate the pronunciation of the speakers.

EMOZIONI E SENTIMENTI	*EMOTIONS AND FEELINGS*
la tristezza	*sadness*
triste	*sad*
la felicità	*happiness*
felice	....
l'ansia	*anxiety*
ansioso/a	....
la nostalgia	*homesickness*
l'entusiasmo	....
entusiasta	....
la paura	*fear*
la vergogna	*shame*
l'agitazione	*nervousness*
agitato/a	*nervous*
la preoccupazione	*worry*
preoccupato/a	....

VERBI ED ESPRESSIONI	*VERBS AND EXPRESSIONS*
temere/avere paura	*to fear/to be afraid of*
sperare	*to hope*
non vedo l'ora che...	*I look forward to ...*
mi manca/mi mancano	*I miss him/her/.....................*
provare (+ sentimento: tristezza)	*to feel (+ feeling, e.g., sadness)*
sentirsi (+ aggettivo del sentimento: triste)	*to feel (+ adjective, e.g., sad)*
preoccuparsi	....
mi dispiace	*I'm sorry*
vergognarsi	*to feel ashamed*

Vocabulary practice 2

Match the expression to the photo.

ho paura	mi sento felice	mi preoccupo
sono entusiasta	sono ansiosa	

a  b  c  d  e 

CONVERSATION 2

Dolceamaro *Bittersweet*

17.07

1 Here are a few words and expressions to help you understand the conversation.

mi sembri *you seem (to me)* luna *moon* ignoto *unknown*

17.08

2 Listen to the conversation without looking at the text. Then listen again and read the text. Note how Annalisa and Cristian express their feelings.

Cristian ha ricevuto un'email molto importante: la sua candidatura al lavoro nella galleria di New York ha avuto successo! Annalisa vuole fare le congratulazioni a Cristian: sicuramente lui è al settimo cielo! (*over the moon, in seventh heaven*). Invece, lo trova un po' preoccupato e ansioso.

Annalisa Congratulazioni! Hai ottenuto il lavoro alla galleria! Ma... mi sembri triste, perché?

Cristian Sono felice ma...

Annalisa Ma?

Cristian Temo che non sia la decisione giusta. Quando penso al futuro provo molta ansia.

Annalisa Mi dispiace che tu ti senta così. Ma forse è solo un po' di paura dell'ignoto... poi sarai entusiasta di New York!

Cristian Spero che tu abbia ragione. Ma ho paura che mi manchino le vie misteriose di Venezia, i canali sotto la luna, le mie montagne...

Annalisa E anche una certa persona che assomiglia al nostro quadro in soffitta?

3 Decide if the statements are vero or falso based on the conversation.

a Cristian non vede l'ora di andare a New York. vero falso

b Secondo Annalisa, Cristian amerà New York. vero falso

c A Cristian mancherà la famiglia. vero falso

d Cristian ama Venezia. vero falso

e Annalisa sa perché Cristian non vuole partire. vero falso

Mi manca / mi mancano works like mi piace / mi piacciono. If the object you are missing is singular, use mi manca: mi manca la famiglia. If plural, use mi mancano: mi mancano i miei amici.

LANGUAGE BUILDER 3

Language discovery 3

Compare the pairs of sentences. How does the verb change in the sentences taken from the conversation?

Non è la decisione giusta	Temo che non sia la decisione giusta.
Hai ragione	Spero che tu abbia ragione.

Expressing personal opinions and feelings with the subjunctive

Some sentences express a subjective statement: how the subject feels about a fact.

Temo che non sia la decisione giusta. *I fear that this is not the right decision.*

Such statements are often introduced by phrases indicating opinion or feeling: sono felice che.., spero che, mi preoccupo che..., sembra che... The statement that is introduced by che must be in a mood called the subjunctive, which indicates that the action expressed by the verb is not objective but subjective, that is, it pertains to the subject's feelings and thoughts. For now, let's look at how three important verbs work in the subjunctive: essere, avere, and stare:

	essere	avere	stare		essere	avere	stare
(che) io	sia	abbia	stia	**(che) noi**	siamo	abbiamo	stiamo
(che) tu	sia	abbia	stia	**(che) voi**	siate	abbiate	stiate
(che)lui/lei/Lei	sia	abbia	stia	**(che) loro**	siano	abbiano	stiano

The singular forms io, tu, lui/lei/Lei are all the same.
The noi form is the same as in the present tense.

Mi preoccupo che si siano persi. *I'm worried they're lost.*

Spero che stiano bene. *I hope they're okay.*

Temo che abbia ragione. *I'm afraid you're right.*

Verbs in the subjunctive never appear alone in a sentence, that is, they always appear in a dependent clause introduced by che.

Language practice 3

Transform the statements below into subjective statements using one of the verbs and expressions that indicate feelings.

temo che	non vedo l'ora che	spero che
sono felice che	mi dispiace che	mi preoccupo che

a È il mio compleanno.

b Tu stai bene.

c Siamo in ritardo per la cena.

d Questo problema non ha una soluzione.

e Voi non avete tempo per un caffè.

f I miei amici sono qui con me.

LANGUAGE BUILDER 4

Language discovery 4

17.09

Listen to the conversation again and repeat each line in the pauses provided. Try to imitate the phrasing and intonation you hear. Look again at the verbs in the subjunctive and compare them with the present tense. Do you notice a pattern?

Mi dispiace che tu ti senta così.	Tu ti senti così. (SENTIRSI)
Ho paura che mi manchino.	Mi mancano. (MANCARE)

The subjunctive for all regular verbs

Now that you are familiar with the concept of subjective statements, let's see how the subjunctive mood works for most verbs. The subjunctive is always based on the present tense io form. Just replace the -o ending with the subjunctive ending: io parlo = (che) io parli; io finisco = (che) io finisca.

Study all the forms in the table. Note that verbs ending in -are take the vowel -i throughout, while verbs ending in -ere and -ire take the vowel -a throughout. The singular forms are all the same for each group.

	parlare	vedere	sentire/finire		parlare	vedere	sentire/finire
(che) io	parli	veda	senta/finisca	(che) noi	parliamo	vediamo	sentiamo finiamo
(che) tu	parli	veda	senta/finisca	(che) voi	parliate	vediate	sentiate finiate
(che) lui/ lei/Lei	parli	veda	senta/finisca	(che) loro	parlino	vedano	sentano finiscano

Does the subjunctive look familiar? If it does, it is because it is the same form used for the formal imperative (see Unit 14).

Language practice 4

1 Cristian keeps talking to Annalisa about his fears. Complete this paragraph with the verbs in the subjunctive.

Ho paura che la mia vita **a** .... (cambiare) radicalmente. Sono felice che la mia carriera **b** .... (crescere, *to grow*). Ma temo che la mia relazione con C. **c** .... (finire) prima di iniziare! Mia sorella Petra teme che a New York io **d** .... (sentirsi) solo e forse ha ragione: io sono un po' introverso e temo che **e** .... (essere) molto difficile per me fare nuove amicizie. Ma ovviamente la mia famiglia mi supporta ed è molto contenta che la galleria mi **f** .... (offrire) questa fantastica opportunità.

17.10

2 Now play Conversation 2 again, but this time you will play Cristian's role. Speak in the pauses provided. Say how he feels about leaving and what he fears.

SKILL BUILDER

1 These are lines from Aicha's chat with her date. Rearrange the messages in the correct order.

1 Ciao! Ecco le informazioni sulla mostra: 10 ottobre al Condominio Arte di Milano.

- **a** Allora forse ci vediamo là. Ci vai con qualcuno?
- **b** Se vuoi ci andiamo insieme...
- **c** Perfetto! Secondo me è una mostra super interessante e spero che ci sia molta gente a vederla. Anche io ci andrò.
- **d** Veramente no... temo che i miei amici non siano interessati all'arte!
- **e** Finalmente me lo hai chiesto! ☺ ☺ benissimo e dopo andiamo a cena fuori!
- **f** Ciao! Ecco le informazioni sulla mostra: 10 ottobre al Condominio Arte di Milano
- **g** Grazie mille! Me le segno e ci andrò sicuramente.

2 Aicha keeps telling Annalisa about her date. Complete the conversation with the correct combined pronouns from the list.

glielo	te lo	me lo

Aicha Ci siamo scritti molti messaggi riguardo alla mostra e non ho capito se voleva andarci con me ma alla fine **a** .... ha chiesto!

Annalisa Dopo molti messaggi! **b** .... ho detto che dovevi farlo tu fin dall'inizio.

Aicha Sì, ma anche io non sono così coraggiosa. E poi lo ho invitato al ristorante.

Annalisa E lui cosa ti ha risposto?

Aicha Ha detto di sì. Ho scelto un buon ristorante e ora **c** .... comunico.

3 **Read these two profiles and decide if the people are compatible. Write a short paragraph to explain why or why not.**

COFFEELOVER91	SEMPREINVIAGGIO87
Caratteristiche: riflessivo, tranquillo, razionale	**Caratteristiche:** dinamico, curioso, ottimista, pragmatico
Hobby: Leggere, vivere nei caffè. Appassionato di cinema	**Hobby:** viaggiare, esplorare, conoscere il mondo. Giocare a pallavolo.
Non ama: il fumo, la vita spartana, le estati calde, le discoteche	**Non ama:** le sigarette, la vita sedentaria, le persone pessimiste.
Ama: l'inverno, le conversazioni intelligenti	**Ama:** la musica latino-americana e uscire con gli amici

17.11

4 **Listen to this voice message and answer the requests using the correct combined pronouns.**

TEST YOURSELF

Complete the following sentences with the subjunctive of the verbs in brackets.

a Temo che Annalisa .... (avere) ragione: questa persona non è molto interessata ad Aicha.

b Petra è felice che Cristian .... (partire) per New York.

c Cristian ha paura che Venezia gli .... (mancare).

d "Mi dispiace che tu non .... (stare) bene!"

e Petra non vede l'ora che Cristian .... (vivere) a New York: così lo andrà a trovare.

La misteriosa donna in soffitta

The mysterious woman in the attic

In questa unità abbiamo parlato di amore e sentimenti, ma qual è il contrario di amore? La lettera iniziale di questa parola è la prossima lettera del nome della donna misteriosa nel quadro.

Remember to use **My review** and **My takeaway** to assess your progress and reflect on your learning experience.

18

In this unit you will learn how to:

- » Tell a story using a wide range of past tenses.
- » Present facts using the passive.
- » Explain cause and effect.
- » Use suffixes for added meaning.

Che storia!

My study plan

I plan to work with Unit 18

- ◯ Every day
- ◯ Twice a week
- ◯ Other ___________

I plan to study for

- ◯ 5–15 minutes
- ◯ 15–30 minutes
- ◯ 30–45+ minutes

My progress tracker

Day / Date					
	◯	◯	◯	◯	◯
	◯	◯	◯	◯	◯
	◯	◯	◯	◯	◯
	◯	◯	◯	◯	◯
	◯	◯	◯	◯	◯
	◯	◯	◯	◯	◯
	◯	◯	◯	◯	◯

My goals

What do you want to be able to do or say in Italian when you complete this unit?

		Done
1	....	◯
2	....	◯
3	....	◯

My review

SELF CHECK

	I can ...
●	... tell a story using a wide range of past tenses, including the pluperfect.
●	... present facts using the passive form.
●	... use suffixes for added meaning.
●	... explain cause and effect.
●	... talk about Italian festivals and cultural events.

CULTURE POINT 1

In viaggio tra le parole *A journey through words*

Ogni anno in Italia è possibile partecipare a molti festival letterari (*literary festivals*) lungo tutta la penisola. Un viaggio attraverso il cuore della letteratura di ogni genere (*genre*): romanzi (*novels*), gialli (*crime stories*), poesia (*poetry*). Da Mantova a Roma, da Lucca a Torino, queste manifestazioni culturali (*cultural events*) conquistano gli amanti delle parole grazie a incontri straordinari con autori nazionali e internazionali. La più importante manifestazione italiana dedicata all'editoria (*publishing industry*) è "Il Salone di Libro" di Torino, dove la magia della narrativa crea dibattiti appassionati che ispirano il dialogo culturale. Non meno famoso, il "festival*filosofia*" di Modena, con eventi dedicati (*dedicated*) al mondo della filosofia. Ma c'è un festival per tutti i gusti (*tastes*) letterari: a novembre troviamo il "Lucca Comics", un paradiso per gli amanti dei fumetti (*comics*), giochi di ruolo e cosplay. È il primo festival in Europa e, nel mondo, è secondo solo al suo collega giapponese, il "Comiket" di Tokyo.

Vai sul sito del festival*filosofia* di Modena.

Esplora le varie pagine e cerca nell'Archivio le Audio Lezioni. Prova a guardare un video su un tema che ti interessa. Quanto italiano riesci a capire?

VOCABULARY BUILDER 1

Look at the words and phrases and complete the missing English words and expressions. Then listen and try to imitate the pronunciation of the speakers.

EVENTI E FESTIVAL	*EVENTS AND FESTIVALS*
affollato/a	*crowded*
la casa editrice	*publishing house*
la copia	*copy*
il costume	....
l'editoria	*publishing industry*
l'esperto	....
l'esibizione	*performance*
il fumetto	....
la gara	*competition*
il genere	....
l'intrattenimento	*entertainment*
la manifestazione	*event*
l'ospite	*guest*
il palcoscenico	*stage*
il pubblico	....
lo spettacolo	*show*
la stampa	*press*

VERBI UTILI	*USEFUL VERBS*
organizzare	....
partecipare	....
produrre	....
promuovere	....
pubblicare	....
stampare	*to print*
travestirsi	*to dress up in costume*

Vocabulary practice 1

Find the word for each definition.

1 .... **a** una persona invitata a partecipare a un evento.

2 .... **b** la parte di un teatro o di un luogo in cui gli attori o gli artisti fanno uno spettacolo davanti al pubblico.

3 .... **c** un evento o una performance pubblica, come un concerto, un film.

4 .... **d** un gruppo di persone che guarda un evento, uno spettacolo.

5 .... **e** un abbigliamento o un abito indossato da una persona in occasioni particolari o come parte di una tradizione culturale o storica.

6 .... **f** un'azienda che pubblica libri, riviste o altri materiali stampati.

CONVERSATION 1

Un nuovo fumetto *A new comic*

1 Here are a few words and expressions to help you understand the following conversation. Note their meanings.

Peccato!	*Shame!*	Fico!	*Cool!*
Non ce l'ho fatta.	*I couldn't make it.*	una ninfa	*a nymph*

2 Listen to the conversation without looking at the text. Then listen again and read the text. Pay attention to how Cristian tells the plot of the comics he has recently discovered.

Cristian è appena tornato dalla Toscana, dove ha partecipato al Lucca Comics, un festival di fumetti internazionale. Durante un aperitivo con Matteo, Cristian racconta qualche dettaglio sull'evento e sulle sue scoperte.

Matteo Allora? Il Lucca Comics? Ti sei travestito?

Cristian Ci avevo pensato, ma ho avuto troppo lavoro.

Matteo Peccato, mi avevi detto di una gara per il miglior costume.

Cristian Sì, ero già andato a informarmi in un negozio specializzato, ma poi non ce l'ho fatta. Però, a Lucca ho scoperto un nuovo fumetto. Viene prodotto da una casa editrice di Kyoto ed è pubblicato dagli autori solo in giapponese.

Matteo Fico, di cosa parla?

Cristian Di una ninfa, che è stata abbandonata dai genitori. Lei non lo sa, ma è la principessa di un mondo parallelo e verrà cresciuta da un orso bianco. Ho una copia, vuoi vederla?

3 Answer the questions in Italian.

- **a** Perché Cristian non si è travestito?
- **b** In che lingue è pubblicato il fumetto che ha scoperto Cristian?
- **c** Cristian ha comprato il fumetto?

LANGUAGE BUILDER 1

Language discovery 1

Look at the sentence pairs.

Una casa editrice lo produce.	Viene prodotto da una casa editrice.
I genitori hanno abbandonato la ninfa.	Una ninfa è stata abbandonata dai genitori.

What's the difference between the first and the second sentence in each pair? Why do you think the second form is used in the conversation?

Passive sentences

The passive voice is used to focus on the action itself or those affected by it, rather than on who's performing it. It's like talking about something that's happening to you, rather than something you're doing. It works very much like it does in English: the direct object becomes the subject, the verb essere carries the tense and is combined with the past participle of the main verb. Additionally, the active subject is introduced by the preposition da (in English, it's *by*).

Gli autori pubblicano il fumetto.	(active form)	*The authors publish the comic.*
Il fumetto è pubblicato dagli autori.	(passive form)	*The comic is published by the authors.*
I romani hanno costruito questa strada.	(active form)	*Romans built this road.*
Questa strada è stata costruita dai romani.	(passive form)	*This road was built by Romans.*
I ladri hanno rubato alcuni quadri.	(active form)	*Thieves stole some paintings.*
Alcuni quadri sono stati rubati (dai ladri).	(passive form)	*Some paintings were stolen (by thieves).*

The verb venire can be used instead of essere; however, only when the active verb is in a simple tense (i.e., consists of a single word, not two, like passato prossimo).

Il fumetto è prodotto da una casa editrice di Kyoto. = Il fumetto viene prodotto da una casa editrice di Kyoto.	*The comic is produced by a publishing house in Kyoto.*
La ninfa è stata abbandonata dai genitori. = La ninfa è venuta abbandonata dai genitori	*The nymph has been abandoned by her parents.*

Remember that the verb venire is irregular in the present tense: vengo, vieni, viene, veniamo, venite, vengono.

Language practice 1

18.04

Listen to the sentences. Five of them are passive—which ones? Write them down, then turn them into active sentences.

.... **I (forma attiva) =** ....

....

.... **I (forma attiva) =** ....

....

.... **I (forma attiva) =** ....

....

.... **I (forma attiva) =** ....

....

.... **I (forma attiva) =** ....

....

LANGUAGE BUILDER 2

Language discovery 2

Listen to the conversation again and repeat each line in the pauses provided. Then complete this sentence you heard.

Ci **a** .... pensato, ma poi **b** .... avuto troppo lavoro.

How do these two verbs differ from each other? What do you think might be the reason? Can you spot the other two similar verb forms in the conversation?

Il trapassato prossimo

The trapassato prossimo is a past tense used to talk about actions that happened before another action or moment in the past. It's like the past of the past. To form it, take the imperfetto form of the verb avere or essere and add the past participle of the main verb.

Mi avevi detto di una gara.	You had told me about a competition.
Ero già andato.	I had already gone.

It's used to make clear the sequence of past events.

Quando sono arrivato in ufficio, Laura era già uscita.	*When I arrived at the office, Laura had already left.*
Ci avevo pensato, ma poi ho avuto troppo lavoro.	*I had thought about it, but then I had too much work to do.*
Ero già andato a informarmi, ma poi non ce l'ho fatta.	*I had already gone to find out, but then I could not make it.*

Language practice 2

1 Match the sentence halves and complete with the correct form of the trapassato prossimo.

1 Quando siamo arrivati in classe
2 .... (comprare) un libro per Mia,
3 Izumi mi ha detto che non conosceva
4 .... già .... (prenotare) i biglietti per il festival
5 Ieri sono tornata a Roma anche se
6 .... appena .... (arrivare - noi) all'ingresso della mostra,

a ma ho scoperto che ne aveva già una copia.
b quando ci hanno detto che i biglietti erano esauriti.
c ci .... già .... (andare) due settimane fa.
d gli esperti che .... (parlare) all'evento.
e la lezione .... già .... (cominciare).
f ma non siamo potute andare.

18.06

2 **Now play Conversation 1 again, but this time you play Cristian's role. Speak in the pauses provided. Try not to refer to the text and make up your own story plot for a comic book. Make sure to use at least a passive form and a trapassato prossimo.**

CULTURE POINT 2

La Mostra del cinema di Venezia *Venice Film Festival*

La Mostra internazionale d'arte cinematografica, anche nota come (*a.k.a.*) Mostra del Cinema di Venezia, è un festival cinematografico annuale che si svolge (*takes place*) tra la fine di agosto e l'inizio di settembre nello storico Palazzo del Cinema e in altri luoghi attorno alla laguna (*around the lagoon*). Organizzato dalla Biennale di Venezia, un famoso festival culturale, questo festival del cinema è più antico al mondo, inaugurato (*launched*) già nel 1932. La Mostra del Cinema di Venezia premia (*awards*) i migliori film con il Leone d'oro, in onore del (*in honor of*) Leone simbolo di San Marco: questo riconoscimento (*recognition*) è molto amato dalla critica (*critics*) ed è paragonabile (*comparable*) ai premi di altri importanti festival europei come la Palma d'oro del Festival di Cannes e l'Orso d'oro del Festival internazionale del cinema di Berlino.

Esplora la sezione cinema del sito web della Biennale di Venezia:

a Quali film saranno presentati quest'anno?

b C'è una premiere in particolare a cui vorresti partecipare?

VOCABULARY BUILDER 2

18.07

Look at the words and phrases and complete the missing English words and expressions. Then listen and try to imitate the pronunciation of the speakers.

CINEMA E ARTE	*CINEMA AND ART*
acclamato/a	*acclaimed*
la capacità	*ability, skill*
la critica	....
il curatore/la curatrice	....
la premiazione	*award ceremony*
il premio/il premio Oscar	..................../*Academy Award*
prestigioso/a	....
la proiezione	*show*
il protagonista/la protagonista	....
il/la regista	*director*
il riconoscimento/il successo	*recognition/success*
il ruolo/la parte	*role, part*

VERBI E PAROLE UTILI	*USEFUL WORDS AND VERBS*
a tal punto	*so that*
applaudire	*to clap*
dirigere	*to manage*
inaugurare	....
interpretare	*to perform*
recitare	*to act*
in modo che	*in order to, so that*
premiare	....
si svolge/ si tiene	*takes place*
valutare	*to evaluate*
incuriosire	*to intrigue*

Vocabulary practice 2

Read the paragraph and complete the gaps with the provided words.

critica	protagonista	capacità	ruoli	ha recitato (x2)
premi	premio	è stata inaugurata		

Sophia Loren è un'icona del cinema italiano. Nata in Italia nel 1934, ha vinto **a** .... prestigiosi e **b** .... accanto a grandi attori, grazie alla sua **c** .... di interpretare **d** .... molto diversi. Nel 1962, ha vinto il **e** .... Oscar come miglior attrice **f** .... per il film *La ciociara*. Nel corso della sua carriera, **g** .... in film molto acclamati dalla **h** .... La sua stella nella Hollywood Walk of Fame **i** .... nel 1994 e, ancora oggi, questa grande attrice continua a ispirare con il suo talento nuove generazioni di artisti.

CONVERSATION 2

Un incontro inaspettato *An unexpected encounter*

18.08

Here are a few words and expressions to help you understand the following conversation. Note their meanings.

potrebbe attivarsi	*might activate*
mi ha incuriosito	*it intrigued me*
non penso ad altro	*I haven't thought of anything else*

18.09

1 Listen to the conversation without looking at the text. Then listen again and read the text.

Durante un evento della Mostra Internazionale del Cinema di Venezia, Cristian conosce Liang Ferretti, il direttore di una famosa galleria d'arte fuori Venezia. La conversazione tra i due sembra portare a qualcosa di interessante.

Cristian Che serataccia!

Liang Vero? Piove così tanto che potrebbe attivarsi il MOSE. Le è piaciuta la proiezione? Il regista è un amico.

Cristian Moltissimo, questo film è stato un successone, molto acclamato dalla critica. La protagonista mi ricorda un dipinto su cui sto lavorando.

Liang Che dipinto?

Cristian Nel mio appartamento ho trovato un antico dipinto di una donna e mi ha incuriosito a tal punto che da mesi non penso ad altro.

Liang È un esperto?

Cristian Un pochino, insegno storia dell'arte.

Liang Lei è troppo modesto. Dirigo una galleria d'arte, perché non mi manda il curriculum, in modo che io possa valutare personalmente le sue capacità? Poi, se vuole, cerchiamo insieme l'identità di questa donna!

2 **Which of the following statements can be inferred from the conversation?**

a È una bella serata.
b Cristian e Liang hanno appena finito di vedere un film.
c La proiezione non è piaciuta molto al pubblico.
d La protagonista sembra la signora del dipinto.
e Liang è un esperto di cinema contemporaneo.

LANGUAGE BUILDER 3

Language discovery 3

Consider these words from the conversation. How do you believe their meaning has evolved? Are they intended to suggest something of lesser, greater, or negative significance?

	Più piccolo	Più grande	Valore negativo
a una serata > una seratacce			
b un successo > un successone			
c un poco > un pochino			

Suffixes for nouns and adjectives

The use of suffixes is a common way to add meaning to nouns and adjectives. Changing the ending of the word can indicate its size or even express a negative opinion. The suffix -ino/-ina, for example, indicates a small size. The noun cucchiaio (*spoon*) becomes cucchiaino (*teaspoon, little spoon*).

È un esperto?–Un pochino.	*Are you an expert?—A tiny bit.*
Ho comprato un nuovo tavolino da caffè.	*I bought a new coffee table* (lit. small table).
Ieri ho trovato una gattina abbandonata.	*Yesterday I found a small, abandoned kitten.*

To indicate largeness, use the suffix -one/-ona. For example, to state that a libro (*book*) is quite big, refer to it as un librone (*a big book*).

Questo film è stato un successone.	*This film was a big success.*
Pilar è una chiacchierona.	*Pilar is a chatterbox.*

Finally, some suffixes convey a negative quality: -accio/-accia. For example, erba (*grass*) becomes erbaccia (*weeds*). And then there's parolaccia (*a bad word, curse word*).

Che serataccia! — *What a miserable evening!*

Andiamo via, questo bar sembra un postaccio. — *Let's leave, this café seems like a bad place.*

There isn't a straightforward rule for knowing when to use these suffixes or when to use words like piccolo or grande. They can be learned by listening to how people speak and observing the different contexts in which these suffixes are used.

Language practice 3

Give the meaning of the following altered nouns.

a un gattone (gatto) = ...

b la mia sorellina (sorella) = ...

c un paesino (paese) = ...

d una vociona (voce) = ...

e un gestaccio (gesto) = ...

f una finestrina (finestra) = ...

g un bacione (bacio) = ...

h un votaccio (voto) = ...

LANGUAGE BUILDER 4

Language discovery 4

Listen to the conversation again and repeat each line in the pauses provided. Then complete the sentences you heard. What meaning do you think they impart to the conversation?

a Piove .... che potrebbe attivarsi il MOSE.

b Mi ha incuriosito .... che da mesi non penso ad altro

c Perché non mi manda il curriculum, che lo possa valutare personalmente?

Consecutive clauses

In Italian, conjunctions like così tanto ... che (*so much ... that*), quindi (*so*) or cosicché, tal punto che (*so that*) are often used to show the logical connection between events. Normally, these conjunctions are followed by the present or past tense or by the conditional.

Piove così tanto che potrebbe attivarsi il MOSE. | *It's raining so much that the MOSE could activate.*

Non so bene cosa è successo, quindi preferisco non parlare. | *I am not sure about what happened, so I prefer not to speak about it.*

Eravamo stanchi a tal punto che ci siamo addormentati sul divano. | *We were so tired (to the point) that we fell asleep on the sofa.*

However, in modo che (*so that, in order to*) requires the subjunctive in the clause that follows.

Perché non mi manda il curriculum, in modo che io possa valutare personalmente? | *Why don't you send me your CV, so that I can evaluate it personally?*

Il regista parla inglese, in modo che tutti lo capiscano. | *The director speaks English so that everyone can understand him.*

Language practice 4

1 Choose the correct phrase to complete the sentece.

a La proiezione ha avuto successo a tal punto che / in modo che il pubblico ha cominciato ad applaudire

b L'attrice era così famosa che / in modo che non sarebbe potuta uscire senza una protezione.

c L'attore protagonista sarà premiato per ultimo a tal punto che / in modo che in sala rimanga un po' di suspence.

d Non ho comprato i biglietti per la premiere quindi / in modo che non posso partecipare.

e La biennale di Venezia si svolge in numerosi luoghi quindi / in modo che i partecipanti possano ammirare la bellezza di tutta la laguna.

f La premiazione è fissata per le 22:00, a tal punto che / in modo che tutti siano pronti.

g Andrea era distratto a tal punto che / in modo che ha perso il momento della sua premiazione.

18.11

2 Now play Conversation 2 again, but this time play Liang's role. Feel free to personalize the conversation and describe your own job instead. Speak in the pauses provided. Try not to refer to the text.

SKILL BUILDER

1 Transform the sentences from present to past, using passato prossimo, imperfetto, and trapassato prossimo.

Example: Jan dice che hai studiato il trapassato prossimo. *Yan ha detto che avevi studiato il trapassato prossimo*

a Oggi finisco la presentazione del libro che ho cominciato la settimana passata.
b Capisco perché quel film non ha vinto il premio.
c Lia non riconosce gli attori che sono entrati.
d Vado alla premiazione, perché Sara mi ha regalato i biglietti.
e Riporto in biblioteca il libro che ho letto.
f Lui mangia meglio, perché glielo ha consigliato il medico.

2 Use the clues to complete the crossword.

1
2
3
4
5
6
7

Orizzontali

2 una gatta piccola
5 un tavolo grande
6 una brutta figura
7 un favore grande

Verticali

1 un libro piccolo
3 un bicchiere piccolo
4 una parola brutta

3 Change these sentences from active to passive form.

a Durante il festival, il regista ha presentato il suo nuovo film. > ....
b Il presentatore ha premiato gli attori più bravi. > ....
c Domenica la pittrice aprirà una nuova galleria in centro. > ....
d Questo cinema dà solo film commerciali. > ....
e Da bambina, mia zia portava sempre me e i miei cugini alle mostre di arte moderna. > ....
f Lo scrittore ha ricevuto molti applausi durante la presentazione. > ....

 4 **Read the article adapted from *Il Corriere della sera* and answer the questions.**

LA MOSTRA INTERNAZIONALE DI ARCHITETTURA DELLA BIENNALE DI VENEZIA VUOLE PROVARE A CAMBIARE LE COSE

«A noi è già successo molto di quanto sta accadendo al resto del mondo. Confrontiamoci per capire dove abbiamo sbagliato finora e come deve essere affrontato il futuro».
Questa affermazione di Lesley Lokko, curatrice della diciottesima Mostra Internazionale di Architettura della Biennale di Venezia 2023, aperta al pubblico da sabato 20 maggio, è una fotografia di cosa aspettarsi da questa edizione. Il 'noi' si riferisce all'Africa e, non a caso, oltre la metà dei partecipanti alla mostra provengono da qui o hanno qui le loro radici. E se il continente africano da anni è spesso menzionato come il posto che guiderà il pianeta negli anni a venire, questa stessa predizione la possiamo ritrovare nel titolo scelto dalla architetta, docente di architettura e scrittrice Lesley Lokko: The Laboratory of the Future.
«Un laboratorio del futuro non può non avere un punto di partenza preciso, o una o più ipotesi in cerca di verifica – ha dichiarato il Presidente della Biennale Roberto Cicutto. La Curatrice parte dal suo continente di origine, l'Africa, per raccontarne tutte le criticità storiche, economiche, climatiche e politiche». I due grandi temi affrontati dai lavori in mostra sono la decolonizzazione e la decarbonizzazione, due processi che sono sicuramente centrali dell'Africa e che riguardano con grande attualità tutti i territori del pianeta su diversi aspetti.
Fuori concorso saranno ci saranno altri artisti, chiamati Guests from the Future (Ospiti dal Futuro), selezionati per il loro lavoro innovativo a tutti i livelli e in molteplici contesti, dal reale all'immaginario perché, come ha ricordato Lesley Lokko, «È impossibile costruire un mondo migliore se prima non lo immaginiamo».

from *Il Corriere della sera*
(https://living.corriere.it/architettura/biennale-architettura-2023/)

a Chi è Lesley Lokko e quale ruolo svolge nella diciottesima Mostra Internazionale di Architettura della Biennale di Venezia 2023?
b Quali sono i due grandi temi affrontati dai lavori in mostra durante questa edizione?
c Cosa significa "The Laboratory of the Future" nel contesto della Mostra?
d Che significato ha l'espressione "Guests from the Future" (Ospiti dal Futuro) in questa manifestazione?
e Qual è il messaggio principale che Lesley Lokko vuole trasmettere attraverso l'idea di un "laboratorio del future"?

18.12

5 **Listen to this piece of news. Then summarize what you hear.**

....

....

....

....

TEST YOURSELF

You are at the Mostra Internazionale del Cinema, after a new show. Take part in the following conversation with Liang Ferretti, following the given prompts.

Liang Le è piaciuto il film?

You **a** (Say yes, it was very interesting, a big success. Add that, before this one, you had already seen other films by the director and they are all great.)

Liang Sono d'accordo. Ho letto che la critica era entusiasta!

You **b** (Say that it's true, the film has already been mentioned by several magazines and news outlets.)

Liang C'è un film in particolare che consiglierebbe?

You **c** (Mention the film "Portrait of a young cat." Say the main actor was so incredible in their role that they won an Academy Award.)

Liang Sembra davvero interessante. Grazie per il consiglio, lo guarderò sicuramente!

La misteriosa donna in soffitta *The mysterious woman in the attic*

Ricordi il nome del luogo principale in cui si svolge la Mostra del Cinema di Venezia? La lettera iniziale di questo posto ti darà una delle lettere finali per costruire il nome della misteriosa donna del quadro. Ci siamo quasi!

Remember to use **My review** and **My takeaway** to assess your progress and reflect on your learning experience.

19

In this unit you will learn how to:

- Discuss civic responsibility and rules.
- Talk about civic duties using **andare** + participle.
- Express opinions, agree or disagree using the subjunctive.
- Express the goal of an action with **per/ affinché**.

Cosa va fatto?

My study plan

I plan to work with Unit 19

○ Every day

○ Twice a week

○ Other ________

I plan to study for

○ 5–15 minutes

○ 15–30 minutes

○ 30–45+ minutes

My progress tracker

Day / Date	Listening	Speaking	Reading	Writing	Conversation
	○	○	○	○	○
	○	○	○	○	○
	○	○	○	○	○
	○	○	○	○	○
	○	○	○	○	○
	○	○	○	○	○
	○	○	○	○	○

My goals

What do you want to be able to do or say in Italian when you complete this unit?

		Done
1	....	○
2	....	○
3	....	○

My review

SELF CHECK

	I can ...
●	... discuss the rules of living together in a city.
●	... express the goal of an action.
●	... express an opinion.
●	... express a duty.

CULTURE POINT 1

Antico o moderno? *Ancient or modern?*

Il patrimonio culturale (*cultural heritage*) dell'Italia è uno dei più grandi al mondo. La tutela (*protection*) di questo patrimonio è difficile e costosa e richiede (*requires*) molta cura e senso civico (*civic sense*). Trasformare l'Italia in un paese completamente moderno spesso è in conflitto con l'idea di preservare (*to preserve*) l'antico. Per esempio, non molte città italiane hanno la metropolitana, o hanno solo poche linee, perché quando si scava (*excavate*), si trovano molti resti archeologici antichi. Alcune stazioni della metropolitana sono dei veri musei sottoterra (*underground*). Inoltre, le città italiane hanno i centri pieni di palazzi storici. Costruire edifici nuovi significa cambiare l'aspetto (*look*) delle città. Per esempio, a Modena, nel 1997, il Comune (*municipality*) ha commissionato una torre moderna e futuristica all'architetto americano Frank Gehry, ma i cittadini hanno firmato una petizione (*signed a petition*) per non costruire questo monumento così architettonicamente disomogeneo (*lack of accord*). È necessario anche proteggere il patrimonio artistico dai frequenti atti di vandalismo (*vandalism*). Un esempio di arte moderna che spesso è interpretato come vandalismo sono i graffiti. In alcuni casi, i graffiti riqualificano (*redevelop*) vecchi edifici, in altri li rovinano (*ruin*).

Guarda il sito del 39C Bolzano Graffiti Jam, organizzato dal gruppo Volontarius.

Qual è l'obiettivo di questo festival?

VOCABULARY BUILDER 1

Look at the words and phrases and complete the missing English words and expressions. Then listen and try to imitate the pronunciation of the speakers.

ANTICO E MODERNO	*ANCIENT AND MODERN*
il patrimonio	....
l'arte di strada	*street art*
lo spazio pubblico	*public space*
la tutela	*protection*
il graffito	*graffiti*
il muro	*wall*
l'iniziativa	....
preservare/ conservare	....
promuovere	*to promote*
la generazione	*generation*
valorizzare	*to enhance*
riqualificare	....
restaurare	*to restore*

The word muro has a regular plural: muri, when talking about, for instance, the walls of a house, or just a number of walls. When referring to the city walls, however, the plural is irregular: mura.

Almost all Italian cities have mura (or the remnants of them), as they were built in the Middle Ages to protect the citizens from the frequent invasions that occurred.

IL SENSO CIVICO	*CIVIC SENSE*
denunciare	*to report*
la polizia	....
l'atto di vandalismo	....
il vandalo/la vandala	*vandal*
il cittadino/la cittadina	*citizen*
sporcare	*to soil*
pulire	*to clean*
trascurare	*to neglect*
il reato	*crime/offense*
rovinare	*to damage*

Vocabulary practice 1

Match the word with their opposites (a–e).

1 pulire
2 valorizzare
3 il reato
4 preservare
5 l'atto di vandalismo

a la tutela
b trascurare
c sporcare
d la polizia
e rovinare

CONVERSATION 1

Arte o vandalismo? *Art or vandalism?*

19.02

1 Here are a few words and expressions to help you understand the following conversation. Note their meanings.

cancellato	*deleted*	intatto	*intact*
è un pugno in un occhio	*it's an eyesore*		

19.03

2 Listen to the conversation without looking at the text. Then listen again and follow along in the text. Pay attention to how the two friends talk about what must be done to preserve the city and protect its cultural heritage.

Matteo e Cristian stanno facendo una passeggiata nel centro di Venezia e Matteo nota un nuovo graffito sul muro di un palazzo.

Matteo Guarda che bello quel graffito! Finalmente un po' di colore su un muro vecchio!

Cristian No! Secondo me, va cancellato subito e il muro va pulito! E i vandali che lo hanno fatto vanno denunciati alla polizia!

Matteo Come sei estremo! Quel muro non è antico, è solo vecchio. Ci sono molti spazi pubblici che vanno valorizzati con arte moderna per riqualificare la città.

Cristian I graffiti non riqualificano: sporcano e rovinano il nostro patrimonio, che va protetto affinché le generazioni future lo abbiano intatto.

Matteo Sí, ma dipende. Dobbiamo preservare l'antico ma anche promuovere le iniziative artistiche nuove.

Cristian Per offrire ai turisti e ai cittadini una bella immagine delle nostre città l'estetica va curata in ogni dettaglio. Quel muro è davvero un pugno in un occhio!

3 Which of the following sentences could have been said by Matteo (M) or Cristian (C)?

- **a** L'arte di strada è spesso brutta. M C
- **b** Le città tutte antiche sono belle. M C
- **c** Mi piace dare spazio agli artisti emergenti. M C
- **d** È importante combinare l'antico e il nuovo. M C
- **e** L'arte di strada rovina il patrimonio culturale antico. M C
- **f** Ci sono tanti modi per riqualificare gli spazi pubblici. M C

LANGUAGE BUILDER 1

Language discovery 1

Look at the sentences from the conversation where Cristian and Matteo talk about what must be done. Can you infer how to express duty in Italian?

Il graffito va cancellato.
Il muro va pulito.
I vandali vanno denunciati alla polizia.
L'estetica va curata in ogni dettaglio.

Cosa va fatto? Expressing duty

In Italian there are a few ways to express that something must be done. One way is to use the expression si deve followed by the infinitive of the verb expressing what must be done.

Si deve rispettare il patrimonio artistico. *The artistic heritage must be respected.*

Another way is to use the verb andare + past participle.

Il muro va pulito. *The wall must be cleaned.*

The past participle agrees in number and gender with the subject.

	Subject	Andare	Participle
Singular	il muro	va	pulito
	la casa	va	pulita
Plural	i vandali	vanno	denunciati
	le persone	vanno	denunciate

Il dipinto va restaurato. *The painting must be restored.*

Piú piste ciclabili vanno realizzati. *More bike lanes must be built.*

In this context, andare can also be used in other tenses, such as the imperfetto, the conditional, and the future: Questo andava/andrà/andrebbe fatto. This had to be/will be/should be done.

Language practice 1

Make sentences with the elements below to express a duty with andare. These sentences constitute a toolkit of civic sense. Sei d'accordo?

a pulire – lo spazio pubblico
b rispettare – il codice della strada
c non – usare – il telefono – in macchina
d pagare – le tasse
e preservare – gli spazi verdi
f non – lasciare – la spazzatura- in strada
g non – sporcare – i mezzi di trasporto

LANGUAGE BUILDER 2

Language discovery 2

19.04

Listen to the conversation again and repeat each line in the pauses provided. Then complete the sentences. How does the speaker express the goal of an action? What tense is used after affinché and per?

a Il patrimonio culturale va protetto affinché le generazioni future lo .... intatto.

b Ci sono molti spazi pubblici che vanno valorizzati per .... la città.

c Per .... offrire ai turisti e ai cittadini una bella imagine della città, l'estetica va curata in ogni dettaglio.

Expressing purpose

To express the purpose or goal of an action, use per with a verb in the infinitive, as long as the subject of both actions is the same:

Lavoriamo per valorizzare la città. — *We work to enhance the city. (we work and we enhance the city)*

Dobbiamo lavorare per proteggere l'ambiente. — *We need to work to protect the environment. (we work and we protect the environment)*

When the subjects are different, use affinché (*so that, in order that*) followed by a verb in the subjunctive, which agrees in number with the new subject:

Lavoriamo affinché la città sia pulita. — *We work so that the city is clean.*

Same subject	per	infinitive
Different subjects	affinché	subjunctive

Language practice 2

1 Attach the correct final clauses (a–e) to the sentences (1–5) by using either per with infinitive or affinché with subjunctive.

1 I cittadini rispettano le leggi
2 Ho telefonato alla polizia
3 Valorizziamo il patrimonio
4 Firmiamo una petizione
5 Promuoviamo gli artisti giovani

a denunciare i vandali
b colorare i muri vecchi
c la società – essere – migliore
d i graffiti – essere – cancellati
e le generazioni future – ereditare – la nostra arte

19.05

2 Now play Conversation 1 again. Express your opinion: what must be done with graffiti?

CULTURE POINT 2

Acqua alta a Venezia *High tide in Venice*

L'acqua alta è un fenomeno normale a Venezia, che fa parte della vita dei veneziani da secoli (*centuries*). L'acqua alta è più frequente nei mesi di novembre e dicembre. Ci sono sirene (*sirens*) che allertano i cittadini dell'arrivo della marea (*tide, flood*) così che le persone possono raggiungere i percorsi pedonali protetti (*protected pedestrian areas*). I servizi di trasporto di navigazione sono comunque garantiti. È importante in ogni caso avere un paio di stivali di gomma (*a pair of rubber boots*) alti fino al ginocchio! Ci sono però alcune aree della città che sono più basse, come la piazza San Marco e il ponte di Rialto, dove ci sono palazzi ed edifici antichi e bellissimi. In queste aree l'acqua alta può essere molto pericolosa. Per questo, dal 2020 è attivo il sistema di barriere del MOSE, che previene (*prevents*) l'allagamento (*flooding*) della città. È l'amministrazione del MOSE che deve decidere quando attivare il MOSE sulla base delle previsioni (*forecasts*) della marea. Spesso una decisione tempestiva (*timely*) può fare la differenza!

Un'alluvione a Venezia, 2019

Se vuoi avere più informazioni sul fenomeno dell'acqua alta guarda i video sul sito della città di Venezia.

VOCABULARY BUILDER 2

Look at the words and phrases and complete the missing English words and expressions. Then listen and try to imitate the pronunciation of the speakers.

ESPRIMERE UN' OPINIONE	*EXPRESSING AN OPINION*
Secondo me	*in my opinion*
supporre	*to suppose*
ritenere	*to maintain*
Mi pare che..	*It seems to me that ...*
da un lato... dall'altro	*on one hand ... on the other hand*
essere d'accordo	....
essere contrario/a/* a qualcosa	*to be against something*
convincere	....
sono convinto/a/*	*I'm convinced*
dubitare	*to doubt*

COME USARE UNA MACCHINA	*HOW TO OPERATE A MACHINE*
accendere	*to turn on*
acceso/a	*on*
spegnere	*to turn off*
spento/a	....
sollevare	*to lift*
abbassare	*to lower*
attivare	....
premere un tasto	*to press the button*
spostare	*to move/to displace*
girare	*to turn/rotate*
attivare	*to activate*
arrestare	*to stop*
la leva	*lever*

Vocabulary practice 2

Complete the following sentences.

a Non c'è elettricità: la macchina è ....

b Per accendere la TV, devi ....

c Per .... il sistema, usiamo il tasto rosso OFF.

d Karima è vegetariana perché .... alla violenza sugli animali.

e .... dobbiamo conservare il patrimonio culturale, ... promuovere l'arte moderna.

f Per attivare il sistema, bisogna .... la leva e per arrestarlo .... la leva.

CONVERSATION 2

Una decisione critica *A critical decision*

19.07

Here are a few words and expressions to help you understand the following conversation. Note their meanings.

andare sott'acqua	*to go underwater*

19.08

1 Listen to the conversation without looking at the text. Then listen again and follow along in the text. Pay attention to how the characters express their opinions.

È un giorno di alta marea a Venezia e il livello dell'acqua aumenterà ancora. Ci vogliono 48 ore per preparare il sistema del MOSE e la decisione dipende dalle previsioni della marea. Molti ingegneri e operai lavorano per abbassare e sollevare le leve. Ascolta la conversazione tra Annalisa e la sua capa. Chi ha ragione? In ogni caso... prepara i tuoi stivali di gomma!

Capa	Annalisa, non credo che faccia nessuna differenza se attiviamo il MOSE.
Annalisa	Mi scusi, ma non sono d'accordo. Le previsioni dicono che domani ci sono 150 cm di alta marea. A questi livelli sono certa che San Marco va sott'acqua e tanti altri edifici antichi nella parte bassa della città. Occorre che lo attiviamo.
Capa	Da un lato le previsioni non sono sempre accurate; dall'altro per attivare il MOSE è necessario che molte persone lavorino per sei ore. Credo che vada fatta solo in casi di vera emergenza.
Annalisa	Sollevare e abbassare il MOSE è la mia competenza e so che è complesso. Ma credo che dobbiamo farlo ora. Penso che sia assolutamente necessario.
Capa	Ne sei proprio convinta? La responsabilità è tua!
Annalisa	Certo. Attiviamo il MOSE!

2 Answer the following questions in Italian.

a Perché Annalisa vuole attivare il MOSE?
b Perché la sua capa è contraria?
c Qual è la decisione finale?

LANGUAGE BUILDER 3

Language discovery 3

Look at the sentences from the conversation. Some of the verbs after che are in the subjunctive, while others are in the present tense. Why are they different?

Non credo che faccia nessuna differenza se attiviamo il MOSE.
Le previsioni dicono che domani ci sono 150 cm di acqua.
Sono certa che San Marco va sott'acqua.
Credo che vada fatta solo in casi di emergenza.
Penso che sia assolutamente necessario.

The subjunctive with verbs of opinion

Unit 17 looked at subjective sentences using the subjunctive. When the action is not perceived as real, but rather as a reflection of the subject's feelings, the verb after che appears in the subjunctive. The same is true for opinions.

The main verbs of opinion are: pensare, credere, supporre, ritenere, immaginare, dubitare. Expressions like mi sembra / mi pare also need to be followed by the subjunctive.

Penso che i graffiti valorizzino la città.	*I think that grafitti enhances the city.*
Sembra che siano in ritardo.	*It seems that they're late.*
Dubito che vengano.	*I doubt they're coming.*

When expressing a certainty, the verb is in the simple present: Sono certo/a/* che è necessario. However, if the subject is not certain, then the subjunctive is needed: Non sono convinto/a/* che sia necessario.

With verbs like dire, annunciare, leggere, which indicate a factual report, the verb is always in the present tense: Dicono che domani piove.

Verbs that end in -porre, like supporre, are irregular in the present tense, inserting -ng- before the ending in the io and loro forms: io suppongo, tu supponi, lui/lei/Lei suppone, noi supponiamo, voi supponete, loro suppongono. Verbs ending in -porre include: comporre (*to compose*) and opporre (*to oppose*), among others. The verb ritenere is a compound of ri + tenere, so it follows the same pattern as tenere: io (ri)tengo, tu (ri)tieni, lui/lei/Lei (ri)tiene, noi (ri)teniamo, voi (ri) tenete, loro (ri)tengono. Notice the -ng- in the io and loro forms, as well as the e/ie stem change in the tu and lui/lei forms. Similar verbs are sostenere (*to sustain*) and contenere (*to contain*).

Language practice 3

1 Complete the sentences with the subjunctive or the indicative.

- **a** Credo che tu .... (essere) molto stanca.
- **b** Non sono certo che tu .... (avere) ragione.
- **c** Annalisa ha letto che domani il tempo .... fare) bello.
- **d** Cristian ha detto che sua sorella .... (andare) a Bolzano.

2 Make sentences using the subjunctive or indicative, as appropriate.

1. Dicono che...
2. La capa di Annalisa non è sicura che...
3. Annalisa pensa che...
4. Mi sembra che...
5. Noi immaginiamo che...
6. Ho letto che...
7. Le previsioni annunciano che...
8. Cristian è convinto che...

- **a** i graffiti e i murales – sporcare – i muri
- **b** il traffico – a Venezia – essere bloccato
- **c** la marea – arrivare – a 150ml
- **d** sollevare il MOSE – non essere – necessario
- **e** Venezia – essere – in pericolo
- **f** attivare il MOSE – essere – una buona idea
- **g** vivere a Venezia centro – non essere facile
- **h** Cristian ha un'opinione un po' estrema

LANGUAGE BUILDER 4

Language discovery 4

Listen to the conversation again and repeat each line in the pauses provided. Then look at the verbs after che in these sentences. Are they subjunctive or indicative? Can you guess why?

È necessario che molte persone lavorino. Occorre che lo attiviamo.

The subjunctive with impersonal expressions

Another instance which requires the subjunctive is following impersonal expressions, such as: è necessario che, bisogna che, occorre che (*it is necessary that ...*), which all indicate a duty. In fact, all expressions that start with è + adjective are usually followed by the subjunctive.

È necessario/bello che tu sia qui. *It is necessary/nice that you are here.*

In the conversation you heard the subjunctive of andare, fare, and dovere. Notice the pattern below.

	fare	andare		fare	andare
io	faccio = faccia	vado = vada	**noi**	facciamo	andiamo
tu	faccia	= vada	**voi**	facciate	andiate
lui/lei/Lei	faccia	= vada	**loro**	facciano	vadano

Remember that the first three persons of the subjunctive are always the same, and the noi form is the same as the present. Notice that fare uses the stem facc- throughout, whereas andare has a different stem in the noi and voi forms. The modal verbs potere and volere behave like fare, and their stems are vogl- and poss-. Dovere behaves like andare: deva, deva, deva, dobbiamo, dobbiate, devano.

Language practice 4

1 Complete the sentences with the verbs in this list.

facciate	vada	deva	andiamo	dobbiate	faccia

a C'è l'acqua alta: credo che .... portare gli stivali di gomma.

b Annalisa crede che il MOSE .... attivato ora.

c Bisogna che voi .... attenzione alle regole.

d Cristian crede che la città .... essere esattamente come era in passato.

e È necessario che tu .... questo esercizio.

f Credi che noi .... in macchina, ma in realtà prendiamo la bicicletta.

19.10

2 Now play Conversation 2 again. Answer the questions: Cosa crede Annalisa? Cosa crede la sua capa?

SKILL BUILDER

1 Complete the sentences with a goal for the action with either per + infinitive or affinché + subjunctive. For a complete list of verbs in the subjunctive see the Grammar Summary.

a È importante che i cittadini rispettino le leggi affinché....

b IL MOSE è attivato per...

c Bisogna leggere le previsioni delle maree per...

d Occorre avere cura del patrimonio artistico affinché....

e Vivere in modo sostenibile è necessario affinché....

2 The conversation below is the continuation of Annalisa's argument with her boss. Complete the conversation with the verbs of opinion in the subjunctive.

vada	possano	premano	funzioni	sia	pensi

Capa Dubito che gli ingegneri **a** .... cominciare a lavorare ora.

Annalisa Secondo me, sì. Mancano ancora 12 ore all'arrivo della marea. Credo che **b** .... totalmente possibile.

Capa **c** .... che il team abbia il tempo di venire? Abitano tutti lontano.

Annalisa Abbiamo attivato il sistema automatico no? È solo necessario che **d** .... il bottone.

Capa Mmm non sono certa che **e** .... già.

Annalisa Ma è importante che proviamo no? Dobbiamo fare tutto il possibile affinché Venezia non **f** .... sott'acqua adesso che abbiamo il sistema per proteggerla.

3 Read the text and choose the most appropriate title.

Nel novembre 2019, a Venezia c'è stata un'altissima marea: l'acqua alta ha raggiunto livelli eccezionali. Le immagini della piazza San Marco sott'acqua e dei negozi sommersi hanno causato preoccupazione a livello globale. Con un picco di 187 centimetri, questa marea eccezionale è stata la seconda più alta registrata nella storia della città. L'allarme è suonato riguardo alla fragilità dell'architettura e dell'ecosistema veneziano. L'evento ha evidenziato l'urgenza di adottare misure concrete per preservare Venezia dal livello del mare che si alza ogni anno di più e la necessità di soluzioni sostenibili e strategie di adattamento per proteggere questa città unica e preziosa. Per fortuna, grazie al sistema del MOSE, dal 2020 la città può proteggersi dall'alta marea. Ma attivare questo sistema è costoso e laborioso ed è necessario che l'amministrazione prenda sempre decisioni tempestive basate sulle previsioni e sulle considerazioni beneficio/rischio.

a Il livello del mare in futuro
b Venezia: una città sul mare
c La sfida di Venezia tra maree e nuova tecnologia

19.11

4 Listen to this interview where an Italian citizen explains what their idea of civic duty is. Write down the things that are mentioned.

....

....

....

....

....

5 **Describe to an Italian friend the idea of civic duty that you have or people in your society/country have. Use the audio in question 4 as a model.**

TEST YOURSELF

Turn the phrases below into sentences expressing a duty. Use andare + participle or expressions such as bisogna che / è necessario che / occorre che followed by the subjunctive.

Example: promuovere il patrimonio artistico

è necessario che le persone proteggano il patrimonio artistico/ il patrimonio artistico va protetto.

- **a** Rispettare l'ambiente.
- **b** Riciclare i rifiuti.
- **c** Pagare le tasse.
- **d** Denunciare gli atti di vandalismo.
- **e** Parcheggiare le macchine negli spazi permessi.
- **f** Non gettare i rifiuti sulla strada.

La misteriosa donna in soffitta *The mysterious woman in the attic*

You probably have guessed the name of the woman in the painting already! If not, here is your next clue. Off the coast of Napoli, Annalisa's hometown, there is a beautiful island known for its amazing beaches and spas. The first letter, as usual, will help you compose the name of the mysterious woman.

Remember to use **My review** and **My takeaway** to assess your progress and reflect on your learning experience.

In this unit you will learn how to:

» Talk about someone's biography, including yours.
» Make hypotheses using the future tense.
» Talk about things that could have happened in the past.
» Express concession.

Che vita!

My study plan

I plan to work with Unit 20

○ Every day
○ Twice a week
○ Other ___________

I plan to study for

○ 5–15 minutes
○ 15 30 minutes
○ 30–45+ minutes

My progress tracker

Day / Date	Listening	Speaking	Reading	Writing	Conversation
	○	○	○	○	○
	○	○	○	○	○
	○	○	○	○	○
	○	○	○	○	○
	○	○	○	○	○
	○	○	○	○	○
	○	○	○	○	○

My goals

What do you want to be able to do or say in Italian when you complete this unit?

		Done
1	....	○
2	....	○
3	....	○

My review

SELF CHECK

	I can ...
●	... talk about my life.
●	... make a hypothesis using the future tense.
●	... talk about what could have happened.
●	... express a concession.
●	... use the pronoun chi correctly.

CULTURE POINT 1

Italiani famosi *Popular Italians*

Margherita Hack

L'Italia, con il suo popolo di esploratori, artisti e scienziati, ha dato i natali a (*gave birth to*) numerosi personaggi che ancora oggi sono ricordati in tutto il mondo. Chi non ha mai sentito almeno (*at least*) menzionare Leonardo Da Vinci, Marco Polo, Giulio Cesare o Lucrezia Borgia? Ma gli italiani famosi non sono solo quelli del passato e negli ultimi anni altri nomi si sono aggiunti (*have been added*) alla lista delle personalità famose a livello internazionale: per la musica, ricordiamo Laura Pausini e Bocelli, per la scienza Enrico Fermi, per l'architettura Renzo Piano, ma potremmo continuare a lungo con educatori come Maria Montessori e imprenditori (*entrepreneurs*) come Enzo Ferrari o Miuccia Prada. Ci sono però moltissimi italiani che rimangono sconosciuti (*unknown*), nonostante (*despite*) il loro contributo a importanti invenzioni moderne. Per esempio, sapevate che la Jacuzzi è stata inventata da un italiano, così come il pianoforte o l'mp3?

Nell'immagine possiamo vedere la famosa Margherita Hack. Ne avete sentito parlare? Se no, provate a scoprire quali sono stati i suoi contributi al mondo scientifico!

Guarda questa galleria creata da Wired.it su cinquanta italiani che hanno contribuito al progresso internazionale, ma che non sono molto conosciuti.

a Quale invenzione ti incuriosisce di più?

b Conosci altri italiani famosi che non abbiamo menzionato? Quali?

VOCABULARY BUILDER 1

20.01

Look at the words and phrases and complete the missing English words and expressions. Then listen and try to imitate the pronunciation of the speakers.

LA MIA BIOGRAFIA	*MY BIOGRAPHY*
assumere	*to hire*
il corso	....
il corso professionale	....
crescere	*to grow up*
il curriculum	....
il diploma	*diploma, certificate*
la facoltà	....
fare ricerca	....
frequentare	*to attend*
iscriversi	*to sign up, to enroll*
laurearsi	*to graduate*
licenziare	*to fire*
licenziarsi	*to resign*
la morte	*death*
nascere	....
la nascita	*birth*
il personaggio famoso	*celebrity*
la promozione	....
seppellire	*to bury*
trasferirsi	*to move, to relocate*

VERBI E PAROLE UTILI	*USEFUL VERBS AND WORDS*
l'archivio	....
approfondire	*to examine in depth*
indicare	....
purtroppo	*unfortunately*
il volume	*book, volume*

Vocabulary practice 1

Try to provide your own description in Italian for the following words from the vocabulary builder.

il corso: ....

il curriculum: ....

laurearsi: ....

nascere: ....

trasferirsi: ....

CONVERSATION 1

La scoperta *The discovery*

20.02

1 Here are a few words and expressions to help you understand the following conversation. Note their meanings.

Dai! *Come on!* Fino a notte inoltrata. *Until late at night.*

20.03

2 Listen to the conversation without looking at the text. Then listen again and read the text. Listen to how Cristian and Annalisa refer to actions that would have occurred in the past if certain circumstances had been different.

È un pomeriggio di gennaio, Annalisa ha appena finito una videochiamata con la direzione generale (*general management*) della sua compagnia che voleva complimentarsi per il suo intervento con il MOSE. Improvvisamente, Cristian entra nella stanza con una grande rivelazione.

Cristian Elena Cornaro Piscopia!

Annalisa Chi?

Cristian La signora del ritratto, Annalisa. Ho finalmente scoperto il suo nome.

Annalisa Dai, chi l'avrebbe mai detto!

Cristian Pensa, era una filosofa italiana che è nata a Venezia nel 1646. Anche senza frequentare l'università, ha studiato filosofia, teologia, greco antico e molto altro. C'è chi pensa che sia stata la prima donna al mondo a laurearsi, anche se non è esattamente la prima.

Annalisa Non è stata l'ultima, per fortuna (*ride*). Racconta.

Cristian Devo ancora approfondire. Stavo facendo ricerca in un archivio, ma purtroppo non c'era chi avrebbe potuto indicarmi i volumi giusti. Credimi, sarei rimasto lì fino a notte inoltrata!

Dai! is a versatile Italian exclamation with various meanings depending on the context. It can be used to encourage or urge someone, expressing motivation or support, as in Dai, puoi farcela! (*Come on, you can do it!*). Alternatively, dai can convey disbelief or surprise, as in Dai, davvero? (*Come on, really?*). In some situations, dai is used to suggest or request something, inviting someone to join in, such as Dai, andiamo a fare una passeggiata! (*Come on, let's go for a walk!*).

3 Summarize the information about Elena Cornaro Piscopia based on the conversation.

....

....

LANGUAGE BUILDER 1

Language discovery 1

Find the pronoun chi in the conversation. Sometimes it can be translated as "those who" but other times not. Can you see when and why?

	Those who	Who
a Chi?		
b Chi l'avrebbe mai detto?		
c C'è chi pensa che sia stata la prima donna al mondo a laurearsi.		
d Non c'era chi avrebbe potuto indicarmi i volumi giusti.		

The pronoun chi

The pronoun chi serves as both a question word (*who?*) and a pronoun. As a question word, chi functions similarly to its English counterpart:

Chi? – La signora del ritratto. *Who? —The woman in the portrait.*

Chi sei? *Who are you?*

Unlike in English, however, chi is also frequently used as a pronoun, meaning ***a person who*** or ***people who***, and substituting for expressions like quello/questo che or qualcuno/una che. Note that chi can also indicate a plural subject (***those who***), but the verb remains singular:

Non c'era chi avrebbe potuto indicarmi i volumi. = Non c'era qualcuno che avrebbe potuto indicarmi i volumi. *There wasn't someone who could point out the books to me.*

Chi non vuole fare l'esame può uscire = Quelli che non vogliono fare l'esame possono uscire. *Those who don't want to take the exam can leave.*

Chi is often employed in proverbs:

Chi va piano, va sano e va lontano! Slow and steady wins the race. (Those who go slowly are healthier and travel further!)

Remember that in relative clauses, che is used instead of chi, even when referring to people.

Era una filosofa che è nata a Venezia. She was a philosopher who was born in Venice.

Language practice 1

Choose the correct pronoun to complete the sentences.

- **a** La donna che / chi sta arrivando è la nostra professoressa.
- **b** Non sopporto che / chi parla a voce troppo alta.
- **c** Ho chiesto a tutte le persone che / chi ho incontrato, ma nessuno sapeva aiutarmi.
- **d** Che / chi non vuole ascoltare la lezione può uscire immediatamente.
- **e** Non capisco che / chi non studia su libri attendibili.
- **f** Ho chiesto le informazioni alla segretaria, che / chi è stata davvero gentile.
- **g** Mio cugino Antonio, che / chi tu non conosci, è appena arrivato.
- **h** Che / chi ha scritto questo curriculum?

LANGUAGE BUILDER 2

Language discovery 2

20.04

Listen to the conversation again and repeat each line in the pauses provided. In the conversation, a new tense is introduced: the conditional perfect. The initial form you come across is avrebbe detto. Can you identify the other two instances? How is this tense formed?

a .... **b** ....

The conditional perfect

The conditional perfect is used to express unreal or hypothetical situations in the past. It allows speakers to discuss imagined outcomes or express regret about events that did not come to pass. It is formed by combining the conditional tense of the helping verb (essere or avere) with the past participle of the main verb.

Chi lo avrebbe mai detto!	*Who would have thought!* (lit. *Who would have ever said it!*)
Sarei rimasto lì.	*I would have stayed there.*

Remember that the past participle agrees with the subject when the auxiliary is essere. When the auxiliary is avere, it agrees with a direct object pronoun if there is one. With modal verbs (potere, dovere, volere), it's the main verb following the modal which determines whether to use essere or avere.

Saremmo rimasti lì.	*We would have stayed there.*
Le avreste comprate, quelle scarpe?	*Would you have bought those shoes?*
Chi avrebbe potuto indicarmi i volumi giusti?	*Who would have been able to point me to the right books?*
Non sarei potuto venire.	*I wouldn't have been able to come.*

Language practice 2

1 Complete the text with the conditional perfect.

La vita di Jasmine è stata molto diversa da come la immaginava. Da adolescente (*studiare*) **a** .... matematica, ma i genitori hanno insistito per giurisprudenza. Al momento di decidere l'università, Jasmine (*frequentare*) **b** .... l'università a Milano, ma poi era troppo lontano e ha deciso di iscriversi all'università di Palermo. Nei suoi sogni, (*sposarsi*) **c** .... con una ragazza straniera, ma sua moglie è italiana, di Bari. (*volere*) **d** .... lavorare in tribunale, ma poi ha trovato lavoro come consulente in una compagnia privata. (*volere*) **e** .... andare all'estero per fare un'esperienza, ma poi ha deciso di rimanere in Italia. (*abitare*) **f** .... volentieri in una casa in campagna, ma poi ha comprato un piccolo appartamento in città. Ogni estate (*andare*) **g** .... al mare, ma la famiglia preferiva la montagna. Insieme a sua moglie Teresa, (*adottare*) **h** .... un cane, ma alla fine hanno preso due gatti.

20.05

2 Now, play Conversation 1 again, taking on the role of Cristian. Speak during the pauses and create your own character for the identity of the woman in the painting.

CULTURE POINT 2

Non solo emigrazione *Not only emigration*

Abbiamo visto come molti giovani italiani decidono di emigrare all'estero per trovare nuove opportunità lavorative. Nonostante questo, l'Italia rimane un polo di attrazione (*center of attraction*) per molti, italiani e non. Numerosi personaggi famosi nel panorama artistico e culturale italiano sono di fatto (*as a matter of fact*) nati in altri Paesi: il regista Ferzan Özpetek, turco di nascita; il ballerino Kledi Kadium, di origine albanese o la politica Cécile Kyenge, originaria della Repubblica Democratica del Congo. Secondo i dati ufficiali, nel 2022 il numero di cittadini di origine non italiana presenti nel Paese erano più di 5 milioni. L'afflusso (*the influx*) di persone provenienti da diverse parti del mondo ha contribuito alla ricchezza culturale e alla diversità della nazione, ma allo stesso tempo ha portato sfide e discussioni connesse all'integrazione, all'identità nazionale e alle risorse sociali ed economiche.

La politica Cécile Kyenge

a Ci sono personaggi italiani famosi nel tuo paese? Cosa fanno?

b Ci sono personaggi del tuo Paese che sono diventati famosi all'estero? In quali campi?

VOCABULARY BUILDER 2

20.06

Look at the words and phrases and complete the missing English words and expressions. Then listen and try to imitate the pronunciation of the speakers.

EVENTI DELLA VITA	*LIFE EVENTS*
affrontare	*to face*
Congratulazioni!	…………………
la decisione	…………………
l'esperienza	…………………
evolvere	…………………
il fallimento	*failure*
fallire	…………………
festeggiare	*to celebrate*
meritarsi	*to deserve*
la sfida	*challenge*
l'obiettivo	…………………
l'ostacolo	…………………
l'opportunità	*chance/opportunity*
raggiungere	*to reach*
succedere	*to happen*
il successo	…………………
superare	*to overcome*
la svolta	*turn, change*
il traguardo	*accomplishment*
il trionfo	…………………
essere all'altezza	*to be worthy*

PAROLE ED ESPRESSIONI UTILI	*USEFUL WORDS AND EXPRESSIONS*
anche se	*even if*
benché	*although*
nonostante	*despite*
sebbene	*albeit*

Vocabulary practice 2

Choose the odd one out.

1 **a** il successo **b** il trionfo **c** il fallimento
2 **a** l'esperienza **b** il traguardo **c** l'obiettivo
3 **a** festeggiare **b** la sfida **c** congratulazioni!
4 **a** fallire **b** la promozione **c** meritarsi
5 **a** affrontare **b** l'opportunità **c** la sfida

CONVERSATION 2

Un brindisi al nostro futuro *A toast to our future*

Here are a few words and expressions to help you understand the following conversation. Note their meanings.

non essere all'altezza	*not being good enough*

1 Listen to the conversation without looking at the text. Then listen again and read the text. Pay attention to how they express a doubt without an immediate answer.

È un grande giorno per Cristian che, dopo un colloquio con Liang Ferretti, ha ricevuto un'offerta di lavoro come consulente per la sua galleria d'arte. Sono successe molte cose nelle ultime settimane, e adesso è il momento di festeggiare!

Aicha Congratulazioni, Cristian!

Cristian Grazie! Sono felicissimo, sebbene abbia anche un po' paura.

Matteo E di cosa avrai mai paura?

Cristian Di non essere all'altezza.

Matteo Stai scherzando? Questo traguardo te lo meriti tutto. Ma... dov'è Annalisa?

Aicha Non so, sarà ancora a lavoro.

Cristian Sapete che ha salvato Venezia dall'acqua alta? Negli ultimi giorni il livello dell'acqua era salito molto e nonostante il MOSE sia un sistema automatico, non si era ancora attivato. Annalisa ha insistito per l'attivazione manuale ed è stato un grande successo!

Aicha Un trionfo, direi! Eccola!

Annalisa Scusate il ritardo. Festeggiamo?

Matteo Certamente! A Cristian e Annalisa!

Cristian ... e alla nostra amicizia e alle belle opportunità!

2 Match each character with an appropriate description based on the conversation.

1 Cristian	**a** rassicura Cristian sulle sue capacità.
2 Annalisa	**b** è felice.
3 Matteo	**c** non sa dove è Annalisa.
4 Aicha	**d** è in ritardo.

LANGUAGE BUILDER 3

Language discovery 3

Matteo uses the future tense when inquiring about Cristian's fears: E di cosa avrai mai paura? Can you identify another form of expressing doubt about the future within the conversation?

....

How would you translate these expressions?

Future of assumption

In Italian, the future tense serves not only to discuss events or actions that will occur in the future but also to express assumptions and hypotheses.

Non so, sarà a lavoro.	*I don't know, she must be at work.*
Quanti anni ha Kim? – Mah, avrà trent'anni.	*How old is Kim?—Well, she is probably thirty.*

In English, this can be conveyed by incorporating words like *probably* or *must*. Using the simple future form of verbs in Italian inherently introduces a level of uncertainty into the sentence. Note that this can also be applied to the present progressive: stare (in the future tense) + gerund.

Cosa sta facendo Lucia? – Starà studiando.	*What is Lucia doing?— She's probably studying.*

Language practice 3

20.09

Listen to the following questions and give an answer using the given verb, making it an assumption.

- **a** Non so, ... (avere) cinquanta anni.
- **b** .... (stare giocando) in giardino.
- **c** .... (avere) fame.
- **d** Chi .... (essere)?
- **e** Il treno .... (essere) in ritardo.
- **f** .... (stare parlando) con qualcun altro.
- **g** Non .... (costare) troppo, ci sono gli sconti.
- **h** .... (arrivare) la settimana prossima.
- **i** Non ho l'orologio, ma .... (essere) le cinque.
- **j** .... (stare facendo) il colloquio di lavoro.

LANGUAGE BUILDER 4

Language discovery 4

Listen to the conversation again and repeat each line in the pauses provided. Can you find two instances of the subjunctive mood? What are the words that precede the subjunctive? Why do you think the subjunctive is needed?

a ....

b ....

The subjunctive after **nonostante, sebbene, benché**

In Italian, the subjunctive mood is often used after certain conjunctions, including nonostante (*despite, in spite of*), sebbene (*although, even though*), and benché (*although, even though*). These conjunctions express a contrast or concession, indicating a situation that is contrary to what might be expected.

Nonostante il MOSE sia un sistema automatico, non si era ancora attivato.	*Despite the MOSE being an automatic system, it didn't switch on yet.*
Sebbene Ana abbia tempo, non riesce partecipare alla riunione.	*Although Ana has time, she cannot make it to the meeting.*
Benché Lia stia per ottenere la promozione, cambierà lavoro.	*Even though Lia is about to get a promotion, she will change jobs.*

In each case, the subjunctive mood is chosen to emphasize the hypothetical or uncertain nature of the situation described. It's a way to convey that the action is not necessarily guaranteed or expected to happen.

While the meaning may be similar, when using anche se (*even if*), the subjunctive is not necessary: Anche se Ana ha tempo... (*Even if Ana has time ...*).

Language practice 4

1 Complete the following sentences using subjunctive or indicative where needed.

a Anche se (essere – io) .... stanca, andrò al lavoro.

b Sebbene Gheorghiu (avere) .... molti ostacoli sul suo percorso, li supererà tutti.

c Nonostante Clara e Bjørnar (studiare) .... molto, non si sentono mai pronti.

d Anche se Annalisa (meritarsi) .... la promozione, non è sicura di ottenerla.

e Benché i giovani (laurearsi) .... molto di più rispetto al passato, le percentuali di laureati sono ancora basse.

f Sebbene il titolo di studio (essere) .... importante, l'esperienza ha un grande valore.

20.11

2 Now play Conversation 2 again, but this time you will play Cristian's role. Try to describe with your own words what Annalisa did and express your feelings about the future events in the pauses provided. Try to use a future of assumption and not to refer to the text.

SKILL BUILDER

1 Read Elena Cornaro Piscopia's biography and respond to the questions.

Elena Lucrezia Cornaro Piscopia è stata una donna straordinaria che ha fatto la storia come una delle prime donne a laurearsi al mondo. Nata a Venezia nel 1646, era la quinta di sette figli. Suo padre, un nobile, ha investito molto denaro per farla riconoscere nel registro della nobiltá. Fino da giovane, Elena si è appassionata agli studi e suo padre l'ha aiutata a migliorarsi, trovando per lei professori che le hanno insegnato molte materie, inclusi latino, greco, teologia e lingue straniere.

Oltre agli studi, Elena aveva anche una forte vocazione religiosa e a diciannove anni è diventata una suora benedettina. Questa scelta non è stata accolta positivamente dai suoi genitori, ma le ha permesso di vivere secondo la regola benedettina senza essere rinchiusa in un monastero. Nonostante il suo desiderio di laurearsi in teologia sia stato inizialmente respinto, Elena è riuscita a ottenere la laurea in filosofia grazie all'aiuto del suo professore Carlo Rinaldini.

Dopo la laurea, Elena si è trasferita a Padova, ma la sua salute era già fragile a causa degli intensi studi e delle pratiche ascetiche: purtroppo, si ammalava spesso e per lunghi periodi. Nel luglio del 1684, Elena è morta e è stata sepolta nella chiesa di Santa Giustina a Padova.

Nonostante la sua importanza storica, la laurea di Elena non ha aperto molte porte per le donne dell'epoca. Solo molti anni dopo, nel 1732, un'altra donna italiana si è laureata. Tuttavia, oggi Elena è ricordata con una statua dedicata a lei nell'Università di Padova, che simboleggia l'emancipazione delle donne e il loro diritto all'istruzione.

Adattato da: https://www.unipd.it/elena-lucrezia-cornaro-piscopia

a Cosa ha fatto di Elena Lucrezia Cornaro Piscopia una donna straordinaria?
b Quali materie ha studiato Elena per ottenere la laurea?
c Dove è stata sepolta Elena dopo la sua morte?

2 Write to a friend about Elena Cornaro Piscopia's life.

....

....

....

....

....

3 Now, let's discuss your own biography. Imagine you're in a job interview and are asked to narrate the story of your life. What would you say?

20.12

4 Listen to the story of Gae Aulenti and complete the missing information.

Data di nascita:		Progetto a Parigi:	
Materia studiata durante il corso di laurea:		Altri progetti su cui ha lavorato:	
Anno di laurea:		Altra passione oltre all'architettura:	
Anno di apertura del suo primo studio:		Anno di morte:	

TEST YOURSELF

1 Complete the sentences with the correct form of the verb in parentheses (subjunctive, conditional past, future for probability).

a Mi dispiace che tu non (venire) .... alla festa.
b Penso che Diana (lavorare) .... anche nel weekend.
c Gli (noi - fare) .... una sorpresa, ma poi Eva e Ivan hanno scoperto tutto.
d Bisogna che le persone (imparare) .... a riciclare correttamente.
e Che ore sono? - Non ho l'orologio, ma più o meno (essere) .... le otto.
f Nonostante (io - studiare) .... molto, non riesco a passare l'esame di cinema.

2 Write a sentence that links to the provided clause. Use the conditional perfect.

a ...., ma ha deciso di non farlo.
b ...., ma poi sono tornate a casa.
c ...., ma mio nonno ha comprato una macchina nuova.
d ...., ma il professore non voleva.
e ...., ma siamo arrivati tardi.
f ...., ma tu mi hai detto di no.
g ...., ma Eva e Ivan hanno scoperto tutto.
h ...., ma vi siete arrabbiati.
i ...., ma ho avuto paura.
j ...., ma non potevamo crederti.

La misteriosa donna in soffitta *The mysterious woman in the attic*

L'identità della signora nel ritratto è stata finalmente scoperta, ma resta ancora un indovinello finale. L'ultima lettera del suo nome corrisponde alla prima lettera della biblioteca dove il ritratto è attualmente. Puoi trovarla? Il dipinto è esposto alla Biblioteca ... di Milano.

Remember to use **My review** and **My takeaway** to assess your progress and reflect on your learning experience.

?

L'identità della signora nel ritratto

Qual è il nome della signora nel ritratto? *What is the name of the woman in the portrait?*

_ _ _ _ _ _ _ _ _ _ _ _ _ _ _ _ _ _ _ _

Answer key

First things first

CULTURE POINT 1 **a** Examples: Milano, Napoli, Torino, Aosta **b** Valle d'Aosta, Trentino Alto-Adige, Lombardia, Umbria, Piemonte **c** 12 **d** Piemonte

VOCABULARY BUILDER 1 good morning, good evening, goodbye, hi/bye

VOCABULARY PRACTICE 1 **1** b **2** a **3** d **4** c

PRONUNCIATION PRACTICE **2 a** cina (*as in English chin*) **b** chimica (*as in English kin*) **c** schema (*as in English skeptical*) **d** ceramica (*cherry*) **e** cappuccino (*chin*) **f** cemento (*cherry*) **g** macchina (*kin*) **h** macchiato (*kin*) **i** eccellente (*cherry*)

CONVERSATION 1 **3 a** Cristian **b** Napoli **c** His last name

LANGUAGE DISCOVERY 1 **1** b/d **2** c **3** b/d **4** e **5** a
I am = io sono; *you are* = Lei è italiano? Sei studente?

LANGUAGE PRACTICE 1 **1 a** sono **b** sei **c** sono **d** è **e** è **f** sono **g** sono **h** è **i** sei **2 a** Lei **b** tu **c** Lei **d** tu **e** Lei **f** tu **3** Students' own answers

VOCABULARY BUILDER 2 apartment

VOCABULARY PRACTICE 2 **a** sette **b** dieci **c** sei **d** otto **e** due **f** quattro

CONVERSATION 2 **2 a** Cristian's flatmate **b** In via Garibaldi 10, in the center of Venice **c** After the street name

LANGUAGE DISCOVERY 3 **a** in **b** a **c** di
We use a with a city. We use in with the address. We use di when we say where we are *from*

LANGUAGE PRACTICE 3 **1 Suggested answers:** Io abito in Via Garibaldi 7, a Venezia. Io abito da solo. Tu sei di Napoli.

LANGUAGE DISCOVERY 4 **a** 3 **b** 1 **c** 2, dove = where, quale = which

LANGUAGE PRACTICE 4 **1 a** Dove **b** Quale **c** Dove **d** Come

SKILL BUILDER **1 a** F **b** F **c** I **d** F **e** I **f** I **g** I **h** F **i** F **2 a** sei **b** sono **c** è **d** sono **e** è **3 a** Tre-tre-sette – quattro-due-sei- uno-nove-sette-sette **b** Tre-quattro-zero – due-uno-otto-due-nove-sette-sei **c** Tre-tre-otto- due-sei-otto- otto-sette-sei-cinque **d** Tre-tre-nove-cinque-quattro-tre-nove-due-uno-sei **e** I

TEST YOURSELF **a** Io abito a Roma. **b** Io abito in via Garibaldi 7. **c** Qual è il tuo numero di telefono? **d** Buongiorno/buonasera signora Rossi! **e** Io abito in piazza Ferretto. **f** Lei è italiano? *or* Tu sei italiano?

Unit 1

CULTURE POINT 1 **a** Answers will vary. Suggested answers: German, Sardinian, Albanian **b** Val d'Aosta **c** Calabria

VOCABULARY BUILDER 1 French, Spanish, German, student

VOCABULARY PRACTICE 1 **a** portoghese **b** tedesco/a **c** britannico/a **d** russo/a **e** statunitense **f** giappponese **g** peruviano/a **h** australiano/a **i** turco/a **j** greco/a **k** canadese **l** messicano/a

PRONUNCIATION PRACTICE **2 a** giraffa (like *jig*) **b** ginnastica (*jig*) **c** geometria (like *gem*) **d** leghe (like *get*) **e** angelo (like *angel*) **f** ghiro (like *gig*) **g** aghi (*gig*) **h** formaggio (*jig*) **i** ghetto (like *ghetto*)

CONVERSATION 1 **2 a** F **b** F **c** T **d** T

LANGUAGE DISCOVERY 1 **a** Questo **b** Questa **c** Questo **d** Questo

LANGUAGE PRACTICE 1 **a** Questo, spagnolo **b** Questa, giapponese **c** Questa, francese **d** Questo, tedesco **e** Questa, canadese **f** Questo statunitense/americano **g** Questa, marocchina

LANGUAGE DISCOVERY 2 **Lui/lei:** the verbs end in -e or -a **Io:** the verb ends in -o **Tu:** the verb ends in -i

LANGUAGE PRACTICE 2 **1 a 1** parlo **2** chiamo **3** vivo **4** leggo **5** abito **6** studio **b 1** lavori **2** parli **3** abiti **4** vivi **5** leggi **c 1** parlate **2** lavorate **3** abitate **d 1** parla **2** lavora **3** vive **4** legge **5** abita **6** studia **e 1** lavoriamo **2** parliamo **3** abitiamo **4** viviamo **5** leggiamo **f 1** parlano **2** vivono **3** lavorano

CULTURE POINT 2 **a** Annalisa grew up near the volcano called Vesuvio and Pompeii **b** The Dolomites **c** Many: Venice, Rome, Padua...

VOCABULARY PRACTICE 2 **a** 75 **b** 18 **c** 61 **d** 32 **e** 38 **f** 71

CONVERSATION 2 **3 a** italiana **b** misterioso **c** venti

LANGUAGE DISCOVERY 3 **a** Ha 20 o 30 anni. **b** E tu, quanti anni hai? **c** Io ho 33 anni. It is not essere. It changes as the subject changes.

LANGUAGE PRACTICE 3 **a** ha **b** hai **c** ha **d** abbiamo **e** avete **f** ha **g** hanno **h** ha

LANGUAGE DISCOVERY 4 **a** un **b** una **c** uno **d** uno With the feminine words we use una. We use un or uno with the masculine words.

LANGUAGE PRACTICE 4 **a** Io (non) ho una macchina **b** Io (non) ho un computer **c** Io (non) ho uno studio (*study room*) **d** Io (non) ho un quadro in soffitta **e** Io (non) un appartamento in centro **f** Io (non) ho uno sguardo misterioso **g** Io (non) ho un coinquilino **h** Io (non) ho una fotografia di gruppo

SKILL BUILDER **1 a** portoghese **b** Quanti **c** Questa **d** parla/ è **e** abitiamo **f** un **g** lavora **h** parla/è **i** vivono **j** ha **2 a** Dove **b** Quanti **c** Dove **d** Chi **e** Dove **f** Quali **3 a** 28 **b** uno **c** ha **d** un'

TEST YOURSELF **1 a** F **b** T **c** F **d** T

LA MISTERIOSA DONNA IN SOFFITTA Etna > E

Unit 2

VOCABULARY BUILDER to dance, to play sports, to scroll on social media, to prefer, movie theater/cinema, concert, gallery, music, theater

VOCABULARY PRACTICE 1 **a** legge **b** giocano **c** mangia **d** guardiamo **e** facciamo

CONVERSATION 1 **3 Aicha e Annalisa:** play volleyball; go to the disco **Cristian:** work; play Dungeons and Dragons

LANGUAGE DISCOVERY 1 libri, gallerie, lezioni; To form masculine plural nouns in Italian, change the ending **-o** to **-i**, and for feminine plural nouns, change the ending -a to **-e**. For Italian nouns ending in **-e**, which can be either masculine or feminine, the plural form changes the ending **-e** to **-i** regardless of gender.

LANGUAGE PRACTICE 1 **a** teatri **b** gallerie **c** concerti **d** social **e** passeggiate **f** televisori **g** stazioni **h** libri **i** scrolling

LANGUAGE DISCOVERY 2 **a** preferisco **b** preferisce **c** capisco

VERB CONJUGATION, VERBS IN -IRE Dormire (*to sleep*): dormo, dormi, dorme, dormiamo, dormite, dormono

LANGUAGE PRACTICE 2 **1** b **2** a **3** d **4** e **5** c

CULTURE POINT 2 **a** Three: aperol, soda, and prosecco **b** Padua, located in the region of Veneto

VOCABULARY BUILDER 2 actor, chef, doctor, mechanic, hospital, restaurant, school

VOCABULARY PRACTICE 2 **1** b **2** a **3** c **4** e **5** d **6** f

CONVERSATION 2 **3 1** b **2** d **3** c **4** a **4** There aren't many cars in Venice.

LANGUAGE DISCOVERY 3 They say faccio il meccanico / faccio la fotografa. They use il and la, definite articles. They are different because il is masculine and la is feminine.

LANGUAGE PRACTICE 3 **a** l' **b** la **c** I **d** la, le **e** gli

LANGUAGE DISCOVERY 4 fai, faccio, fa Faccio and fa mean *I do* and *he does*.

LANGUAGE PRACTICE 4 **a** fate **b** fa, faccio **c** fanno, fa, fa **d** fai, faccio **e** facciamo **f** fanno **g** fate **h** facciamo **i** fa

SKILL BUILDER **1** Students' own answers. **2 a** fa **b** amici **c** officina **d** parla **e** lo **f** gli **g** il **h** fa **i** dorme **3 a** vero **b** falso **c** vero **d** falso

TEST YOURSELF **1 a** Noi leggiamo i libri. **b** Voi fate gli influencer?. **c** Loro preferiscono gli uffici. **d** Loro capiscono lo spagnolo. **2 1** c **2** a **3** c **4** b **5** b **6** a

LA MISTERIOSA DONNA IN SOFFITTA i libri > L

Unit 3

VOCABULARY BUILDER 1 mother, son/daughter, couple, divorced

VOCABULARY PRACTICE 1 **a** nipote **b** genitori **c** sorella **d** cognata **e** compagna **f** zia **g** moglie/marito

CONVERSATION 1 **3 a** F **b** V **c** F **d** F **e** V

LANGUAGE DISCOVERY 1 **a TU** La tua famiglia **b NOI** I nostri nonni **c VOI** I vostri genitori **d LORO** Loro hotel

LANGUAGE PRACTICE 1 **a** Ecco la nostra macchina! **b** Ecco la sua famiglia piccola! **c** Ecco il loro B&B a Bolzano! **d** Ecco il tuo computer nuovo! **e** Ecco la tua amica fotografa! **f** Ecco la sua casa grande! **g** Ecco il loro quadro in soffitta! **h** Ecco il suo piano!

LANGUAGE DISCOVERY 2 Words that describe family relations

LANGUAGE PRACTICE 2 **1 a** Suo padre e` di Bolzano. **b** Sua madre vive a Bolzano. **c** Lui ha una sorella. **d** I suoi cugini studiano all'università. **2 Model answer:** Ecco la mia famiglia: mio padre; mia madre (= i miei genitori) mio fratello, mia sorella (= i miei fratelli), Ecco la tua famiglia: tuo padre, tua madre (= i tuoi genitori) tuo fratello, tua sorella (= i tuoi fratelli), Ecco la sua famiglia: suo padre, sua madre (= i suoi genitori) suo fratello, sua sorella (= i tuoi fratelli), Ecco la nostra famiglia: nostro padre, nostra madre (= i nostri genitori), nostro fratello, nostra sorella (= i nostri fratelli), Ecco la vostra famiglia: vostro padre, vostra madre (= i vostri genitori), vostro fratello, vostra sorella (= i vostri fratelli), Ecco la loro famiglia: il loro padre, la loro madre (= i loro genitori), il loro fratello, la loro sorella (= i nostri fratelli)

CULTURE POINT 2 **a** Cinque: Primavera, Nascita di Venere, Annunciazione, Madonna con Bambino, Pallade **b** Otto

VOCABULARY BUILDER 2 hair, blond(e), long, blue, introverted, calm

VOCABULARY PRACTICE 2 **a** ricci **b** biondi **c** occhi

CONVERSATION 2 **3 1 b** La famiglia di Annalisa è curiosa. **2 a** Cristian non è a casa. **3 d** La donna misteriosa ha i capelli neri. **4 c** Gina è la zia di Niccolò.

LANGUAGE DISCOVERY 3 The adjectives' ending matches that of the noun.

LANGUAGE PRACTICE 3 un appartamento grande/piccolo, una famiglia grande/piccola/seria/intelligente/turca, una faccia seria/intelligente, gli amici spagnoli/intelligenti/seri, le amiche serie/intelligenti/spagnole

LANGUAGE DISCOVERY 4 Sometimes it starts with a **v**: loro vanno, lei va. Sometimes it has the same stem as the -are form: noi andiamo, voi andate

LANGUAGE PRACTICE 4 **1 a** va **b** vanno **c** vanno **d** va **e** va **f** vai **g** vado **2 a** Cristian non è a casa / è via. **b** Cristian è alto, hai capelli castani e gli occhi azzurri. **c** Lui ha 29 anni. **d** Lei ha i capelli neri e ricci e ha una faccia seria e triste.

SKILL BUILDER **a** Vengono da Firenze **b** Loro sono banchieri/fanno i banchieri **c** Sandro Botticelli, Michelangelo, Donatello e Leonardo da Vinci. **d** È una nobile signora alla corte dei Medici. **e** Ha i capelli lunghi e biondi, ha una faccia regolare e ha gli occhi azzurri.

TEST YOURSELF **1 a** artistica **b** famoso **c** importanti **d** belle immortali **e** serena **f** biondi **2 a** La mia **b** Mio **c** Mia **d** I miei **e** Mia **f** la sua **g** Il loro **h** i suoi **i** i miei **3 a** va **b** sta **c** fa **d** facciamo/andiamo **e** vado **f** vanno

LA MISTERIOSA DONNA IN SOFFITTA Estroversa > E

Unit 4

CULTURE POINT 1 Fontana di Trevi

VOCABULARY BUILDER 1 morning, night, dinner (to have dinner), to get ready

VOCABULARY PRACTICE 1 **a** svegliarsi (mattina) **b** vestirsi (mattina) **c** mangiare (mattina/pomeriggio/sera) **d** divertirsi (sera)

CONVERSATION 1 **3 a** Lunedì **b** antipatica (i.e., "not nice") **c** Si fa una doccia

LANGUAGE DISCOVERY 1 **a** mi **b** mi **c** si **d** ti

LANGUAGE PRACTICE 1 **a** riposarsi **c** farsi **d** sposarsi **f** divertirsi

LANGUAGE DISCOVERY 2 They both mean "to know"; here in the dialogue more precisely, "do you know?" Conoscere is followed by a noun (Sandra), sapere by a verb or by an entire sentence (cosa facciamo).

LANGUAGE PRACTICE 2 **1 a** sappiamo **b** sa **c** Conoscete **d** d sanno **e** conoscono **f** Conosco **g** Sai

VOCABULARY BUILDER 2 rarely, February, August, October, November, fall

VOCABULARY PRACTICE 2 **1 0** mai **1** raramente **2** qualche volta **3** spesso **4** di solito **5** sempre **2 a** Raramente **b** marzo, aprile, maggio, giugno **c** settembre, ottobre, novembre, dicembre **d** Es. il 18 novembre **e** Es. L'autunno, perché bevo il tè e i colori nel parco sono belli

CONVERSATION 2 **2 a** At eight. **b** Twenty past nine.

LANGUAGE DISCOVERY 3 **1 a** al **b** delle **c** alle **2 a** a + il **b** di + le **c** a + le

LANGUAGE PRACTICE 3 **a** alle **b** degli **c** alla **d** nel **e** sul **f** dagli **g** degli **h** al

LANGUAGE DISCOVERY 4 **a** A che ora chiude il supermercato? **b** Ma che ore sono? The questions specifically ask about the time.

LANGUAGE PRACTICE 4 **1 a** Alle diciassette e cinquanta/Alle sei meno dieci (17:50) **b** Alle dodici (12:00) **c** Alle sedici e trenta/alle quattro e mezzo (16:30) **d** Alle ventuno e cinque (21:05) **e** Alle venti e venti (20:20) **f** Alle sette e quindici/Alle sette e un quarto (07:15) **2 a Time:** 21:10 **Date:** 2 gennaio **b Time:** 16:15 **Date:** 30 luglio **c Time:** 14:25 **Date:** 27 ottobre **d Time:** 08:45 **Date:** 11 maggio

SKILL BUILDER **1 a** ogni giorno **b** sette **c** si veste **d** otto **e** sei **f** qualche volta **g** spesso **h** si riposa **i** venerdì **j** sempre **k** ci divertiamo **2 a** Mi faccio **b** mangia **c** ballano **d** Ti alzi **e** studio **f** vi divertite **3 a** conosco **b** A che ora? **c** Finisco **d** finisce **e** Perfetto!

TEST YOURSELF **1 a** Sono le due e un quarto/le quattordici e quindici **b** Sono le undici e quarantacinque **c** Sono le sei e venti/le diciotto e venti **d** È l'una/sono le tredici **e** Sono le nove e mezza/trenta **f** Sono le quattro meno venti/sono le quindici e quaranta **g** Sono le cinque meno venti/sono le sedici e cinquanta **h** Sono le dodici e trenta/è mezzogiono e mezza **2 Example:** 07:00 – Mi sveglio e mi alzo. 07:30 – Mi lavo i denti e mi faccio la doccia. 08:00 – Mi vesto e faccio colazione. 09:00 - Vado in ufficio. 12:30 – Pranzo con i colleghi. 13:30 – Torno a lavorare. 18:00 – Faccio sport. 19:30 - Mi faccio una doccia e mi rilasso. 20:00 – Ceno con la mia famiglia. 21:00 – Guardo un film o una serie TV. 23:30 – Mi addormento.

LA MISTERIOSA DONNA IN SOFFITTA November > N

Unit 5

VOCABULARY BUILDER 1 croissant, sandwich, glass of milk, standing

VOCABULARY PRACTICE 1 **a** spremuta **b** spremuta **c** tramezzino **d** primo

CONVERSATION 1 **2 Cristian** mangia il muesli e lo yogurt, il pane e il formaggio e beve l'espresso. **Matteo** mangia il cornetto alla marmellata, il tost e il tramezzino.

LANGUAGE DISCOVERY 1 **a** Cosa volete? **b** E tu Cristian, cosa vuoi? **c** Anche io voglio bere un caffé forte.

LANGUAGE PRACTICE 1 **a** volete? **b** vorrei **c** vuoi un antipasto? **d** vorrei **e** volete **f** vorrei **g** voglio **h** vuoi **i** voglio **j** vorrei

LANGUAGE DISCOVERY 2 We use mi piace followed by singular objects or a verb in -are/-ere/-ire. We use mi piacciono with plural objects.

LANGUAGE PRACTICE 2

1

MI = A ME / TI = A TE PIACE	MI = A ME / TI = A TE PIACCIONO
l'aperitivo	gli spaghetti
la bruschetta	i biscotti
andare al ristorante	le lasagne
la colazione dolce	i cereali
il pane	i funghi
la spremuta d'arancia	
fare colazione al bar	
lo yogurt	
l'omelette	
studiare l'italiano	
il latte	

VOCABULARY BUILDER 2 fruit, potato, olive oil

VOCABULARY PRACTICE 2

LA PIZZA NAPOLETANA	IL TIRAMISU	IL RISOTTO ALLA MILANESE
ci vogliono 5 grammi di lievito	ci vogliono 15 biscotti	ci vogliono 2 etti di riso
ci vuole il basilico	ci vuole un bicchiere di caffe	ci vuole un cucchiaino di zafferano
ci vuole il pomodoro	ci vogliono 750 grammi di mascarpone	ci vuole una cipolla
ci vogliono 500 grammi di farina	ci vuole un etto di zucchero	ci vuole un cucchiaio di olio d'oliva
ci vuole l'acqua	ci vogliono 5 uova	ci vuole un cucchiaio di burro
		ci vuole il sale
		ci vuole un litro di brodo vegetale

CONVERSATION 2 **3 a** patate **b** maccheroni **c** chilo **d** cipolle **e** sale

LANGUAGE DISCOVERY 3 **a** Si, lo metto. **b** Si, le preparo. **c** Si, li preferisco. **d** No, non la serviamo.

LANGUAGE PRACTICE 3 **a** la **b** lo **c** le **d** li **e** li **f** lo **g** la **h** la **i** le **j** lo voglio **k** Lo invitiamo? **l** le

LANGUAGE DISCOVERY 4 **a** Quante cipolle (mettiamo?) Mio padre ne mette una o due **b** Quanta pasta mettiamo? Ne mettiamo un chilo

LANGUAGE PRACTICE 4 **1 1** d **2** a **3** e **4** g **5** f **6** c **7** b

SKILL BUILDER **1 a** Quante **b** ne **c** lo **d** lo **e** le **f** le **g** la

TEST YOURSELF **1 a** piace **b** piacciono **c** piacciono **d** piace **e** piace **2 a** si le preparo **b** ne bevo uno **c** si lo metto **d** ne metto uno **e** si li mangio **f** si lo compro **3** Students' own answers. **4** Italians tend to eat a sweet breakfast, although in some parts of Italy, like in the Alps, you can find items like bread and cheese. You can expect your host family to serve tea and coffee (coffee made with stovetop moka) with bread, jam, butter, or cereal and milk.

Cookies are very common for breakfast. If you go to a bar you can have a croissant with barista drinks. You can also have something savory like a sandwich or a toasted sandwich called tost. It is almost impossible to find eggs for breakfast, let alone beans and sausage.

LA MISTERIOSA DONNA IN SOFFITTA Aceto > A

Unit 6

CULTURE POINT 1 Tutti i giorni 09:00 – 19:00 **c** Sala del Maggior Consiglio

VOCABULARY BUILDER 1 fountain, market, monument, to the left (of)

VOCABULARY PRACTICE 1 **a** lontano **b** scuola **c** semaforo **d** mangiare **e** dritto **f** museo

CONVERSATION 1 uscire dalla libreria, girare a sinistra, arrivare in una strada lunga, continuare per venti metri, davanti al negozio di artigianato girare a sinistra, girare a destra

LANGUAGE DISCOVERY 1 **a** devo **b** dobbiamo **c** devi

EXPRESSING NEEDS AND DUTIES WITH THE VERB DOVERE **a** devo **b** devi **c** dobbiamo

LANGUAGE PRACTICE 1 Deve comprare i biscotti, non deve preparare le lezioni, devono preparare i costumi per il cosplay, non devono pagare l'affitto, devono scoprire il nome della signora nel dipinto, deve chiamare Petra, non deve scrivere un'e-mail per la candidatura, non devono organizzare una riunione con gli amici dell'università

LANGUAGE DISCOVERY 2 **a** vicino **b** dietro

LANGUAGE PRACTICE 2 **1**

2 **a** No, è vicina. **b** Deve attraversare il ponte e girare a destra. Alla fontana grande, deve girare a destra e andare dritto. **c** Sì, è vicina al mercato, di fronte alla biblioteca.

CULTURE POINT 2 **a** Caserta **b** 130.000 m²

VOCABULARY BUILDER 2 ice cream parlor, hospital, park, pizza restaurant, station, bus, bicycle, taxi, train

VOCABULARY PRACTICE 2 **1 c** in pizzeria **2 d** dal fruttivendolo **3 e** in palestra **4 a** in piscina **5 f** in gelateria **6 b** in stazione

CONVERSATION 2 **3 b** fruttivendolo

LANGUAGE DISCOVERY 3 C'è (*there is*) is used with singular nouns, ci sono (*there are*) with plural nouns.

LANGUAGE PRACTICE 3 **1 a** c'è **b** ci sono **c** ci sono **d** c'è **e** c'è **f** ci sono **g** c'è **h** ci sono **i** ci sono **j** c'è **k** ci sono **l** c'è **2** Example. Nella mia città c'è una piazza grande, ci sono molti parchi e molti teatri. Non c'è un cinema, ma ci sono molti teatri.

LANGUAGE DISCOVERY 4 Possibility, to be able to do something.

EXPRESSING POSSIBILITY AND ASKING FOR PERMISSION WITH POTERE **a** posso **b** puoi **c** possiamo

LANGUAGE PRACTICE 4 **1 a** possiamo **b** possono **c** posso **d** può **e** potete

SKILL BUILDER **1 a** F **b** V **c** F **d** V **e** V **2 a** possono **b** lontano **c** in centro **d** vicino a **e** c'è **f** in palestra **g** deve **3** Students' own answers.

TEST YOURSELF **1 1** e **2** a **3** d **4** b **5** c **2 a** c'è **b** può **c** devo

LA MISTERIOSA DONNA IN SOFFITTA Caserta > C

Unit 7

CULTURE POINT 1 **b** Lago means *lake*; collina means *hill*; pianura means *plain/valley.*

VOCABULARY BUILDER 1 swimming pool, countryside, farm, mountain, sea, to visit

VOCABULARY PRACTICE 1 **1** f **2** b **3** a **4** d **5** c **6** e

CONVERSATION 1 **3 c** Il Sole del Sud

LANGUAGE DISCOVERY 1 **1** d **2** a **3** e **4** b **5** c

LANGUAGE PRACTICE 1 **1 a** ha mangiato **b** ho dormito **c** abbiamo lavorato **d** hai preparato **e** hanno telefonato **f** avete ballato **2** Aicha ha lavorato tutta la settimana. Annalisa e le sue amiche hanno video-telefonato a Aicha. Nel pomeriggio loro hanno dormito in spiaggia. Il proprietario dell'agriturismo ha preparato il pane fatto in casa. Annalisa dice: La sera noi abbiamo prenotato in un ristorante tipico.

LANGUAGE DISCOVERY 2 **a** siamo **b** siete **c** siamo **d** siamo

LANGUAGE PRACTICE 2 **1** Ieri Annalisa e le sue amiche hanno avuto un giorno molto intenso. La mattina sono andate in barca per visitare una spiaggia lontana e particolarmente bella. Quando sono arrivate alla spiaggia, loro hanno nuotato nell'acqua blu e cristallina. Alle 13 hanno pranzato con focaccia e burrata, un tipo di mozzarella tipica della

Puglia. Carlotta è vegana quindi non ha mangiato la mozzarella ma ha preparato un panino con verdura. Il pomeriggio hanno visitato un villaggio vicino. Qui Paola ha comprato molti souvenir per la sua famiglia. Annalisa ha fotografato le case tipiche della Puglia e ha postato le fotografie su Instagram. Immediatamente è arrivato un messaggio di Aicha: "Dove siete andate???" E Annalisa risponde: "Abbiamo visitato la Città Bianca." Le amiche sono tornate alla masseria alla sera e sono uscite ancora per andare al ristorante.
2 a Ieri ho mangiato **b** Ieri ho bevuto **c** Sono andato/a/* **d** Ho visitato

VOCABULARY BUILDER 2 hot, cold, sunny, humid/wet, climate

VOCABULARY PRACTICE 2 **a** è nuvoloso **b** c'è il sole/fa bello **c** piove **d** c'è il temporale **e** fa freddo **f** fa caldo

CONVERSATION 2 **3 a** F **b** F **c** F **d** V

LANGUAGE DISCOVERY 3 **1** a **2** g **3** e **4** b **5** d **6** c **7** f

LANGUAGE PRACTICE 3 **a** abbiamo fatto **b** sei stata? **c** ha scritto **d** ho detto **e** avete letto **f** è rimasto **g** hai speso? **h** hanno preso

LANGUAGE DISCOVERY 4 **a** very **b** many **c** many

LANGUAGE PRACTICE 4 **1 a** troppe **b** un po' di **c** molte **d** molto **e** poco **f** alcuni

SKILL BUILDER **2 a** 32 = trentadue **b** nuvoloso **c** piove/temporali **d** bello **e** nevica
3 a RECENSIONE 1 **b** RECENSIONE 1 **c** RECENSIONE 2 **d** RECENSIONE 3
4 An agriturismo is a *farm stay*, or a style of vacationing in farmhouse resorts. You can expect beautiful rural surroundings, homemade food, and simple but comfortable rooms, although some can be quite luxurious.

TEST YOURSELF **1 a** Cristian ha = **è** a Roma. **b** I turisti hanno visitati = **visitato** i monumenti e i musei. **c** A che ora ha = **è** partito il treno? **d** Hai veduto = **visto** i quadri di Villa Borghese? **e** Aicha è rimasto = **rimasta** in ufficio. **f** Avete mangiati = **mangiato** i dolci tipici di questa regione? **g** Hai prenduto = **preso** il biglietto dell'autobus?
2 a Venezia è molto bella. **b** Ho molti amici in Italia **c** Bevo poco caffè ma molta acqua. **d** A Venezia ci sono troppi turisti in estate.

LA MISTERIOSA DONNA IN SOFFITTA Ostuni > O

Unit 8

VOCABULARY BUILDER 1 blouse, jacket, sandals, dress, blue, red, large, long

VOCABULARY PRACTICE 1 **a** gialla **b** viola **c** verde **d** verde **e** neri

CONVERSATION 1 **3** A - Perché indossa un completo verde con scarpe rosa.

LANGUAGE DISCOVERY 1 **a** Prova questo. **c** Non esagerare! **d** Metti anche le scarpe.

LANGUAGE PRACTICE 1 **1 a** Scegli **b** Compra **c** Vesti **d** Prepara **e** Cerca **2** Non scegliere, non comprare, non vestire, non preparare, non cercare

LANGUAGE DISCOVERY 2 **1 b** Annalisa **2** Mi, ti, vi

LANGUAGE PRACTICE 2 **1 a** Ti **b** gli **c** Vi **d** le **e** Ci **f** gli **2 a** No, è troppo stretta per te. **b** No, è troppo corta. Ti piace la giacca blu, vicino ai pantaloni bianchi? **c** Chiama la commessa e chiedi dov'è il camerino. **d** Ti sta bene, è perfetta.

VOCABULARY BUILDER 2 t-shirt, classic, elegant, young-looking, cotton, linen

VOCABULARY PRACTICE 2 **ESTATE:** il costume, i sandali, la maglietta, la gonna di lino **INVERNO:** i guanti, i calzini di lana, il maglione, la sciarpa, il cappotto

CONVERSATION 2 **3 a** F **b** F **c** F **d** V **e** F

LANGUAGE DISCOVERY 3 The pronouns connect to the end of the verb. In the first form the letter M doubles itself.

LANGUAGE PRACTICE 3 **a** Ascoltami **b** non dimenticare **c** Guarda **d** Chiamalo **e** Chiamali **f** Senti **g** portalo **h** ricordati **i** telefonami

LANGUAGE DISCOVERY 4 **a** bella **b** quei **c** quella **d** bel **e** quel **f** quelle. Both the adjectives bello and quello change following the definite article of the noun they refer to.

LANGUAGE PRACTICE 4 **1 1** quel vestito **2** bell'abbigliamento **3** quello sport **4** bella gonna **5** quell'arancione **6** bei calzini **7** quegli stivali **8** belle scarpe

SKILL BUILDER **1** Ciao Fabio! Per un matrimonio in Italia ti consiglio un completo elegante. Prendilo nero, blu o marrone, ma di cotone o di lino, perché a giugno fa caldo. Metti una bella camicia bianca o azzurra e scarpe eleganti, di un colore simile a quello del completo. Non dimenticare la cravatta e l'orologio! **2 a** bel **b** quel **c** le **d** divertiti **e** mi **f** le **3** La ragazza porta una camicia bianca di cotone e una maglia rosa. Ha una gonna nera e verde, forse di lana, e scarpe con il tacco rosa. Il ragazzo indossa una giacca marrone, un maglione bianco e pantaloni marroni di cotone. Porta scarpe nere e calzini rosa.

TEST YOURSELF

1 a le **b** ci **c** mi **d** Gli **e** Gli **f** ti **2 a** Mettila! **b** Non indossarli **c** dimmi **d** comprale **e** Non spendere **f** cambialo

3

Articolo		QUELLO	BELLO
il	completo	**Quel** completo è elegante.	È un **bel** completo.
la	giacca	**Quella** giacca è alla moda.	È una **bella** giacca.
gli	stivali	**Quegli** stivali sono di pelle	Sono dei **begli** stivali.
le	gonne	**Quelle** gonne sono lunghe	Sono delle **belle** gonne.
lo	zaino	**Quello** zaino è di cotone	È un **bello** zanino.
i	vestiti	**Quei** vestiti sono blu	Sono dei **bei** vestiti.
l'	orologio	**Quell'**orologio è moderno	È un **bell'**orologio.

LA MISTERIOSA DONNA IN SOFFITTA Rosa > R

Unit 9

VOCABULARY BUILDER 1 palace, detached house, terraced house, bedroom, bathroom, garden, balcony

VOCABULARY PRACTICE 1 **a** la cucina **b** la camera da letto **c** l'ingresso **d** il bagno **e** il salotto/soggiorno/sala da pranzo **f** il salotto/soggiorno/sala da pranzo

CONVERSATION 1 **3 a** F **b** F **c** V **d** V **e** V **f** V

LANGUAGE DISCOVERY 1 **a** io, abitare **b** loro, avere **c** lui, essere **d** tu, avere **e** noi, dividere

LANGUAGE PRACTICE 1 **a** piaceva **b** amavo **c** costruivo **d** eri **e** aveva **f** leggeva **g** suonava **h** eravamo **i** giocavamo **j** sognavo

LANGUAGE DISCOVERY 2 An ongoing situation

LANGUAGE PRACTICE 2 **1 a** Da giovane **b** piaceva **c** andava **d** non... mai **e** di solito **f** A 25 anni **g** spesso **h** una volta

CULTURE POINT 2 **b** School is compulsory until students are 16 years old.

VOCABULARY BUILDER 2 kindergarten, student/schoolchild, mathematics, literature, science, to teach

VOCABULARY PRACTICE 2 **a** la matematica **b** la letteratura **c** le scienze **d** le lingue straniere **e** l'educazione fisica

CONVERSATION 2 **3 a** A **b** C **c** A **d** C **e** A

LANGUAGE DISCOVERY 3 **a** sto leggendo = leggere **b** cosa sta succedendo? = succedere **c** stai ancora pensando? = pensare **d** ci penso tutti i giorni = pensare. The verbs involved are stare + (leggere, succedere, pensare). Sentence 3 indicates that the person is thinking in this very moment, sentence 4 indicates that the person thinks of something not in this moment (ongoing action) but usually (habitual action).

LANGUAGE PRACTICE 3 **a** sta guardando **b** sta leggendo **c** stanno andando **d** stiamo frequentando **e** state facendo **f** stai studiando

LANGUAGE DISCOVERY 4 **1** b **2** c **3** a The common element is that replacement elements start with the preposition a.

LANGUAGE PRACTICE 4 **1 a** Ci pensa tutti i giorni. **b** Non ci va volentieri. **c** Ci lavora spesso. **d** Ci lavora da lunedì a venerdì. **e** Ci vanno per 5 anni. **f** Ci andava in treno. **2 a** Sì, ci andavo volentieri/ no, non ci andavo... **b** Ci andavo... **c** Sì ci penso/ no, non ci penso... **d** Ci vado...

SKILL BUILDER **1 1** c **2** b **3** a **4** d **2** Students' own answers **3 a** Ci vado spesso, qualche volta, sempre **b** Ci vado spesso, qualche volta, sempre **c** Sì, ci lavoro spesso, sempre, qualche volta / no, non ci lavoro mai **d** Sì, ci vado spesso, qualche volta, sempre / no, non ci vado mai **4 a** Da bambin* io andavo **b** L'anno scorso sono andat*... **c** Da bambin* mi piaceva... **d** io abitavo...

TEST YOURSELF **1 a** abitavo/vivevo **b** era **c** vivevamo/abitavamo **d** lavoravano **e** andavamo **f** piaceva **2 a** Cristian sta leggendo un libro. **b** Zhuang sta telefonando a Lisa. **c** Voi state scrivendo un'email. **d** Io sto cucinando il pranzo. **e** Tu stai lavorando in ospedale. **f** Sandra e Pablo stanno uscendo.

LA MISTERIOSA DONNA IN SOFFITTA Notizie > N

Unit 10

VOCABULARY BUILDER 1 to start, incredible, aggressive, enormous, dog, cat, species

VOCABULARY PRACTICE 1 **a** Uccello **b** Gatto **c** Cavallo **d** Piccione **e** Cane

CONVERSATION 1 **3 a** Kubo **b** Tre **c** Pausa pranzo **d** Un panino **e** Le ha rubato il panino

LANGUAGE DISCOVERY 1 **a** Mentre mangiavo, è arrivato **b** Mentre correvo dentro, mi ha rubato Mentre introduces the sentences.

LANGUAGE PRACTICE 1 **a** era, siamo rimasti **b** tornavo, ho trovato **c** era, siamo andate **d** ho visto, aspettavo

LANGUAGE DISCOVERY 2 veramente > vero; probabilmente > probabile

LANGUAGE PRACTICE 2 **1 a** aggressivamente **b** enormemente **c** incredibilmente **d** allegramente **e** freddamente **f** felicemente **g** sportivamente **h** formalmente **i** informalmente **j** correttamente

VOCABULARY BUILDER 2 coast, forest, lake, territory, volcano

VOCABULARY PRACTICE 2 **Orizzontali 1** vulcano **4** fiume **5** lago **7** costa **8** foresta **Verticali 2** aquila **3** collina **6** orso

CONVERSATION 2 **3** d, a, c, b

LANGUAGE DISCOVERY 3 In the first example, the duration of the action is precisely known: two minutes. In the second example, the duration is uncertain.

LANGUAGE PRACTICE 3 **a** Abbiamo studiato **b** è andato, era, indossava **c** giocavano **d** passeggiavamo, ha cominciato **e** hai abitato **f** hanno finito **g** siete entrati, parlava

LANGUAGE DISCOVERY 4 **a** L'ho seguita **b** Li ha messi per terra. The direct object pronoun is the shared element.

LANGUAGE PRACTICE 4 **1 a** Sì, l'ho comprata. **b** Sì, le ho viste. **c** Sì, li ho letti. **d** Sì, l'ho guardato. **e** Sì, l'ho mangiato. **f** Sì, li ho prenotati. **g** Sì, l'ho pulita. **h** Sì, l'ho chiamata. **i** Sì, le ho preparate. **j** Sì, le ho prese.

SKILL BUILDER **1** Il cane, il somaro, il pipistrello, il mulo, il coccodrillo, i serpenti, l'agnellino, cani, la scimmia, i pesci **2 a** F **b** F **c** V **d** F **e** V **3 Example:** Il cucciolo di orso sembrava terrorizzato e solo. Il lupo si è avvicinato con curiosità e gentilezza. Gli altri lupi hanno deciso di prendere l'orso nel gruppo. Con il tempo, il cucciolo di orso è diventato amico con i lupi, ha imparato le loro abitudini e è diventato parte della comunità. Insieme, lupi e orso, hanno vissuto la vita nella foresta. La loro unione ha dimostrato che, anche in mezzo alla natura, l'amicizia e la solidarietà possono superare ogni differenza.**4** **a** la montagna **b** ovviamente **c** l'ha scoperta **d** l'ha più abbandonata **e** amava **f** ha scoperto **g** li ha amati **h** giocava **i** si è trasferito **j** ero **k** fortunatamente

TEST YOURSELF **1** **a** Sono arrivati **b** è cominciata **c** mi facevo la doccia **d** ho sentito **e** si è rotta **f** mi lavavo **g** ho chiamato **h** aspettavo **i** ha telefonato **j** ho finito **k** sono uscito **l** ho dimenticato **2** **1** d **2** a **3** f **4** g **5** b **6** c **7** e **3** **b** aggressivamente **c** felicemente **e** correttamente

LA MISTERIOSA DONNA IN SOFFITTA Aquila > A

Unit 11

VOCABULARY BUILDER 1 program, newscast, documentary, thriller, TV license, episode

VOCABULARY PRACTICE 1 **a** drammatico **b** gioco a premi **c** poliziesco **d** documentario **e** dibattito politico **f** cartoni animati **g** commedia romantica

CONVERSATION 1 **3** **a** A **b** C **c** C **d** A **e** C **4** Students' own answers

LANGUAGE DISCOVERY 1 **1** b **2** c **3** a Verbs in -are and -ere end in -erei; verbs in -ire end in -irei.

LANGUAGE PRACTICE 1 **a** guarderebbe **b** smetterei **c** mangeremmo **d** annoierebbe **e** uscirebbero

LANGUAGE DISCOVERY 2 These verbs don't follow the pattern of regular verbs. The stem of the verb is different.

Would you want/like to subscribe to SkyTV?	Vorresti fare l'abbonamento a SkyTV?	VOLERE
I would not be able to sleep.	Non potrei dormire	POTERE
I would go to bed.	Andrei a letto	ANDARE
It would be perfect to fall asleep on the couch.	Sarebbe perfetta per addormentarsi sul divano	ESSERE

LANGUAGE PRACTICE 2 **1** **a** potrei... **b** andrei **c** vorrebbe **d** dovrebbe **e** gatto starebbe **2** **a** Io mangerei... **b** Si, mi piacerebbe / no, non mi piacerebbbe... **c** Si, vorrei... / no, non vorrei... **d** Io guarderei... **e** Si, lo farei... / no. non lo farei... **f** Si, io Andrei / No. no andrei...

VOCABULARY BUILDER 2 newspaper, article, society, to play the lottery, to dream, two hundred (three hundred...), one million, two million

VOCABULARY PRACTICE 2 **1 a** 2000.000 = due milioni **b** 8790 = ottomilasettecentonovanta **c** 6923 = semilanovecentoventitre **d** 348 = trecentoquarantotto **e** 4000.000.000 = quattro miliardi **f** 7560.000 = settemilioni e settecentocinquantamila **2 a** il giornalista **b** il giornalaio/la giornalaia **c** in edicola **d** il titolo

CONVERSATION 2 **3 a** Uno studente vince 500.000 euro e compra una casa al mare = li dá in beneficenza. **b** I giornalisti scrivono articoli noiosi. = sensazionali **c** Annalisa vorrebbe lavorare di più = meno **d** Aicha aprirebbe un negozio a Berlino = uno studio di fotografia **e** In edicola Aicha e Annalisa comprano una rivista. = un Gratta e Vinci / un biglietto della lotteria

LANGUAGE DISCOVERY 3 **a** P; potere **b** W; volere **c** S; dovere **d** P; potere

LANGUAGE PRACTICE 3 **1 a** Potresti chiudere la porta. **b** Scusi, Lei mi potrebbe dire dove è l'autobus? **c** Aicha vorrebbe visitare Berlino. **d** Io vorrei ordinare un caffé. **e** Cristian vorrebbe fare una maratona di serie TV. **f** Noi vorremmo vivere in campagna. **g** Non dovresti telefonare in treno.

LANGUAGE DISCOVERY 4 Giornalista has two plurals, one for masculine and one for feminine. Città does not change. Dramma has a plural ending in -i like all masculine nouns although it ends in -a.

LANGUAGE PRACTICE 4 **1 a** giornalista **b** caffé **c** problemi **d** città **e** pianista **f** atlete **g** drammi **h** maratoneti

SKILL BUILDER **1** ORRORE/THRILLER – Curon; DOCUMENTARIO – Caffé sospeso; GIALLO/POLIZIESCO – La legge di Lidia Poet; COMMEDIA ROMANTICA – Sotto il sole di Riccione **2 a** tennisto = tennista **b** citte – città **c** I programma = i programmi **d** caffí = caffè **3 a** Caldissimo **b** 750.000 euro **c** dibattito **d** gli atleti **e** sogna

TEST YOURSELF **1 a** compreresti **b** deciderei **c** piacerebbe **d** studiereste **e** avremmo **f** Sarebbe **g** verrebbero **h** faresti **2 a** Le città italiane sono belle. **b** I giornalisti sono giapponesi. **c** Mi piacciono i programmi. **d** I teoremi sono difficili. **3 a** Potresti **b** Dovresti **c** Vorresti **d** Potrei **e** Vorreste

LA MISTERIOSA DONNA IN SOFFITTA Roberto Benigni > R

Unit 12

VOCABULARY BUILDER 1 lamp, possibility, vase, metal, plastic, colorful, design, functional, modern

VOCABULARY PRACTICE 1 **a** lampada **b** poltrona **c** sedia **d** libreria **e** caffettiera **f** vaso

CONVERSATION 1 **2 a** To make coffee **b** Moka – caffettiera **c** Because it's modern and has a stylish design.

LANGUAGE DISCOVERY 1 **1 a** meno – di **b** più – che **2** Piú and meno before the adjective and di/che to introduce the second word.

LANGUAGE PRACTICE 1 **a** Londra è più grande di Roma. **b** Cucinare le lasagne è meno veloce che cucinare la pasta. **c** Le poltrone sono più comode delle sedie. **d** La tua lampada è meno moderna della mia.

LANGUAGE DISCOVERY 2 **a** Che cos'è? – *What* **b** La caffettiera che ho comprato ieri. – *That* **c** Forse scopri che fare il caffè è più facile. – *That*

LANGUAGE PRACTICE 2

1

	What? / Which?	That (conjunction)	That/which (relative)	Who	Than	How
a					x	
b		x				
c				x		
d						x
e		x				
f						x
g	x					
h			x			
i					x	
j			x			

2 **1** e **2** a **3** f **4** d **5** b **6** c

CULTURE POINT 2 **a** Ferrari > Modena/Maranello **b** Lamborghini > Bologna/Sant'Agata Bolognese **c** Maserati > Modena **d** Ducati > Bologna/Borgo Panigale **e** Dallara > Parma/ Varano dè Melegari

VOCABULARY BUILDER 2 second hand, app, mobile phone, computer, notification, digital watch, selfie, social media, tablet, television, to click, to google, to zoom in/out

VOCABULARY PRACTICE 2 **a** contapassi **b** motorino **c** computer **d** auricolari **e** cellulare

CONVERSATION 2 **3** **a** F **b** V **c** F **d** V **e** F

LANGUAGE DISCOVERY 3 **a** With which **b** Next to which **c** On which **d** That/which Cui is always preceded by a preposition.

LANGUAGE PRACTICE 3 **1** **a** in cui **b** di cui **c** in cui **d** a cui **e** per cui **2** **a** che **b** in cui **c** che **d** con cui **e** che

LANGUAGE DISCOVERY 4 **a** ne hai già persi **b** Ne ho vista The past participle changes according to the noun ne is referring to.

LANGUAGE PRACTICE 4 **1** **a** ne ho persi **c** ne hanno comprata **d** ne hanno riparati **e** ne ho comprato

SKILL BUILDER **1 b** Il mio amico con cui ho fatto una videochiamata abita in Colombia. / Ho fatto una videochiamata con il mio amico che abita in Colombia. **c** La poltrona su cui mio nonno si siede sempre è di design. / Mio nonno si siede sempre sulla poltrona che è di design. **d** Sei andato all'evento del Salone del Mobile che era alle 5 pm? **e** In città circolo solo con la Vespa che ho comprato di seconda mano. **f** Gli amici con cui mi hai visto sono i miei compagni di cosplay. / Tu mi hai visto con gli amici che sono i miei compagni di cosplay. **g** L'ufficio in cui Felipe e Tatiana lavorano è in centro. / Felipe e Tatiana lavorano nell'ufficio che è in centro. **2 a** Sì, ne ho comprati due per mia sorella. **b** Sì, ne ho comprate quattro. **c** Ne ho ricevute almeno venti. **d** Sì, ne ho comprata una molto moderna. **e** Ne ho vista molta. **f** Sì, ne ho comprata una di seconda mano. **g** Sì, ne ho scaricate almeno cinque o sei. **3 a** Questa lampada è meno antica di quella lampada. **b** Questi auricolari sono più moderni di quegli auricolari. **c** Lamborghini è più veloce della Fiat 500.

TEST YOURSELF **1** h **2** a **3** e **4** j **5** c **6** f **7** i **8** b **9** g **10** d

LA MISTERIOSA DONNA IN SOFFITTA Orologio digitale > O

Unit 13

VOCABULARY BUILDER 1 connection, connected, microphone, video camera, video call, to connect, to disconnect, remote working, I can't see you/I can't hear you, I can see you/I can hear you

VOCABULARY PRACTICE 1 **a** connettermi **b** connessione **c** videochiamata **d** connesso **e** ti vedo **f** non ti sento **g** attivare

CONVERSATION 1 **3 a** a casa **b** Una cattiva connessione, difficoltà con la condivisione dello schermo, ha dimenticato di disattivare il microfono. **c** no

LANGUAGE DISCOVERY 1 They have essere as an auxiliary and the reflexive pronouns.

LANGUAGE PRACTICE 1 **a** ti sei alzato/a **b** ci siamo divertiti/e **c** mi sono dimenticato/a **d** si è arrabbiata **e** si sono lamentati **f** vi siete lavati/e

LANGUAGE DISCOVERY 2 **a** sto per impazzire **b** Stavano per attaccare **c** Sto per cominciare. The verb stare is followed by per + infinitive.

LANGUAGE PRACTICE 2 **1** e **2** c **3** d **4** f **5** b **6** a

VOCABULARY BUILDER 2 bye/see you soon, for your availability, thank you (informal), I'm writing to you (informal), I would like to ask, reference letter, via

VOCABULARY PRACTICE 2

	INFORMAL	FORMAL
How to address the recipient	Caro/a	Gentile, egregio/a
How to introduce the reason of contact	ti scrivo per	le scrivo per
How to start a question	vorrei chiederti	vorrei chiederle
How to say you are waiting for an answer	fammi sapere!	in attesa di una sua risposta
How to thank the recipient	ti ringrazio	la ringrazio
Final greetings	ciao/a presto	distinti/cordiali saluti

CONVERSATION 2 a, d

LANGUAGE DISCOVERY 3 **a** vorrei chiederle **b** Mi hanno chiesto **c** potrebbe scriverla **d** La può mandare. The pronoun precedes a conjugated verb, and it is joined to the verb when in the infinitive form.

LANGUAGE PRACTICE 3 **a** può darmi un secondo **b** non le voglio rubare **c** devo scriverla **d** la può scrivere **e** la può mandare **f** posso chiederle

LANGUAGE DISCOVERY 4 **a** le **b** le (chiederle) **c** la

LANGUAGE PRACTICE 4 **1 a** lo **b** le **c** gli **d** lo **e** la **f** gli **g** li **2 a** Sì le ho scritto **b** Sì, la compro **c** Lo chiamo domani **d** Gli regaliamo una lampada **e** Le vedo domani **f** Sì, l'ho visto **g** Le ho detto che sto male

SKILL BUILDER **1 a** mi sono svegliata alle 7 **b** mi sono alzata solo alle 7:30 **c** mi sono fatta una doccia **d** mi sono pettinata **e** alle 08:30 mi sono vestita **f** mi sono connessa **2 a** ci siamo svegliati/e alle 7 **b** ci siamo alzati/e solo alle 7:30 **c** ci siamo fatti/e una doccia **d** ci siamo pettinati/e **e** alle 08:30 ci siamo vestiti/e **f** ci siamo connessi/e **3 Example:** Gentile Dott. Steiner, le scrivo per dirle che ieri ho mandato la lettera alla galleria. Ho scritto le informazioni che mi ha detto e ho già ricevuto conferma. Buona fortuna! Federico Padoan **4** b, e, f, g, i

TEST YOURSELF **1 a** La riunione è cominciata in anticipo. **b** Le scrivo perché vorrei chiederle un favore. **c** Puoi disattivare il microfono? **d** Preferisco fare una videochiamata, perché lavoro da casa. **e** La ringrazio in anticipo per la disponibilità. **2 a** Eva è svegliata **b** Paolo e Mariam si sono connessi **c** Io mi sono comportato/a **d** Noi ci siamo fatti/e la doccia **e** Jonas si è vestito **f** Voi vi siete lamentati/e **3 a** Può provarle? **b** Possiamo parlargli? **c** Puoi pagarlo? **d** Potete chiamarla? **e** Può scrivergli? **f** Puoi usarlo?

LA MISTERIOSA DONNA IN SOFFITTA Posta > P

Unit 14

VOCABULARY BUILDER 1 torso, doctor's, hospital/emergency room, allergy, medicine, pharmacy

VOCABULARY PRACTICE 1 **1 a** ho mal di pancia **b** ho male ai piedi **c** ho mal di testa **d** ho la febbre **e** soffro di allergia **f** ho il raffreddore

CONVERSATION 1 **2 BENE:** fare una passeggiata; un po' di attività fisica **MALE:** guardare la televisione o il computer prima di dormire; il caffé e le bevande con caffeina; troppo lavoro

LANGUAGE DISCOVERY 1 When using the expression fa bene / fa male, the verb fare agrees with the thing that does good/harm. If this thing is singular, we use fa, if it is plural we use fanno.

LANGUAGE PRACTICE 1 **a** fa **b** fa **c** fa **d** fanno

LANGUAGE DISCOVERY 2 The doctor is prescribing something. Previously, you have learned the imperative to command.

LANGUAGE PRACTICE 2 **a** Beva... **b** Non guardi... **c** Faccia... **d** Vada **e** Prenda **f** Telefoni... **g** Stia... **h** Non fumi... **i** Scriva... **j** Non compri...

VOCABULARY BUILDER 2 stressful, relax, mind, mental health, to go to the psychologist, to meditate

VOCABULARY PRACTICE 2 **a** calma **b** stress **c** tranquillo **d** camminare **e** respirare **f** rilassarvi **g** palestra **h** yoga **i** si prendono cura

CONVERSATION 2 **2 c** Aicha ed Annalisa vogliono andare all'hotel Belvedere ma Cristian dice che il B&B di sua sorella è un'opzione migliore.

LANGUAGE DISCOVERY 3 **a** Il servizio è decisamente superiore. **b** La qualità è peggiore che in posti meno cari. **c** Hai un'idea migliore? **d** Vi potrebbe offrire un prezzo inferiore. **e** Mia sorella minore All the underlined words end in -ore.

LANGUAGE PRACTICE 3 **a** maggiore **b** meglio **c** superiore **d** inferiore **e** inferiore **f** migliore **g** peggio

LANGUAGE DISCOVERY 4 They are encouraging or ordering. The pronoun is attached at the end of the verb.

LANGUAGE PRACTICE 4 **1 a** respiriamola! **b** riposatevi! **c** pratichiamolo! **d** la faccia! **e** andiamoci! **f** bevila! **g** non guardiamola! **h** guardalo! **i** gli telefoni! **2 Sample answer:** Chiama il numero/chiamalo! Prenota una vacanza/prenotala! Rilassati!

SKILL BUILDER **1 a** Signora, è molto stressata, si rilassi. **b** Il corso di yoga è bellissimo, facciamolo! **c** L'hotel è economico, prenotiamolo! **d** Dottore, mi dica, cosa devo fare? **e** Compri questa medicina e la prenda tutti i giorni. **2 a** V **b** V **c** F **d** F **e** V **3 IL PAZIENTE HA:** mal di stomaco; la febbre; mal di testa; sono stanco **IL MEDICO SUGGERISCE:** mangi pasti leggeri; beva molta acqua; si riposi; non vada al lavoro; una medicina

TEST YOURSELF **1 a** Dorma **b** Non guardi **c** Faccia **d** Mangi **e** Beva **f** Prenda **g** Vada **2 a** le gambe **b** la febbre **c** la panica/lo stomaco **d** i denti **e** la testa

LA MISTERIOSA DONNA IN SOFFITTA Rotula > R

Unit 15

CULTURE POINT 1 **a** Valle d'Aosta, Piemonte, Lombardia, Emilia Romagna, Liguria, Toscana, Lazio **b** Canterbury, Reims, Losanna, Passo San Bernardo, San Gimignano, Siena, Roma

VOCABULARY BUILDER 1 pajamas, sunglasses, hiking boots, shampoo, path/road, ...to, foot

VOCABULARY PRACTICE 1 **a** caricatore **b** il pettine **c** lo zaino **d** attraverso

CONVERSATION 1 **3 a** F **b** F **c** V **d** V **e** F

LANGUAGE DISCOVERY 1 **a** Di solito si parte la mattina presto **b** Si percorrono circa 30 km al giorno **c** Si fa lo zaino leggerissimo **d** certo non si portano i trucchi. These sentences express a general habit or a custom. They are built with si + singular verb in the he/she form or plural in the loro form. It depends on the verb being associated with an activity/singular object on the one hand, or a plural object on the other.

LANGUAGE PRACTICE 1 **a** In Italia si fa sempre colazione al bar. F **b** In Italia si mangia molta pasta. V **c** In Italia ci si veste elegante per andare ai matrimoni. V **d** In Italia si mangiano antipasto, primo, secondo e dolce tutti i giorni. F **e** In Italia si va in vacanza solo al mare. F **f** In Italia ci si mette il costume per la festa di Carnevale. V

LANGUAGE DISCOVERY 2 **Matteo:** La Via degli Dei è sentiero **più** corto del mio programma... **Aicha:** Sarebbe **il** viaggio a piedi più lungo della mia vita...

LANGUAGE PRACTICE 2 **1 a** il **b** dell' **c** la **d** la **e** della **f** il **g** dei **h** la **i** più **j** dell'

VOCABULARY BUILDER 2 to explore, to go shopping, to take a walk, to sleep, village, museum

VOCABULARY PRACTICE 2 **una persona che ama la natura:** camminare nel bosco, salire su una montagna, dormire in tenda, guardare le stelle, andare a funghi **una persona che ama il cibo:** degustare i prodotti tipici, andare a funghi **una persona che ama l'arte e la storia:** andare a una rievocazione storica, visitare un castello, scoprire una chiesa antica, fare una visita guidata

CONVERSATION 2 **3 a** Bello ma non lo rifarebbe **b** Dormire in tenda **c** i castelli e la rievocazione storica **d** Sandra

LANGUAGE DISCOVERY 3 **a** piaciuta **b** piaciuti **c** piaciuto; The endings after **piaciut-** follow the subject in gender and number: **-o** for singular masculine, **-a** for singular feminine; **-i** for plural masculine; **-e** for plural feminine. The helping verb is **essere**.

LANGUAGE PRACTICE 3 **1 a** Annalisa sono piaciuti i borghi. **b** Mi è piaciuto pernottare nell'albergo diffuso **c** Ti sono piaciute le visite guidate? **d** A Aicha non è piaciuto salire sulla montagna. **e** Vi sono piaciuti molto i prodotti tipici.

LANGUAGE DISCOVERY 4 **1 a** Abbiamo **b** abbiamo **c** Abbiamo **d** siamo **e** voluto **2** We use avere when the verb after potuto, voluto, dovuto requires avere in the passato prossimo. We use essere when the verb after potuto, voluto, dovuto requires essere in the passato prossimo.

LANGUAGE PRACTICE 4 **1** Ieri Aicha ha voluto passare una giornata in totale relax. Prima però ha dovuto fare alcune cose in ufficio poi finalmente è potuta uscire. È voluta andare al museo per vedere una mostra di fotografia e ha voluto anche fare un giro in centro per fare un po' di shopping prima di incontrare un'amica per un aperitivo. Purtroppo però la sua amica non è potuta venire perché ha dovuto lavorare fino a tardi e così Aicha ha dovuto bere uno spritz da sola in piazza. **2 Model answers:** (Non) mi è piaciuto/a; (Non) mi sono piaciuti/e; La cosa più bella è stata...

SKILL BUILDER **1 a** abbiamo **b** voluto **c** è **d** piaciuta **e** abbiamo **f** potuto **g** i abbiamo **h** dovuto **i** sono **j** voluto/a **k** Ho **l** potuto **m** ho **n** dovuto **o** siamo **p** potuti **q** abbiamo **r** voluto **s** abbiamo **t** potuto **u** è **v** piaciuto **2 a** Si prenotano i musei nelle grandi città in anticipo (*advance*). **b** Nel Centro e Sud Italia, non si mangia prima delle otto di sera. **c** Normalmente nei ristoranti e nei bar non si dà la mancia (*tip*). **d** In Italia si guida a destra. **e** Negli alberghi si paga la tassa di soggiorno. **f** Si paga per guidare in autostrada. **3 a** Il viaggio in Italia è stato il più/meno bello dell'anno. **b** La vacanza al mare è stata la più/meno lunga dell'anno. **c** Lucy è la più meno/alta del gruppo. **d** Pablo è il più meno/giovane della classe. **4** Students' own answers

TEST YOURSELF **Example answers: a** Il Lago di Garda è il più grande dei laghi della Lombardia. L'Etna è il più alto dei vulcani d'Italia. Terni è la città più piccola dell'Umbria.

LA MISTERIOSA DONNA IN SOFFITTA Sicilia > S

Unit 16

CULTURE POINT 1 **a La carta:** venerdì, mercoledì **b I rifiuti organici:** lunedì, martedì, mercoledì, giovedì, venerdì **c Il vetro:** lunedì, mercoledì, giovedì, venerdì

VOCABULARY BUILDER 1 metal, plastic, something, general waste, to collect, to recycle

VOCABULARY PRACTICE 1 **a** raccolta plastica **b** raccolta metalli **c** raccolta indifferenziato **d** raccolta vetro **e** raccolta carta e cartone **f** raccolta organico.

CONVERSATION 1 **3 a** Sta per mettere la plastica nel bidone del vetro. **b** Non ha gli occhiali. **c** Riceve una multa. **d** Non hanno il bidone del vetro in casa.

LANGUAGE DISCOVERY 1 Ne consegue: From this (referring to what has been said before, if you make a mistake you receive a fine); Ne abbiamo solo tre: the bins; Non ne ho sentito parlare: of this (referring to what has been said before about getting a fine

LANGUAGE PRACTICE 1 **a** Ho letto un articolo sulla raccolta differenziata in Trentino e ne sono stato molto impressionato. **b** Hanno cambiato il modo di fare la raccolta. Secondo me ne viene fuori un grande caos! **c** Hai visto cosa ha fatto il primo ministro? Tutti ne parlano. **d** Abbiamo finito le carote. Ne compri un chilo, per favore? **e** Quel ristorante è molto rumoroso. Ne sono uscita con il mal di testa!

LANGUAGE DISCOVERY 2 Niente means *nothing* and qualcosa means *something*. Niente is preceded by a negative form (non) placed before the verb. Qualcosa has the preposition di afterwards.

LANGUAGE PRACTICE 2 **1 a** Qualcuno **b** qualcosa **c** niente **d** Qualcuno **e** Qualcuno nessuno **f** qualcosa

CULTURE POINT 2 **a** 14 maggio 2003 **b** Modulo Sperimentale Elettromeccanico, abbreviato con l'acronimo Mo.S.E. **c** Consorzio Venezia Nuova

VOCABULARY BUILDER 2 environmental change, erosion, level, renewable, system, sustainable, to monitor, to protect

VOCABULARY PRACTICE 2 **a** mondo **b** ambiente **c** cambiamento climatico **d** inquinamento **e** risorse **f** sostenibile **g** proteggere **h** ambiente **i** risorse

CONVERSATION 2 **3 1** e **2** c **3** a **4** d **5** b

LANGUAGE DISCOVERY 3 The sentences provided contain a future tense and indicate actions or events that will happen at some point after the moment of speaking. The verbs' stem is the same as the one built to form the conditional mood.

LANGUAGE PRACTICE 3 **a** comincerò **b** andranno **c** Scriveremo **d** dovrà **e** finirete - verrano **f** sarà **g** potremo **h** rimarrà

LANGUAGE DISCOVERY 4 dei problemi = *some problems*. Qualche problema is an equivalent in the conversation. Alcune funzioni is a way to express an indefinite quantity, referring to a different noun.

LANGUAGE PRACTICE 4 **1 a** del **b** delle/alcune **c** qualche **d** qualche **e** alcuni/dei **f** Alcune/delle **g** qualche

SKILL BUILDER **1 a** del, del **b** alcune **c** Nessuno **d** Qualcosa **e** Alcuni **f** qualcosa **g** qualcosa, delle **h** Niente **i** Qualcuno **j** niente **2** Il MOSE di Venezia è un sistema di dighe mobili che sono posizionate in diversi punti. Ne troviamo alcune all'ingresso delle bocche di mare principali che collegano la laguna di Venezia al Mar Adriatico. Le dighe si trovano sul fondo del mare e ne escono solo quando è necessario evitare inondazioni. Perché questo sistema? Perché Venezia ne ha molto bisogno. Quando le dighe sono alzate, creano una barriera contro l'acqua. La città ha avuto molte inondazioni nel passato, ma il MOSE è stato creato per proteggerla.

TEST YOURSELF **1 a** Le temperature globali cresceranno. **b** Questo porterà condizioni climatiche più estreme. **c** Nei prossimi decenni, le inondazioni diventeranno più frequenti. **d** Le siccità saranno più comuni in alcune regioni. **e** L'innovazione tecnologica ci aiuterà a adattarci ai cambiamenti climatici. **f** Le energie rinnovabili, come il sole e il vento, diventeranno sempre più importanti. **g** La cooperazione internazionale sarà cruciale per affrontare gli effetti dei cambiamenti climatici. **h** Il nostro futuro dipenderà dalle azioni che cominceremo oggi. **i** Ridurre le emissioni, promuovere la sostenibilità e adattarci ai cambiamenti saranno attività essenziali. **2 Example:** Il futuro del nostro pianeta

dipenderà dalle scelte che faremo oggi. Il riscaldamento globale e gli eventi climatici estremi rappresentano una sfida globale che richiede azioni urgenti. Le energie rinnovabili e l'innovazione tecnologica offrono strumenti per adattarci e mitigare questi effetti. Penso però che la cooperazione internazionale e la promozione della sostenibilità siano indispensabili per un futuro migliore. Investire ora in soluzioni sostenibili è essenziale per proteggere il nostro ambiente e garantire la sopravvivenza delle prossime generazioni.
3 a andremo **b** studieranno **c** avremo, berremo **d** Partirete **e** Farà **f** scriverà **g** riceveranno

LA MISTERIOSA DONNA IN SOFFITTA Barriera di Chioggia > C

Unit 17

CULTURE POINT 1 a Liguria **b** 1951 **c** Nilla Pizzi. La canzone era "Grazie dei Fiori"

VOCABULARY BUILDER 1 unpleasant, impulsive, reserved, shy, love, love story, attraction, to be single

VOCABULARY PRACTICE 1 a permaloso **b** esce **c** convivono **d** riservata **e** si sono lasciati **f** antipatica

CONVERSATION 1 3 a Perché Aicha dice che ogni volta ha trovato la persona giusta. **b** Perché la parola non indica attrazione/amore. **c** Aicha dovrebbe chiedere alla persona di andare alla mostra insieme.

LANGUAGE DISCOVERY 1 1 c **2** b **3** a **4** a The pronouns agree with the thing **1 a** andremo **b** studieranno **c** avremo, berremo **d** Partirete **e** Farà **f** scriverà **g** riceveranno they replace. The first pronoun changes the final vowel.

LANGUAGE PRACTICE 1 a Sì, te lo ho già detto / No, non te lo ho detto. **b** Sì, te lo do / No, non te lo do. **c** Sì, glielo scrivo/ No, non glielo scrivo. **d** Sì, te la mando / No, non te la mando. **e** Sì, glielo ho detto / No, non glielo ho detto. **f** Sì , ve lo scrivo. / No, non ve lo scrivo. **g** Sì, ce li mandi / No, non ce li mandi. **h** Non me lo compro / Sì, me lo compro, **i** Sì, te lo compro / No, non te lo compro. **j** No, non glielo ho mandato/ Sì, glielo ho mandato.

LANGUAGE DISCOVERY 2 1 a **2** c **3** b Ogni does not agree with volta

LANGUAGE PRACTICE 2 1 a tutti **b** ognuno/a/* **c** ogni **d** tutte **e** ognuna **f** uno/a/*

VOCABULARY BUILDER 2 happy, anxious, enthusiasm, enthusiastic, worried, I miss, to worry

VOCABULARY PRACTICE 2 a sono entusiasta **b** ho paura **c** mi sento felice **d** sono ansiosa **e** mi preoccupo

CONVERSATION 2 3 a F **b** V **c** F **d** V **e** V

LANGUAGE DISCOVERY 3 è turns into sia.

LANGUAGE PRACTICE 3 a Non vedo l'ora che sia il mio compleanno. **b** Spero che tu stia bene. **c** Mi dispiace che siamo in ritardo per la cena. **d** Mi preoccupo che questo problema non abbia una soluzione. **e** Mi dispiace che non abbiate tempo per un caffè. **f** Sono felice che i miei amici siano qui con me.

LANGUAGE DISCOVERY 4 Sentire ends in -a and mancare has an ending in - (-ino).

LANGUAGE PRACTICE 4 **1 a** cambi **b** cresca **c** finisca **d** mi senta **e** sia **f** offra

SKILL BUILDER **1** g, c, a, d, b, e **2 a** me lo **b** te lo **c** glielo **3 Example answer:** CoffeeLover91 e Sempreinviaggi0 87 sono compatibili perché loro Non sono compatibili perché uno/a/* ama / odia... e uno/a/* **4** Si, te lo compro. Si, glielo mando.

TEST YOURSELF **a** abbia **b** parta **c** manchi **d** stia **e** viva

LA MISTERIOSA DONNA IN SOFFITTA Odio > O

Unit 18

VOCABULARY BUILDER 1 costume, expert, comic, genre, public/audience, to organize, to participate, to produce, to promote, to publish

VOCABULARY PRACTICE 1 **a** l'ospite **b** il palcoscenico **c** lo spettacolo **d** il pubblico **e** il costume **f** la casa editrice

CONVERSATION 1 **3 a** Non ha avuto tempo **b** Solo in Giapponese **c** Sì

LANGUAGE DISCOVERY 1 In the first sentence, the subject performs the action on an object. In the second one, the object becomes the subject, and the action is carried out on it by someone or something. This construction is employed to emphasize the action rather than the subject.

LANGUAGE PRACTICE 1 **2** Il Salone del Libro di quest'anno ha ospitato numerosi autori famosi. **4** Il concerto di ieri sera ha attirato un pubblico numeroso ed entusiasta. **5** Il festival cinematografico di Cannes presenterà una grande selezione di film internazionali **7** Ieri sera gli organizzatori del festival teatrale di Bologna hanno presentato sul palcoscenico nuovi spettacoli. **8** Alla presentazione del nuovo libro, il pubblico ha applaudito l'autore.

LANGUAGE DISCOVERY 2 **a** avevo **b** ho The auxiliary verb is in the imperfect tense for the first one and normal present tense for the second one. Although both actions happened in the past, the first action took place before the second. The other two forms in the conversation are mi avevi detto; ero andato a informarmi.

LANGUAGE PRACTICE 2 **1 e** era cominciata **2 a** avevo comprato **3 d** avevano parlato **4 f** avevamo prenotato **5 c** ero andata **6 b** eravamo arrivati/e

VOCABULARY BUILDER 2 critics, curator, award/prize, prestigious, protagonist/main actor, to inaugurate, to award

VOCABULARY PRACTICE 2 **a** premi **b** ha recitato **c** capacità **d** ruoli **e** premio **f** protagonista **g** ha recitato **h** critica **i** è stata inaugurata

CONVERSATION 2 **2 b** *Cristian e Liang hanno appena finito di vedere un film.* **d** La protagonista sembra la signora del dipinto.

LANGUAGE DISCOVERY 3 **a** valore negativo **b** più grande **c** più piccolo

LANGUAGE PRACTICE 3 **a** un gatto grande **b** la mia sorella più piccola **c** un paese piccolo **d** una voce alta **e** un gesto brutto **f** una finestra piccola **g** un bacio grande **h** un voto brutto

LANGUAGE DISCOVERY 4 **a** così tanto **b** a tal punto **c** in modo che. They highlight a consequence of what happened in the previous sentence.

LANGUAGE PRACTICE 4 **a** a tal punto che **b** così famosa che **c** in modo che **d** quindi **e** in modo che **f** in modo che **g** a tal punto che

SKILL BUILDER **1 a** ho finito, avevo cominciato. **b** Ho capito, aveva vinto. **c** ha riconosciuto, erano entrati. **d** Sono andato/a, aveva regalato **e** Ho riportato, avevo letto. **f** ha mangiato, aveva consigliato **2 Orizzontali 2** gattina **5** tavolone **6** figuraccia **7** favorone **Verticali 1** librino **3** bicchierino **4** parolaccia **3 a** Durante il festival, il nuovo film è stato presentato dal regista. **b** Gli attori più bravi sono stati premiati dal presentatore. **c** Domenica una nuova galleria in centro sarà/verrà aperta dalla pittrice. **d** Solo film commerciali sono/vengono dati da questo cinema. **e** Da bambini, io e i miei cugini eravamo/venivamo sempre portati alle mostre di arte moderna da mia zia. **f** Molti applausi sono stati ricevuti dallo scrittore durante la presentazione. **4 a** Lesley Lokko è la curatrice della diciottesima Mostra Internazionale di Architettura della Biennale di Venezia 2023 Gioca un ruolo fondamentale nell'organizzazione e nella definizione di questa mostra. **b** I due temi principali affrontati dai lavori in mostra durante questa edizione sono la decolonizzazione e la decarbonizzazione. **c** Nel contesto della Mostra, 'Il Laboratorio del Futuro' ; simboleggia un luogo in cui vengono sviluppate e testate idee e soluzioni innovative per il futuro. **d** L'espressione 'Ospiti dal Futuro' fa riferimento ad artisti innovativi e visionari il cui lavoro va oltre diversi contesti, dalla realtà all'immaginario. **e** Il messaggio principale che Lesley Lokko intende trasmettere attraverso il concetto di un 'laboratorio del futuro' è che immaginare un mondo migliore è un passo fondamentale per costruirlo. **5 Example answer:** Oggi è stata inaugurata la nuova edizione del Salone del libro a Torino, nel centro congressi Lingotto Fiere. Ci sono molte sorprese in arrivo, come la presentazione del nuovo libro di Niccolò Ammaniti il 7 maggio, a cui seguirà un'opportunità di fare domande. Altre sorprese saranno svelate nei giorni successivi. Non perdetele!

TEST YOURSELF **a** Sì, era molto interessante! **b** È vero, il film è già stato citato da diverse riviste e notiziari. **c** Sì, "Ritratto di un giovane gatto". L'attore/attrice protagonista era così incredibile nel suo ruolo da vincere un premio Oscar.

LA MISTERIOSA DONNA IN SOFFITTA Palazzo del Cinema = P

Unit 19

CULTURE POINT 1 L'obiettivo è organizzare un incontro di tutte le persone che amano la street art.

VOCABULARY BUILDER 1 heritage, initiative, preserve/safeguard, requalify/develop, police, act of vandalism

VOCABULARY PRACTICE 1 **1** c **2** b **3** d **4** e **5** a

CONVERSATION 1 **3 a** C **b** C **c** M **d** M **e** C **f** M

LANGUAGE DISCOVERY 1 We use the verb andare plus the participle of the verb indicating the action that must be done.

LANGUAGE PRACTICE 1 **a** Lo spazio pubblico va pulito. **b** Il codice della strada va rispettato. **c** Il telefono non va usato in macchina. **d** Le tasse vanno pagate. **e** Gli spazi verdi vanno preservati. **f** La spazzatura non va lasciata in strada. **g** I mezzi di trasporto non vanno sporcati.

LANGUAGE DISCOVERY 2 The speaker uses either per or affinché to introduce the goal of an action. Sometimes the verb is an infinitive; sometimes it is a subjunctive. **a** abbiano **b** riqualificare **c** offrire

LANGUAGE PRACTICE 2 **1 1 c** affinché la società sia migliore **2 a** per denunciare i vandali **3 e** affinché le generazioni future ereditino la nostra arte **4 d** affinché i graffiti siano cancellati **5 b** per colorare i muri vecchi

VOCABULARY BUILDER 2 to agree, to convince, switched off, to activate

VOCABULARY PRACTICE 2 **a** spenta **b** premere un tasto **c** accendare **d** è contraria **e** da un lato... dall'altro **f** sollevare... abbassare

CONVERSATION 2 **2 a** perché c'è l'alta marea **b** perché va fatta solo in caso di emergenza; molte persone devono lavorare; le previsioni non sono sempre accurate **c** attivare il MOSE

LANGUAGE DISCOVERY 3 The sentences containing a subjunctive indicate a subjective opinion. The others report information or facts that are sure or certain.

LANGUAGE PRACTICE 3 **1 a** sia **b** abbia **c** fa **d** va **2 a** Dicono che vivere a Venezia in centro non è facile. **b** La capa di Annalisa pensa che attivare il MOSE non sia necessario. **c** Annalisa pensa che attivare il MOSE sia una buona idea. **d** Mi sembra che il traffico a Venezia sia bloccato. **e** Ho letto che Venezia è in pericolo. **f** Noi immaginiamo che Cristian abbia un'opinione estrema **g** Le previsioni annunciano che la marea arriva a 150 metri **h** Cristian è convinto che **i** graffiti e i murales sporchino i muri.

LANGUAGE DISCOVERY 4 Subjunctive. The sentences indicate not a fact but something seen as necessary.

LANGUAGE PRACTICE 4 **1 a** dobbiate **b** vada **c** facciate **d** deva **e** faccia **f** andiamo **2** Annalisa crede che attivare il MOSE sia necesssario. La sua capa crede che non sia una buona idea.

SKILL BUILDER **1 Example answers: a** la società sia migliore. **b** proteggere/preservare Venezia. **c** attivare il MOSE. **d** le generazioni future lo abbiano. **e** le persone vivano in un ambiente migliore. **2 a** possano **b** sia **c** pensi **d** premano **e** funzioni **f** vada **3 c 4** rispettare lo spazio pubblico, proteggere l'ambiente, avere delle leggi chiare, non sporcare gli spazi comuni, riciclare **5** Students' own answers.

TEST YOURSELF a È necessario rispettare l'ambiente / l'ambiente va rispettato. **b** È necessario che le persone riciclino i rifiuti / i rifiuti vanno riciclati. **c** Pagare le tasse. **d** Denunciare gli atti di vandalismo. **e** Parcheggiare le macchine negli spazi permessi. **f** Non gettare i rifiuti sulla strada.

LA MISTERIOSA DONNA IN SOFFITTA Ischia = I

Unit 20

VOCABULARY BUILDER 1 course, professional course, CV, faculty, to do research, to be born, promotion, archive, to indicate/to point

VOCABULARY PRACTICE 1 Suggested answers: Il corso: Un corso è un insieme di lezioni per insegnare qualcosa. Ad esempio, potrebbe essere un corso di matematica, di cucina o di informatica. **Il curriculum**: Il curriculum è un elenco delle esperienze di studio e di titoli che una persona ha fatto in un determinato periodo. Può anche includere esperienze lavorative, abilità acquisite e altri dettagli. **Laurearsi**: Laurearsi significa completare con successo un corso di studi, normalmente un'università, ottenendo una laurea. Ad esempio, laurearsi in medicina significa completare con successo gli studi necessari per diventare un medico. **Nascere**: Nascere è l'atto di venire al mondo. Quando una persona nasce, inizia la sua vita. **Trasferirsi**: Trasferirsi significa spostarsi da un luogo a un altro. Ad esempio, una persona può decidere di trasferirsi in una nuova città per lavoro o per motivi personali. La parola si riferisce al cambio di residenza o posizione.

CONVERSATION 1 3 Example answer: Elena Cornaro Piscopia è nata a Venezia nel 1646 Anche se non ha frequentato l'università, ha studiato filosofia, teologia e greco antico. È stata una delle prime donne al mondo a laurearsi, anche se non esattamente la prima.

LANGUAGE DISCOVERY 1 a who **b** who **c** those who **d** those who. Sometimes it means simply who, sometimes a person who, or people who.

LANGUAGE PRACTICE 1 a che **b** chi **c** che **d** chi **e** chi **f** che **g** che **h** chi

LANGUAGE DISCOVERY 2 a avrebbe potuto **b** sarei rimasto. Conditional of the auxiliary (essere or avere) and past participle

LANGUAGE PRACTICE 2 1 a avrebbe studiato **b** avrebbe frequentato **c** si sarebbe sposata **d** avrebbe voluto **e** sarebbe voluta **f** avrebbe abitato **g** sarebbe andata **h** avrebbero adottato

VOCABULARY BUILDER 2 congratulations!, decision, experience/expertise, to evolve, to fail, promotion, objective, obstacle, success, triumph

VOCABULARY PRACTICE 2 1 c **2** a **3** b **4** a **5** b

CONVERSATION 2 1 b **2** d **3** a **4** c

LANGUAGE DISCOVERY 3 Non so, sarà ancora a lavoro. What are you possibly afraid of? I don't know, she is probably at work.

LANGUAGE PRACTICE 3 **a** avrà **b** staranno giocando **c** avrà **d** sarà **e** sarà **f** starà parlando **g** costeranno **h** arriverà **i** saranno **j** starà facendo

LANGUAGE DISCOVERY 4 **a** sebbene abbia anche un po' paura **b** nonostante il MOSE sia un sistema automatico. They convey a sense of contrast or concession, signifying a situation that goes against the anticipated expectation.

LANGUAGE PRACTICE 4 **1 a** sono **b** abbia **c** studino **d** si merita **e** si laureino **f** sia

SKILL BUILDER **1 a** Elena Lucrezia Cornaro Piscopia è stata una delle prime donne a laurearsi al mondo. **b** Elena ha studiato molte materie, inclusi latino, greco, teologia e lingue straniere. **c** Elena è stata sepolta nella chiesa di Santa Giustina a Padova. **2 Example:** Elena Lucrezia Cornaro Piscopia era la prima donna al mondo a laurearsi e sapeva tante cose interessanti. Elena amava studiare fin da piccola e suo padre l'ha aiutata molto. Ha imparato molte lingue diverse e era anche brava in musica. Ma non era facile per Elena dimostrare la sua intelligenza come donna. Non poteva competere con gli uomini nel campo intellettuale. Anche se ha ottenuto una laurea importante, tutto è tornato come prima. Solo molti anni dopo, un'altra donna italiana si è laureata. Oggi, c'è una statua di Elena all'Università di Padova. È un omaggio alla prima donna laureata al mondo e un simbolo di libertà per le donne. Elena Lucrezia Cornaro Piscopia sarà sempre ricordata per la sua intelligenza e il suo coraggio. **3** Students' own answers.

4

Data di nascita:	4 dicembre 1927	**Progetto a Parigi:**	la trasformazione della stazione ferroviaria di Gare d'Orsay nel Musée d'Orsay
Materia studiata durante il corso di laurea:	architettura	**Altri progetti su cui ha lavorato:**	musei, teatri e spazi espositivi
Anno di laurea:	1953	**Altra passione oltre all'architettura:**	design industriale
Anno di apertura del suo primo studio:	Negli anni Sessanta	**Anno di morte:**	2012

TEST YOURSELF **1 a** venga **b** lavori **c** avremmo fatto **d** imparino **e** saranno **f** studi **2 Example answers: a** Avrei tagliato i capelli **b** Anna e Serra sarebbero andate in discoteca **c** Avrei chiesto la macchina in prestito a mio cugino **d** Avrebbero portato una torta in classe **e** Saremmo andati all'opera **f** Ti avrei sposato **g** Avrebbero organizzato una festa a sorpresa **h** Vi avremmo chiesto aiuto **i** Sarei salito sulle montagne russe **j** Ci hai detto la verità

LA MISTERIOSA DONNA IN SOFFITTA A > Ambrosiana

L'IDENTITÀ DELLA SIGNORA NEL RITRATTO

Elena Cornaro Piscopia

Index of grammatical topics

Notes